Preface Books

A series of scholarly and critical studies of major writers intended for those needing modern and authoritative guidance through the characteristic difficulties of their work to reach an intelligent under-standing and enjoyment of it.

General Editor: JOHN PURKIS
Founding Editor: MAURICE HUSSEY

Cover (and frontispiece): Allegorical portrait of Swift by Francis Bindon, *c.* 1730, private collection. Photo: Roy Hewson.

Bindon painted a number of portraits of Swift after the success of the *Drapier's Letters*. This one shows him, holding the Fourth Letter, being crowned with a laurel by Fame and being acknowledged by Fortune, who blows her trumpet and scuds on a sphere, representing the precarious opportunity she affords. At his feet grovels a mad Bedlamite who bites his arm resting on a crumpled schedule for Wood's halfpence. (Swift represented the unreason of Man in *Gulliver's Travels* and also set up a hospital for the insane.)

A Preface to Swift

Keith Crook

LONGMAN
LONDON AND NEW YORK

Addison Wesley Longman Limited
Edinburgh Gate
Harlow
Essex CM20 2JE
United Kingdom
and Associated Companies throughout the world

*Published in the United States of America
by Addison Wesley Longman, New York*

First published 1998

ISBN 0 582–28978–5 (ppr)
      0 582–28977–7 (csd)

British Library Cataloguing-in-Publication Data

A catalogue record for this book is available from the British Library

Library of Congress Cataloging-in-Publication Data

Crook, Keith.
   A preface to Swift / Keith Crook.
      p.   cm. — (Preface books)
   Includes bibliographical references (p.   ) and index.
   ISBN 0–582–28978–5 (ppr). — ISBN 0–582–28977–7 (csd)
   1. Swift, Jonathan, 1667–1745 — Criticism and interpretation.
I. Title.
PR3727.C79   1998
828′.509—dc21   98–10984
                                                          CIP

Set by 35 in 10½/11pt Mono Baskerville
Produced by Addison Wesley Longman Singapore (Pte) Ltd.,
Printed in Singapore

Contents

Contents

List of Illustrations

Acknowledgements

Swift scholarship is generously supplied and in common with many others I am indebted to the community of writers who have shared their findings and perceptions concerning this 'Incomparable Man' whose works 'are absolutely Original, unequald, unexampled'. In particular I have benefited from two. Irvin Ehrenpreis in his three volume biography and Harold Williams in his edition of the letters effortlessly present Swift in rich detail and I hope their works will once more become available for students to read first hand. Other scholars are acknowledged in the course of the book. I also wish to thank the Chief Librarian of Cambridge City Library for an unusually extended loan of Swift's *Letters*. And I am grateful to Roy Hewson for taking the cover photograph.

For the opportunity to write on Swift I am thankful to Professor Ian Gordon who suggested I might write in this series and to John Purkis, an ever helpful editor who let me have my head when I wanted. The direction of my study owes much to the acute questioning and shared enjoyment of Swift I experienced with the students of English literature on degrees that have flourished at the Cambridge campus of APU since 1971. And I have a special debt to Nora Crook for encouragement, scholarly companionableness and critical judgement. Both she and Harry Browne took on the task of reading this work through in various drafts and have helped me with valuable suggestions. I freely confess my errors for I have proceeded on conjecture, as all men must do – as Swift said.

KC

Part One
The Writer and His Setting

Chronological chart of Swift's life and contemporary events

Date	Monarch	War	Visits England	Swift's life (**bold**) & *works* *(ital)* – dates of writing unless otherwise indicated
1660	Chas II 29 May			
1661				
1662				
1663				
1664				
1665		2nd Anglo Dutch		
1666				
1667				**Birth Swift, 30 Nov., Dublin.**
1668				
1669				**Nurse takes him to Whitehaven.**
1670				
1671				

Context Births/deaths; events; arts
Restoration of British monarchy.
Birth Harley.
Royal Society incorporated. Quaker's Act. Act of Uniformity. Britain sells Dunkirk to France.
Marriage of Swift's father and mother, Jonathan Swift and Abigail Erick.
Birth Jas Butler 2nd Duke Ormonde. Great Plague.
Birth Jane Swift. Great Fire of London. 1st Duke Ormonde re-endows Kilkenny School.
Death Swift's father, Jonathan, March or April. Treaty of Breda. Sprat, *History of Royal Society*.
Treaty of Aix-la-Chapelle: Fr. gets Belgian border towns. Triple Alliance Brit., UP, Sweden.
(Secret) Treaty of Dover w Fr. to pull out of Triple Alliance.

Chronological chart of Swift's life and contemporary events (cont'd)

Date	Monarch	War	Visits England	Swift's life (bold) & *works* (*ital*) – dates of writing unless otherwise indicated
1672		3rd Anglo Dutch		**Age 5.**
1673				**Enters Kilkenny School.**
1674				
1675				
1676				
1677				**Age 10.**
1678				
1679				
1680				
1681				
1682				**Age 15. Enters Trinity Coll. Dublin.**
1683				
1684				
1685	James II 6 Feb			
1686				**BA ex speciali gratia.**
1687				**Age 20.**

Context Births/deaths; events; arts
Birth Addison and Steele. Declaration of Indulgence. Franco-Dutch war-79.
Test Act in England.
Treaty of Westminster.
Rochester, *A Satire Against Mankind*.
Birth St John. 1678–81 Popish Plot (Titus Oates). Treaty of Nymwegen 78/9: France gets Franche Comté.
Habeas Corpus Amendment Act.
Sir Wm Temple buys Compton Hall (Moor Park), Farnham.
Birth Stella. Execution of Oliver Plunket, RC Abp Armagh. Dryden, *Absalom and Achitophel*.
Dryden, *Mac Flecknoe* (pirated edn).
John Sobieski drives Turks from Vienna (stems spread of Islam). Rye House Plot to assassinate Charles II & James II.
Monmouth Rebellion. Jeffreys Bloody Assize. Revocation of Edict of Nantes causes emigration of Huguenots (Protestants) from France.
Declaration of Indulgence.

Chronological chart of Swift's life and contemporary events (cont'd)

Date	Monarch	War	Visits England	Swift's life (bold) & *works* *(ital)* – dates of writing unless otherwise indicated
1688				
1689	Wm III & Mary II 3 Feb	League of Augsburg	Mar to May.	**Becomes secretary to Sir Wm Temple; tutor to Stella (8 yrs old); onset Ménière's disease.**
1690				**Brief return to Ireland.**
1691				**Back at Moor Park.**
1692			Oct to	**Age 25. Hart Hall MA.** *Ode to the Athenian Society.*
1693				
1694	Wm III 28 Dec		Aug.	**Ordained deacon in Ireland, 28 Oct.**
1695				**Priest, 13 Jan; prebend Kilroot, Belfast, 28 Jan.**
1696			Jun to	**Proposal to Varina, 19 Apr; returns to Temple;** writing *A Tale of a Tub.*

Context
Births/deaths; events; arts

Birth Pope, Vanessa. Death John Temple. Flight of James II.

Bill of Rights declares James II to have abdicated.
Locke, *An Essay Concerning Human Understanding.*

Battle of Boyne, 1 July.

Treaty of Limerick.

National debt incurred.
Locke, *Some Thoughts Concerning Education.*

Birth Voltaire.
Triennial Act.

Expiry of Licensing Act.

Toland, *Christianity not Mysterious.*

Chronological chart of Swift's life and contemporary events (cont'd)

Date	Monarch	War	Visits England	Swift's life (**bold**) & *works (ital)* – dates of writing unless otherwise indicated
1697				**Age 30.**
1698				
1699			Jul.	*A Tale of a Tub* finished by this date.
1700				**Vicar Laracor, 20 Feb; prebend St Patrick's Cathedral, 22 Oct;** ed. Temple's *Letters i & ii.*
1701			Apr to Sep.	Edits Temple's *Miscellanea, iii;* writes *A Discourse of the Contests & Dissensions in Athens & Rome.*
1702	Anne 8 Mar	Span. Succsn		**Age 35. DD Trinity Coll.**
1703				
1704			Nov. to May.	pub. *A Tale of a Tub & The Battle of the Books.*
1705				
1706				

Context
Births/deaths; events; arts

Birth Hogarth.
Treaty of Ryswick.
Dampier, *A New Voyage Round the World.*

Death Temple, 27 Jan.

Deaths Dryden, Charles II: K. of Spain.

Stella and Dingley to Dublin, Aug.
Act of Settlement.

Bill against Occasional Conformity fails.
Dampier, *Voyage to New Holland.*

Death Locke.
Tisdall's proposal to Stella. Test Act in Ireland.
Battle of Blenheim. Harley Sec. State (north), 1704–06.
Newton, *Opticks.*

Birth Benjamin Franklin. Death Leopold I: H.R. Emperor.

Battle of Ramillies.

Chronological chart of Swift's life and contemporary events (cont'd)

Date	Monarch	War	Visits England	Swift's life (**bold**) & *works (ital)* – dates of writing unless otherwise indicated
1707				**Age 40. Negotiates first fruits;** *Bickerstaff Papers 1707?–09; Baucis & Philemon*
1708			Dec to	**Addison, Steele friendship;** *The Sentiments of a Church-of-England Man; An argument to prove that the Abolishing of Christianity . . .*
1709			May.	*A Project for the Advancement of Religion; A Description of the Morning.*
1710			Sep to	**1710–13 visitor at Vanhomrigh's (Vanessa 20); Harley & St John friendships;** *Memoirs relating to that change . . . ; Journal to Stella 1710–13; The Examiner nos 14–45, 1710–11; A Description of a City Shower.*

Context
Births/deaths; events; arts

Act of Union with Scotland, 6 Mar, adds 45 members to existing 513 in Commons.

Battle of Oudenarde.

Birth Sam Johnson.
Battle of Malplaquet.

Death Swift's mother, 24 Apr.
Trial of Sacheverell, March. Harley Lord Treasurer, 23 Aug 1710–14. St John Sec State (north) 1710–12.
Berkeley, *Principles of Human Knowledge*.

Chronological chart of Swift's life and contemporary events (cont'd)

Date	Monarch	War	Visits England	Swift's life (**bold**) & *works* (*ital*) – dates of writing unless otherwise indicated
1711				**Cooling Addison, Steele friendship;** *The Conduct of the Allies; The Windsor Prophecy.*
1712				**Age 45. Pope, Gay, Arbuthnot friendships.**
1713			May.	**Dean of St Patrick's Cathedral, 13 Jun;** *The Importance of the Guardian Considered; Cadenus & Vanessa; Epi VII Bk i to Oxford.*
1714	Geo I 1 Aug		Sep to Jul.	**Scriblerus Club,** *The Publick Spirit of the Whigs; Author upon Himself.*
1715				
1716				**Supposed marriage, w Stella; proposes 'Newgate pastoral' to Gay.**
1717				**Age 50.**

Context
Births/deaths; events; arts

Guiscard attacks Harley, 8 Mar. Harley created 1st Earl Oxford, 23 May. Charles VI, Holy Roman Emperor, 12 Oct. Marlborough dismissed, Dec. Act against Occasional Conformity. Pope, *Essay on Criticism.*

Birth Rousseau. Death Frederick I: K. of Prussia. St John created 1st Viscount Bolingbroke, June. Bandbox plot, 4 Nov. Pope, *Rape of the Lock* (2 cantos).

Birth Diderot. Treaty of Utrecht, 9 Apr. Bolingbroke Sec State (south). Pope, *Windsor Forest.*

Dismissal Oxford, 27 July, & Bolingbroke, 31 Aug. Walpole Chancellor of Exchequer, 1714–17. Vanessa to Cellbridge, Ireland. Newton, *Principia* (with *General Scholium*). Mandeville, *Fable of the Bees.*

Death Louis XIV, K. of France. Bolingbroke & Ormonde join Pretender, 27 March & 20 July. Oxford in Tower, 16 July. Jacobite Rising.

Septennial Act. Gay, *Trivia.*

Release of Oxford, 1 July.

Chronological chart of Swift's life and contemporary events (cont'd)

Date	Monarch	War	Visits England	Swift's life (bold) & works (ital) – dates of writing unless otherwise indicated
1718		Quadruple Allce		**Thos Sheridan, Patrick Delany friendships;** *Letter to Mr Delany; Mary the Cook Maid's. . . .*
1719				*Answer to Mr Sheridan; Stella's Birthday.*
1720				*A Proposal for the Universal Use of Irish Manufacture.*
1721				MS first part *Gulliver's Travels.*
1722				**Age 55.**
1723				
1724				*Drapier's Letters 1724–5; To Stella.*
1725				
1726			Mar to Sep.	pub. *Cadenus & Vanessa and Gulliver's Travels.*
1727	Geo II 11 Jun		Apr to Sep.	**Age 60.** *Pope–Swift Miscellanies.*
1728				*Ireland.*

Context
Births/deaths; events; arts

Birth Pitt Elder (Chatham).
Britain intervenes in Austro-Spanish war in a Quadruple Alliance.

Birth Garrick.
Defoe, *Robinson Crusoe*. Watts, *Psalms of David*.

South Sea Bubble. Declaratory Act.

Walpole Chancellor of Exchequer, 1721–42.

Impeachment Atterbury.

Death Vanessa, 2 June.
Bolingbroke returns to England.
Defoe, *Journal of the Plague Year and Moll Flanders*.

Death Oxford, 21 May.

Birth Clive.
Bolingbroke's bribes regain him his title. Order Bath instituted.

Stella ill. Famine in Ireland.

Death Newton. Births Gainsborough, Adam Smith.
Famine in Ireland.
Pope, 1727–29 *var edns The Dunciad (3 books)*.

Death Stella, 28 Jan.
Gay, *Beggar's Opera*.

Chronological chart of Swift's life and contemporary events (cont'd)

Date	Monarch	War	Visits England	Swift's life (bold) & works (ital) – dates of writing unless otherwise indicated
1729				*A Modest Proposal*; *A Grand Question Debated*; *?Lady Acheson weary of the Dean.*
1730				*Death & Daphne*; *A libel on Rev DD.*
1731				*Verses on the Death of Dr Swift*; *?A riddling Letter*; *?Strephon & Chloe*; *A love song from Dick Bettesworth.*
1732				**Age 65.**
1733		Polish Succsn		*Love Song in the Modern Taste.*
1734				**Deafness ends hopes of returning to England;** *On Poetry: A Rhapsody*; *On his deafness.*
1735				
1736				*The Legion Club.*
1737				**Age 70.**
1738				*Polite Conversation.*
1739				

Context
Births/deaths; events; arts

Birth Cook. Death Abp Wm King.

Birth Lessing.

Birth Erasmus Darwin.
Hogarth, *The Harlot's Progress*. Cave (ed.) *The Gentleman's Magazine*.

Death Gay, 4 Dec. Births Washington, Cowper, Haydn.

Birth Fragonard.
Pope, *Essay on Man*.

Death Arbuthnot, 27 Feb.
Bolingbroke returns to France.
Hogarth, *The Rake's Progress*.

Porteus riots in Edinburgh.

Death Caroline Anspach. Birth Gibbon.

1739–41 great famine in Ireland; a fifth die.

Chronological chart of Swift's life and contemporary events (cont'd)

Date	Monarch	War	Visits England	Swift's life (**bold**) & *works* *(ital)* – dates of writing unless otherwise indicated
1740		Austrn Succsn		
1741				
1742				**Age 75. 'of unsound mind & memory', 17 Aug.**
1743				
1744				
1745				**Death Swift, 19 Oct;** *Directions to Servants* (found with his will).

Context
Births/deaths; events; arts

Birth Francis Towne.

Battle of Dettingen, 27 June.

Death Pope, 30 May. Birth Lavoisier.
Johnson, *Life Savage.*

Death 2nd Duke of Ormonde.
Battle of Fontenoy, 22 Jun–20 Sep '46. '45' rebellion.

Chronological chart of ministers, 1702–1715, spanning the reign of Queen Anne

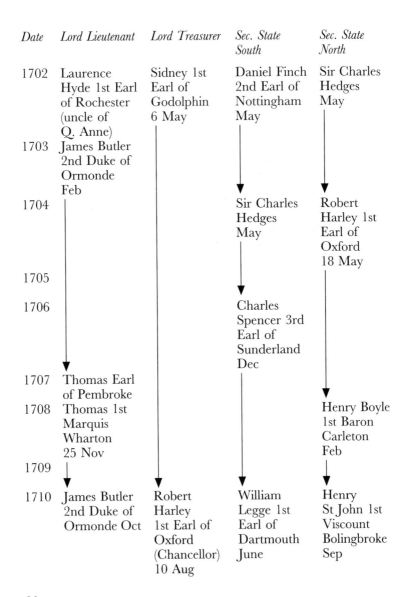

Date	Lord Lieutenant	Lord Treasurer	Sec. State South	Sec. State North
1702	Laurence Hyde 1st Earl of Rochester (uncle of Q. Anne)	Sidney 1st Earl of Godolphin 6 May	Daniel Finch 2nd Earl of Nottingham May	Sir Charles Hedges May
1703	James Butler 2nd Duke of Ormonde Feb			
1704			Sir Charles Hedges May	Robert Harley 1st Earl of Oxford 18 May
1705				
1706			Charles Spencer 3rd Earl of Sunderland Dec	
1707	Thomas Earl of Pembroke			
1708	Thomas 1st Marquis Wharton 25 Nov			Henry Boyle 1st Baron Carleton Feb
1709				
1710	James Butler 2nd Duke of Ormonde Oct	Robert Harley 1st Earl of Oxford (Chancellor) 10 Aug	William Legge 1st Earl of Dartmouth June	Henry St John 1st Viscount Bolingbroke Sep

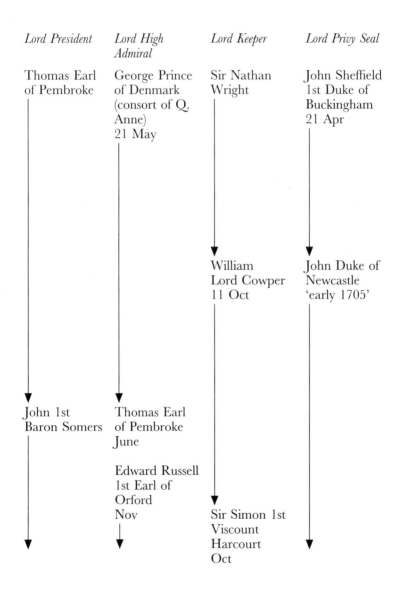

Lord President	Lord High Admiral	Lord Keeper	Lord Privy Seal
Thomas Earl of Pembroke	George Prince of Denmark (consort of Q. Anne) 21 May	Sir Nathan Wright	John Sheffield 1st Duke of Buckingham 21 Apr
		William Lord Cowper 11 Oct	John Duke of Newcastle 'early 1705'
John 1st Baron Somers	Thomas Earl of Pembroke June		
	Edward Russell 1st Earl of Orford Nov	Sir Simon 1st Viscount Harcourt Oct	

Chronological chart of ministers, 1702–1715, spanning the reign
of Queen Anne (cont'd)

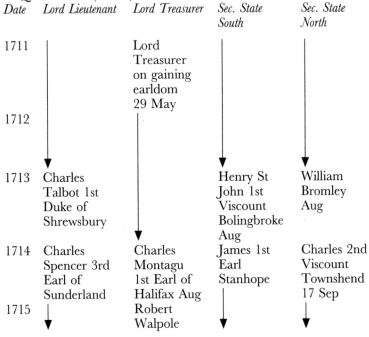

Date	Lord Lieutenant	Lord Treasurer	Sec. State South	Sec. State North
1711		Lord Treasurer on gaining earldom 29 May		
1712				
1713	Charles Talbot 1st Duke of Shrewsbury		Henry St John 1st Viscount Bolingbroke Aug	William Bromley Aug
1714	Charles Spencer 3rd Earl of Sunderland	Charles Montagu 1st Earl of Halifax Aug	James 1st Earl Stanhope	Charles 2nd Viscount Townshend 17 Sep
1715		Robert Walpole		

Lord President	Lord High Admiral	Lord Keeper	Lord Privy Seal
John Sheffield 1st Duke of Buckingham 12 Jun		Commissioners	John Robinson Bishop of London 29 Aug
	Thomas Wentworth Baron Raby 'summer'	Commissioners	
		Sir Simon 1st Viscount Harcourt	William Legge 1st Earl of Dartmouth Aug
Daniel Finch 2nd Earl of Nottingham	Edward Russell 1st Earl of Orford Oct	William Lord Cowper Sep	Thomas 1st Marquis of Wharton Aug
			Charles Spencer 3rd Earl of Sunderland

1 A brief life of Swift

A sketch of the man and of some significant issues

A man of overwhelming intellect and power goes scourged through life between the dread of insanity and the wrath of his own soul warring with a brutal age. He exhausts mind, heart, and brain in that battle: he consumes himself, and perishes in utter desolation. Out of all his agony remains one little book, his dreadful testament against his fellow-kind, which to-day serves as a pleasant tale for the young under the title of *Gulliver's Travels*. That, and a faint recollection of some baby-talk in some love-letters, is as much as the world has chosen to retain of Jonathan Swift, Master of Irony. Think of it! It is like tu[r]ning-down the glare of a volcano to light a child to bed!

Rudyard Kipling, *'Fiction'* (1926), *A Book of Words*

Kipling's passionate outburst against contemporaries who valued Swift only as a comfortable story-teller for children attempts to reclaim a writer who is exhilarating to read: a heroic and dangerous energy which burned itself out in combating enemies without and within. This is the satirist whose power to disturb we recall when we speak of the 'Swiftian' savagery of a political cartoon and the 'Lilliputian' littleness of some example of meanness of spirit. And this is the master of irony we recognise whose play on meanings in *Gulliver's Travels* goes beyond the range of the normal children's book of outlandish adventures. And yet the over-simple view persists. That Gulliver is a matter-of-fact reporter of his own marvellous adventures. Perhaps this is what the Irish Tourist Board is trading on when it invites enquirers to telex 'Gulliver' for travel information, overlooking the ironies that its hero was often unreliable: off-course, shipwrecked, degradingly at variance with the natives and that he returned home to disenchantment with his wife. Such a 'misreading' happens because there is a truth, which Kipling dismisses, in seeing *Gulliver's Travels* as a 'pleasant tale'. It has a fanciful and inventive side which charms and engages us in a story well-told with episodes that catch the imagination as though they might have happened. This as well as the 'dreadful testament' is part of Swift's creation.

To concentrate on one or the other has often had the effect of treating *Gulliver's Travels* as though it were in two parts. Preference for one aspect has led to the exclusion of the other from appreciative consideration. However, *Gulliver's Travels*, like Swift's other writings, is a more integrated creation than this in which the dangerous energy, irony and charm work together. Partial judgements on Swift's creative work occur since his viewpoint is elusive. His satires often invite us to live in a country of appearances of truth, half truth and lie, each of which may be attractive or repellent, where meanings have to be teased out to reveal wisdom, private jokes or nonsense. And his mordancy, humour and inventiveness constantly alert us to his tone of voice as a way of encouraging an intellectual suppleness in reading his satire where we must discriminate with care and neither edit out nor overlook anything.

Many readers continue to have the same limitation Kipling criticised: of knowing him mainly by 'one little book', the world-famous *Gulliver's Travels*. And yet there is much more, prose and poetry, to admire and to enjoy. In addition we may be less equipped than Kipling's readers with respect to our knowledge of Swift's life. It is probable that many of us don't know the *Journal to Stella* to which he also refers (unfairly) as 'baby-talk' or much of the detail of Swift's personal life hinted at in 'warring with a brutal age'. But not knowing Swift's life and context denies us another way of coming to terms with him, for there seems to be a strong connection between Swift's behaviour as a man and his satiric method as an author. Fortunately many of his letters have been preserved where we may see him writing with a clear sense of his reader and presenting a different face to each. This leads to great variety: for example, on one hand, wit, wordplay, irony and outrageousness founded in a secure sense of friendship and on another, political acumen and adroitness in addressing an untrustworthy schemer. What we do discover of him reveals a fascinating, perceptive, congenial, dominating and fastidious personality.

Swift's writing is particularly relevant to the history of politics and Ireland. He wrote with the first-hand knowledge that came from being at the centre of political intrigue in London and in Dublin. How did he resist with integrity and intelligence the deceptions of party and survive in a self-serving and duplicitous political world? Was he master or tool of contemporary political power games and intrigue? The decade in which he became close to government policymakers is discussed in the next chapter and his later political activity in Ireland is a part of Chapter 3.

As a writer he was admired by the greatest poet of the age, Alexander Pope, who paid him this tribute in a letter to a mutual friend:

> My sincere Love for this most valuable, indeed Incomparable Man will accompany him thro Life, & pursue his memory were I to live a hundred lives, as many as his Works will live, which are absolutely Original, unequald, unexampled. His Humanity, his

Charity, his Condescension, his Candour, are equal to his Wit,
& require as good and true a taste to be equally valued.

To read Swift is to become acquainted with a group of individuals
whose literary works have been considered as significant productions of the period: Pope, Addison, Steele, Arbuthnot and Gay, and
to raise issues of the value of their mainly moral and satiric writing
and the nature of the reading public. How Swift interacted with this
community of writers and drew on their support even when separated from them by the Irish Sea is the subject of Chapter 3.

Swift's relationships with intelligent women and the attitudes to
feminine qualities represented in his poems have become an important focus of interest. His lack of inhibition has been seen as clearing
away male/female stereotyping and also as verging on a patholo-
gical fear of bodily functions, decay and death. In Chapter 4 these
matters receive attention, raising the issue of the relevance of biography to literary judgement.

The sequence of these thematic discussions is broadly chronological, leading up to an examination in Chapter 5 of Swift's most
famous work, *Gulliver's Travels*, published just before his 59th birthday. It discusses how in *Gulliver's Travels* Swift reflects on previous
political events, contemporary science, and theories of education, of
government and of human understanding and develops into a consideration of the nature of Swift's satire.

These phases of Swift's literary activity reveal different aspects of
a man who was born an Anglo–Irishman and for forty years was a
clergyman, ordained in the Church of Ireland. His nationality and his
calling moulded his characteristic sense of separateness and of human
fallibility. One encouraged his unruly wit and the other his uncom-
promising judgements. The following sketch of Swift's life will show
how important both experiences were to him and will also give us a
context for the later more detailed examination of his writings.

The Anglo–Irish 'Ascendancy'

The formative context for Swift

Swift was born in Dublin on 30 November 1667, the second child
of an Englishman who had emigrated to Ireland in 1660 and of a
first generation Irishwoman, Abigail Erick, whose father came over
in 1634. So he was of Anglo–Irish stock which was the ruling or
'ascendant' community in Ireland, but often divided in its allegiance
to England and Ireland. A glance at the chronological chart on page
2 shows that he was only a year old when he was taken away from
his mother to England for three years by his nurse and that from
1689 to 1714 he was constantly crossing the Irish Sea. A recent

study, following the work of Harold Williams,[1] has also shown him extensively travelling across Ireland, particularly in the years after 1714. Like Gulliver, he was constantly on the move and wedded to no particular place.

Late in his life, in 1737, he complained that his stay in Ireland had been enforced as a result of an influential friend's[2] fall from power in 1714 just when he might have advanced Swift's career:

> having been driven to this wretched Kingdom (to which I was almost a Stranger) by his want of power to keep me in what I ought to call my own Country; though I happened to be dropped here, and was a Year old before I left it, and to my Sorrow did not dye before I came back to it again.

But as we shall see this extreme expression of the misery of living in Ireland does not tell all. Swift's support for certain sections of the Irish community varied during his career and he established many fulfilling friendships in Ireland. However, London had offered him an active adult career in politics and intimacy with major literary figures. He was split between the two countries. His sense of not belonging was heightened by being fatherless (his father died before his birth) and the disruption to family life caused by his unaccountable three-year separation from his mother at such an early age.

The term 'Anglo–Irish' embraces a connection of Ireland with England that goes back to the Norman invasion of Ireland in the twelfth century. So it requires further qualification to describe Swift's condition. As a general description, its meaning is a matter of a current debate, which is particularly concerned to rescue the Gaelic tradition which pre-dates the twelfth century. Only a partial account is necessary for our understanding of Swift here.[3] The 'new Anglo–Irish' to which Swift belonged were part of a wave of sixteenth/seventeenth-century immigrants who entered Ireland following the Tudor settlements and Cromwell's brutal suppression of Ireland and confiscation of lands to reward his soldiers and 'adventurers' (English investors). The effect of the Cromwellian settlement was to set against each other Catholics, Anglicans and Non-conformists (Protestants who did not adhere to the Church of England – in the North of Ireland these were mainly Presbyterian). Contemporary writers contrasted the supposed harmony of the 'old Anglo–Irish' settlement with the dissension caused by the 'new Anglo–Irish'. Lord Anglesey, who had been a puritan parliamentarian under Cromwell but later enjoyed royalist confidence, wrote in 1681 of this earlier time as one where 'there never was more Unity, friendship, and good Agreement, amongst all sorts and degrees'.[4]

By birth, Swift belonged to a class of people who could be seen as usurpers of what had become in Tudor times a largely Catholic nation. Also he spent his boyhood during a time when fundamental changes were shaking religious and political stability in England, which would fuel his scepticism about human impartiality and reason and which he would see with the eyes of a detached 'outsider'. In England, Catholicism came near to becoming the established religion; wars on the continent of Europe involved England in radical changes of alliances (siding with former enemies); and a revolution occurred which toppled its reigning king. The 'Restoration' of the royal House of Stuart in 1660, after the puritan and republican 'Commonwealth' established by Cromwell, continued the struggle between the Church of England and the Church of Rome. Under Charles II, who reigned from 1660–1685, England fought two wars with the Dutch. In the following reign, it was plunged into civil war ending in the overthrow of Charles's successor, James II, in the Revolution of 1688 which placed William of Orange (the Stadtholder of the United Provinces which included Holland) and his wife, Mary Stuart, on the throne as William III and Mary II.

Ireland had a subsidiary nation status and its political life was determined by these events in England. Poyning's Law of 1494 had effectively shackled the Irish Parliament, since its decisions did not become law until they had been approved by the English Parliament. So it could not act independently when, during the Restoration, England fought for naval supremacy in order to have a commercial monopoly in trade with colonies. England passed the Navigation Acts (1663, 1670), which placed restrictions on Irish trade in order to privilege that of England. Legislation in England advanced the pre-eminence of the minority Anglican community in Ireland. This was a consequence of the religious struggle, which gave rise to a series of acts discriminating against non-members of the Church of England, i.e. Non-conformists and Catholics. Three of the most important were as follows: the Corporation Act (1661) confined municipal office to Anglicans; the Act of Uniformity (1662) ejected Non-conformists from their livings and excluded them from teaching in schools and universities; and the Sacramental Test Act (1673) barred Non-conformists and Catholics from civil and military offices – unless they accepted the Church of England communion and declared against 'transubstantiation', the belief that the bread and wine became the same substance as the body and blood of Christ. This legislation was not immediately effected in Ireland. For example, the Sacramental Test only came into force in 1704. But Ireland's dependence ensured that individuals and corporations took account of what was happening in England and operated within the spirit of the acts, although inconsistently and sporadically, until they became law in Ireland. In essence, the legislation gave Anglicans political pre-eminence and weighted arguments in their favour.

Protestant land-owning of good cultivable Irish property rose from one-third in 1641 to two-thirds after 1665. In England a fever of anti-Catholicism was fuelled by fears of a 'Popish Plot' to establish a Roman Catholic monarchy. This allowed for five years (1678–1681) the cunning and unscrupulous Titus Oates to send Roman Catholic sympathisers to the gallows with false accusations of treason. The plot was said to have a branch in Ireland. The Roman Catholic Archbishop of Armagh, Oliver Plunkett, was imprisoned on perjured testimony and was executed by hanging, drawing and quartering.

During this time Swift went to the Anglican Kilkenny School, 60 miles south-west of Dublin, where he was sent by his uncle Godwin in 1673. At the same time, his mother went to stay with relatives in Leicester, where she remained for the rest of her life. While only a few anecdotes tell of Swift's eight years here, the place itself (see Plate 1) unavoidably brought him into contact with central features of Irish history and politics. At Kilkenny stood the ancestral castle of the Ormondes, an old Anglo–Irish family of grand distinction originally from Caen in Normandy and called 'Fitzwalter'. Thomas Butler, the twelfth Earl and first Duke, Viceroy of Ireland, who was royalist and Protestant, had re-endowed the school in 1666. Later his grandson, James Butler, the second Duke, was to receive William of Orange at the castle after his victory at the Battle of the Boyne, which routed James II and his followers (1679). More than 30 years after that, he was to help secure Swift's appointment as Dean of St Patrick's Cathedral, Dublin (1713). As a counterpoise to the twelfth-century castle's symbol of great secular power (despite one tower reduced to rubble by Cromwell's artillery in 1650) stood three Catholic religious foundations (a Franciscan friary and St John's Priory, both in ruins, and the restored but abandoned Dominican Black Abbey) and the Anglican cathedral, St Canice's, which had also been despoiled by Cromwellians. Here were visible signs of the threat to Anglican faith from Protestant Non-conformists and of the powerful presence of temporarily restrained Catholicism.

In 1683, Swift entered the Protestant Trinity College, Dublin. While he did not excel, he established a coterie of friends and accumulated experiences there which were later to become grist for his mill. Irvin Ehrenpreis, the author of the standard and most detailed biography of Swift,[5] tells us his tutor St George Ashe, whom he liked well, was a prominent member of the Dublin Philosophical Society, which went in for scientific observations with similarities to those seen in the voyages of Gulliver. Ashe had made 'a collection of curiously shaped stones and fossils (including one "taken out of the bladder of the noble man's cook in the country who lately dyed of it")', another member put odd substances into dogs and one constructed Lilliputian models of a road haulage carriage and a fleet of ships. One of the logical exercises invented by the provost, Narcissus Marsh, may have suggested a theme for the fourth voyage of *Gulliver's Travels.*

> Man is a rational animal. No horse is rational. Only rational animals are capable of discipline.[6]

Swift did not apply himself to his studies and spent most of the time reading poetry and history. He was frequently punished by the college authorities for indiscipline and on one occasion when he insulted the junior dean he had to beg pardon publicly on bended knee. For his uneven academic performance he was awarded a 'special' degree (i.e. by special dispensation) in 1686. In February 1689 he left for England, before completing the residence requirement for an MA, in order to avoid the civil war which followed the invasion of Ireland by James II in his attempt to win back the crown from William of Orange.

Secretary to Temple, 1689–1699

Literary and priestly ambitions

Swift's journey to England brought him into close contact with two of the most important influences on his life. He became secretary to Sir William Temple, who was acquainted with the Swift family (through the friendship of his father with Swift's uncle, Godwin Swift), and acted as tutor to a member of his household, a girl, 14 years younger, called Esther Johnson but whom he nicknamed 'Stella'. At first, Sir William was the more significant of the two in forming Swift's behaviour but, later, Stella would have a central role. Sir William was, like Swift, 'new Anglo–Irish' but of the second generation and his career reinforces the sense that members of this group occupied a privileged position, by virtue of the 'ascendancy', and yet had an uneasy allegiance to Ireland. He also ended up as a detached observer of political life. His family's contacts with Ireland were strong, dating from 1600, and his grandfather became provost of Trinity College, Dublin, in 1609. Sir William was a career diplomat, travelling between Ireland and England, and for a short time he resided in Ireland becoming the member for Carlow in 1661. He soon left the country and when, in 1677, he inherited the Irish position of Master of the Rolls, he filled the post as an absentee, eventually appointing a deputy and relinquishing it altogether in 1696. He knew the centre of political gravity was at the court of the king of England, from where he was sent abroad during the second Anglo–Dutch War (1665–1667) on the king's business. He much impressed the Dutch courtier and politician, de Witt, and in 1667 negotiated with great speed the treaty which brought about in 1668 a Triple Alliance of England, Holland and Sweden to block the expansion of France. He did not know, until 1670, that King Charles II was secretly in contact with Louis XIV, the long-reigning French 'Sun King' (1643–1715), and that all his efforts would be undermined.

In 1670 his sense of misplaced trust and his disappointment at unintentionally deluding de Witt made him go into semi-retirement. He was recalled (1674) to negotiate the peace of the third Anglo–Dutch War and the marriage of the future William III with Charles II's niece, the future Mary II, which took place in 1677. In 1680 he had become dissatisfied with Charles II's growing absolutism yet could not ally himself to those who believed in the Popish Plot. So he bought for his final retirement Compton Hall near Farnham, Surrey, which he renamed Moor Park. Here he attempted to live in a distinguished and honourable manner, modelled on Horace (Quintus Horatius Flaccus) the Roman poet and adviser of Augustus. He intended to be consulted as an elder statesman and to reach the thinking reading public through his literary productions. Much of his time was spent writing essays, his memoirs and a history of recent events. When William III became king in 1688, he sought Temple's advice but was unable to tempt him back into office. Instead William took on Temple's son, John, who almost immediately made the mistake of recommending the freeing of an Irish general, Hamilton. He had thought that Hamilton would persuade the rebel, Tyrconnel, to lay down his arms but he sided with the rebel instead. In remorse, John drowned himself in the Thames. When Swift joined Temple's service in 1689, he came at a time when his patron was still distressed by an acute sense of the loss of his son. The next ten years show Temple's growing care for Swift and dependence on him as secretary. In these years Swift expressed admiration for Temple and for a time modelled himself on his patron. But it was a period of interrupted employment and later he would remember the cold looks he sometimes received from Temple, since Swift's ambition to gain preferment either as a writer or a cleric did not suit the needs of an otherwise congenial employer.

In 1689 the first serious attack of disabling giddiness and headaches afflicted Swift. He was suffering from what is now known to be Ménière's disease which began in his left inner ear and caused him to become deaf late in his life. In June 1690, with the vain hope of restoring his health by a change of air, he returned to Ireland and so was in the country when William defeated James II at the Battle of the River Boyne, confirming the fall of the Stuart monarchy. As the stay in Ireland did not bring about a cure he went back to England in October 1691 and at the end of the year to Moor Park to continue as secretary and tutor with an eye to political or other advancement.

With his limited funds, middling social status and Anglo–Irish educational background, few openings were available for Swift and the influence of his patron could be decisive in both the secular and religious spheres. Many ecclesiastical appointments were made as 'preferments' – the choice of an influential person who often had no great religious concern. Except where the post was in the sole gift of a patron, the candidates were dependent on how determined was the support of their patrons and at the mercy of those who neglected an opportunity or took too casual a line. In view of the petty politics, it was important to have secured the right person to apply pressure from without and to circumvent the power-seeking promotions from within the church. In much of Swift's subsequent career he was to experience the truth of this at first hand.

To further his hopes of securing a position in holy orders or a university fellowship, in 1692 Swift took his MA at Hart Hall, Oxford University. Then, Temple's esteem for him seemed to suggest there were opportunities for him at court. Showing some confidence in Swift's abilities, in 1693 Temple sent him to present William III with his arguments about holding elections every three years. But Temple probably wished to keep so excellent a young man as his secretary rather than to advance his career. Swift was shrewd enough to see something of this but felt that he had been promised more. He returned to thinking of the church as a career and he imagined it might combine with his role in Temple's household. He wrote to his uncle, William Swift, in November 1692: 'I am not to take orders till the King gives me a Prebendary: and Sir William Temple, tho' he promises me the certainty of it, yet is less forward than I could wish; because, I suppose he believes I shall leave him, and upon some accounts, he thinks me a little necessary to him.'

Prebends were usually sinecures[7] attached to cathedrals. If, as might naturally be expected, this referred to an English cathedral, such as Westminster or Canterbury, the position would be a valuable source of income and require no duty of residence. He could even belong to a gentleman's family as a chaplain and have time for writing. In high spirits he wrote a letter in 1692 which shows that the literary world was most congenial to him. He twitted his cousin Thomas as a fellow poet in self-congratulatory prose which rattled on, pretended to a familiarity with the court, which he did not yet have, and offered unsolicited advice. He had just been successful in having his own *Ode to the Athenian Society* printed by the Society and also quoted with approbation in another book 'so that perhaps I was in good humor all the week'. He felt he had written not only as Temple's man but also as one who was independently convinced of the society's worth: 'at least S[r] W[m] T speaking to me so much in [the Society's] Praise made me zealous for their cause, for really I take that to be a part of the Honesty of Poets that they cannot write well except they think the subject deserves it.' Probably his declaration of his warm affection for Temple and his high estimation of his works owes something to his belief that he had been promised his patronage, for he added a self-deflating comment to his praise: 'I never read his writings but I prefer him to all others present in England, Which I suppose is all but a piece of selflove.' At this time the trade of writing definitely seems Swift's chosen path and he felt that the poet, Abraham Cowley,[8] would be his role model.

> I have a sort of vanity, or Foibless,[9] I do not know what to call it, and which I would fain know if you partake of it, it is (not to be circumstantial) that I am overfond of my own writings, I would not have the world think so for a million, but it is so, and I find when I have writt what pleases me I am Cowley to my self and can read it a hundred times over.

In this confidence he could advise Thomas to give his poem 'another wipe, and then it will be one of my Favorits'. And he could wish Thomas well in the path that Jonathan was not going to take: 'All that I can say is that I wish to God you were well provided for thô it were with a good living in the Church.'

However, nothing matching the prebendary in the gift of the king was offered in the next year and a half, so in May 1694 Swift left Temple's service and on 25 October 1694 was ordained deacon in the Church of Ireland (Anglican) and was made prebend of Kilroot, near Belfast in Ulster, on 13 January 1695. This was not a sinecure and gave him the responsibility of living in the parish which was also linked with two others. The church at Kilroot was ruined and the tiny congregation neglected, while being hemmed in by a thriving Presbyterian (Non-conformist) community. By the investigation of an ecclesiastical commission, the Bishop of the diocese, Down and Connor, had been deprived of his incumbency and a number of clergymen were made subject to 'suspensions, excommunications, and deprivations for such varied offences as drunkenness, fornication, adultery, neglect of cures, pluralism, diversion of funds, excessive procuration and visitation fees, non-residence, illegal use of the bishop's seal, and simony'.[10] The isolation of the living and the unglamorous prospect of the work it would entail was very different from the future as a writer that Swift had entertained in 1692.

Now there came a reversal of fortunes. While Swift was at Kilroot, his cousin Thomas filled his place as Temple's right hand, was ordained priest at Puttenham, Surrey, and got married. For nearly two years Swift was out of the fashionable and literary centre, unable to preen himself on his noble acquaintance and minor celebrity. He could not even claim to have achieved the minimum he had recommended to Thomas: 'a good living in the Church'. Even so, he might have stayed in Kilroot had his proposal of marriage been accepted by Jane Waring, a young woman of good family from the region near Carrickfergus, whose brother he had met at Kilkenny school. Her rejection of him was the turning point for his return to Temple.

Only two letters (dated 1696 and 1700 respectively) survive of this courtship of Jane Waring (Latinised by Swift into 'Varina') and it is clear that both are preceded by an interchange of letters which irritated Swift. So there is little to help form a judgement on the nature of their relationship, but they do have significance for understanding Swift's development as a writer, particularly of *A Tale of a Tub* which is discussed later in this chapter. In the first letter (19 April 1696), Swift struck the self-admiring pose he had with Thomas with all its rattle and cocksureness. Wise aphorisms about the nature of lovers, love, liberty, philosophy, ambition and friendship are surrounded with balanced antitheses, apostrophising questions and patterned climaxes. It is all very literary and reads more like the mannered writing of the Elizabethan court of 100 years before.[11] After this artfulness, pretending not to know what to say next, he tells an anecdote: 'Two strangers, a poet and a beggar went to cuffs yesterday in this town . . . best of all, the poet got the better . . . This was of great comfort to me, till I heard the victor himself was a most abominable bad rhymer . . . It is a pity he has not also the qualifications to recommend himself to your sex.'

This looks suspiciously like dramatising his own predicament in the poses of the lover as writer of verses and the lover as begging for reward for his devotion. Swift would rather bandy words (even in 'abominable bad rhymes') than sue for love. Typically, when Swift's feelings are involved, he expresses himself obliquely and here his wounded pride produces an awkward posturing. His discomfiture leads, immediately afterwards, to a very clear message which has been behind the awkwardness. It comes over all the more finally in its bluntness: 'You have now had time enough to consider my last letter, and to form your own resolutions upon it. I await your answer with a world of impatience, and if you think fit I should attend you before my journey, I am ready to do it.'

In June 1696 he was back at Moor Park and rising in Temple's esteem. Stella was now 15. Swift's close friendship with her now became established and was to last for the rest of her life. The nature of their attachment will be treated more fully in Chapter 4. As tutor to her and a dependent of Temple, Swift could be said technically to have a subservient role. But her regard for him and his character tipped the balance the other way. An example from a letter to her (1698) gives some idea of the blend of affection and wittiness in their bond. Already he had gained her understanding and affection, so that he was able to express a gentle mockery first of her and then of himself, making fun of their roles. Being left on his own at Moor Park he wrote to her as though he had assumed the position of lord of the manor. He adopted a high-flown language to describe the strong wind as though it were a classical god of whom he was in awe: '*Æolus* has made a strange revolution in the rooks nests; but I say no more, for it is dangerous to meddle with things above us.' Instead of wishing her present in the polite formula of the dependent tutor he impudently expressed pleasure in her staying away: 'I desire your absence heartily; for now I live in great state, and the cook comes in to know what I please to have for dinner: I ask very gravely what is in the house, and accordingly give orders for a dish of pigeons, or, &c.' While this appears to refuse to show affection, indirectly the specific detail presents an amusing picture to delight her and they both know he is putting on airs. And through an empty threat he tells her he wishes to hear from her too: 'You shall have no more ale here, unless you send us a letter.' Swift's fun with his own self-image emphasises the security he felt in an employment that satisfied. At this time he was writing two works: *A Tale of a Tub* out of his experience of the meanness of Kilroot and the threat to Anglicanism of the Presbyterian Non-conformists and also *The Battle of the Books* in defence of his patron, who had praised the writings of the ancients and had fallen into controversy. At last he was back in the literary and aristocratic world he had described to Thomas but the death of Sir William on 27 January 1699 launched Swift into the political tide washing between Ireland and England.

First satiric works: *The Battle of the Books* and *A Tale of a Tub*

While both of Swift's works were not published until 1704, they belong to the phase of political apprenticeship under Temple. *The Battle of the Books* joins in the pamphlet war which Temple's work 'An Essay upon Ancient and Modern Learning' (1690) had stirred up. Temple had incautiously added his voice to an ongoing debate among European intellectuals about whether classical (ancient) literature was superior to modern literature. He had praised certain examples of ancient literature and lucklessly damaged his credibility by incorrectly including the *Epistles of Phalaris* and Aesop's *Fables* as productions entirely of the sixth century BC. Richard Bentley, the foremost classical scholar, exposed these mistakes and William Wotton attacked Temple's view of history. In reply, a collection of ghost writers at Trinity College, Cambridge, defended Temple under the name of the Honourable Charles Boyle. Swift then entered the fray, using an incident reported of Bentley as his cue. It was said that

Bentley as the Keeper of the Royal Library in St James had refused to admit readers on the grounds that the books were in disarray. Swift imagined that this physical disarray symbolised the discontinuity and disorder of modern learning over which Bentley presided. In *The Battle of the Books* he presents the library as a battlefield in which the volumes, taking on the actual lives of their authors, chaotically fight over the merits of Temple's arguments and tumble about the shelves.

A Tale of a Tub was a more substantial and significant satire and is considered by many to be Swift's greatest achievement. It probably drew Swift's usefulness as a polemicist to the attention of the politicians scrambling for power and at the same time offended Queen Anne who had succeeded William III in 1702. Swift presented it as an attempt to dampen the fires of bigoted religion. (In *Gulliver's Travels*, the *Tale* is represented as the giant Gulliver's pissing on a palace fire, causing the Empress to have perpetual malice against him 'on account of that infamous and illegal Method you took to extinguish the Fire in her Apartment'.) *A Tale of a Tub* works as an allegorical fable of the history of the Christian church represented through the 'adventures' of three brothers: Peter (Catholic), Martin (Anglican), and Jack (Non-conformist). What happens to them follows in broad outline the progress of organised Christianity from apostolic to contemporary days but their behaviour is undignified and vain.

Swift never used the style of *A Tale of a Tub* again and its energy has much in common with the exuberant language of his letters to Thomas Swift and to Varina, as though the creative act was necessary to celebrate and purge his youthful excess in order to move on to his mature style. The posturing and inventive experimentation of the letters is the matrix from which he shaped this early artistic 'voice'. For example, the image of the poet and beggar as aspects of a split in one's personality becomes transformed into one of imagination sparring ('at cuffs') with reason. 'But when a man's fancy gets astride on his reason, when imagination is at cuffs with the senses, and common understanding as well as common sense, is kicked out of doors, the first proselyte[12] he makes is himself.' And the breathless succession of ideas is similarly matched. In the story of the brothers' first encounter with town life Swift's account tumbles out in a scurry of verbs revealing insider knowledge of young arrogance, metropolitan behaviour and the places-to-be-at.

> On their first appearance our three adventurers met with a very bad reception, and soon with sagacity guessing the reason, they quickly began to improve in the good qualities of the town: they writ, and rallied, and rhymed, and sung, and said, and said nothing; they drank, and fought, and whored, and slept, and swore, and took snuff; they went to new plays on the first night, haunted the

chocolate-houses, beat the watch, lay on bulks, and got claps;[13] they bilked hackney-coachmen, ran in debt with shopkeepers, and lay with their wives; they killed bailiffs, kicked fiddlers down stairs, eat at Lockets, loitered at Wills; they talked of the drawing-room and never came there; dined with lords they never saw; whispered a duchess, and spoke never a word; exposed the scrawls of their laundresses for billets-doux of quality; came ever just from court and were never seen in it; attended the Levee *sub dio*; got a list of the peers by heart in one company, and with great familiarity retailed them in another.

Their quarrels about their father's will concerning the clothes they should wear parallel the division between the churches' interpretation of the scriptures. The way Swift introduces this provides an example of how his satire also has a charming and attractive fancy. It was a well-known conceit that the make-up of the universe (the 'macrocosm') was mirrored in the composition of man (the 'microcosm'): the body politic is reflected in the human body; the king is the head of state; the head is the king of the body and so on. Swift takes up the metaphoric quality of this by imagining the world and the body in terms of dress.

Look on this globe of earth, you will find it to be a very complete and fashionable *dress*. What is that which some call *land*, but a fine coat faced with green? or the sea, but a waistcoat of water-tabby?[14] Proceed to the particular works of the creation, you will find how curious *Journeyman* Nature hath been, to trim up the *vegetable* beaux; observe how sparkish a periwig adorns the head of a *beech*, and what a fine doublet of white satin is worn by the *birch*. To conclude from all, what is man himself but a *micro-coat*, or rather a complete suit of clothes with all its trimmings?

In the course of the fable, Swift scores some lampooning hits. Jack's enthusiasm for self-abasement and mortification of his flesh comes over comically in the dignified entreaties which end in Anglo–Saxon bluntness and slap-stick situation. 'He would stand in the turning of a street, and calling to those who passed by, would cry to one, "Worthy sir, do me the honour of a good slap in the chaps." To another, "Honest friend, pray favour me with a handsome kick on the arse."'

Swift asserted that he was thus satirising extremism rather than the *via media* of the moderate Anglican church. Certainly he memorably united the ceremonious garments of Catholicism with the threadbare hair shirt of Non-conformism, for 'it is the nature of rags to bear a kind of mock resemblance to finery, there being a sort of fluttering appearance in both which is not to be distinguished at a distance, in the dark, or by short-sighted eyes.' But his criticism did not seem to stop there.

The title '*A Tale of a Tub*' contained a multiple pun which played on the idea of a pulpit as a tub and the notion of a trivial story. Not only did church history lose respect but also human morality appeared suspect. A wonderfully apt series of metaphors relating dress to character follows the passage quoted earlier, including the question that '[is not] conscience a *pair of breeches* which, though a cover for lewdness as well as nastiness, is easily slipped down for the service of both?' Human nature appears as basic appetite: sexual and digestive, unsanitised by abstractions, in the rapid and telling image of 'easily slipped down'. Similar and more extended passages occur elsewhere in the book, for example, with the description of the Æolists whose 'inspiration' is a matter of drawing in and expelling wind. (This is another case of metaphor stretched to cover a surprising application. The literal meaning of 'inspiration' is that of '[divine] breathing in [to the soul]'. However the association with burping and farting expunges the spiritual application.) Enough has been said here to show how the 'method' of the satire is one in which human individuals appear increasingly ignoble while also standing for 'god-given' church institutions. Churchmen, such as Wotton, already wounded by *The Battle of the Books*, were quick to pounce on the author's impropriety and turn it to impiety. (At the time, Swift's hand in writing *A Tale of a Tub* he did not know.) 'God and religion, truth and moral honesty, learning and industry are made a May-game, and the most serious things in the world are described as so many several scenes in a *Tale of a Tub*.' Swift could be seen to be attacking the divine ordination of the institution of the church rather than its manifestation as communities of Christians. Wotton wrote that he 'strikes at the very root . . . 'tis all with him a farce'. His ironies were misread as plain statements of scepticism and showed 'at the bottom his contemtible opinion of everything which is called Christianity'. And his indecency encouraged the disapproving, averted eye. Wotton argued he would show little regard for his reader 'if I should barely repeat after [the author] what is there'. And such an eye was also able to blink at the greater immorality of 'drunkenness, fornication, adultery, neglect of cures, pluralism, diversion of funds, excessive procuration and visitation fees, non-residence, illegal use of the bishop's seal, and simony' which Swift encountered in the actual church of Kilroot.

The fecundity of *A Tale of a Tub* does not stop with the account so far given. It begins with advertisements, an apology, two dedications, a bookseller's comment on the text, a preface and an introduction, and then five digressions interrupt the fable of the brothers in which are heard a number of voices congratulating themselves on their modernity and verging on madness. This reproduces the babble of contemporary learning, reliant on print for its fame, and enacts the competitiveness and disorder of the Moderns satirised in *The Battle of the Books.* Also it glances at John Dryden, the great satiric poet, translator and dramatist of the latter half of the seventeenth century. He eased his poetry into the world with self-defending prefaces. (An extended example of *A Tale of a Tub* is discussed in the final section of this book.)

Although Swift published these two works anonymously, the tattling world of Grub Street[15] was soon assigning them to him but it also credited some of *A Tale of a Tub* to Thomas. In 1710 Swift suspected that 'this little Parson-cousin of mine' had encouraged the belief and advised his bookseller how to handle him. Angus Ross and David Woolley have concluded his part in the work was marginal. 'Ideas or "hints" Thomas may well have contributed. In the seven years before publication it appears that he did not even see the work.'[16] But the balance of fortunes had tipped once more and Swift was now in his element of letters and controversy and polite society. He felt restored to a high position with potential for success and could look down on Thomas as a 'little Parson-cousin'.

The wit and the ministers, 1700–1714

The pull of England

Four years intervene between the death of Temple and the celebrity of *A Tale of a Tub*. The prebend in the gift of the king did not materialise despite Swift's petition. On the 20 February 1700 he was presented as vicar of Laracor, a village near Trim, County Meath, 28 miles NNW of Dublin, and, on 22 October 1700, installed as prebend of St Patrick's Cathedral, Dublin. Jane Waring seems to have renewed contact, reopening the matter of marriage, but the only surviving letter of this correspondence is Swift's and it is plain and factual, answering point by point what seem to be her 'particulars wherein you desire satisfaction': that he felt her health and good spirits suffered in her present circumstances; that she had no rival in his thoughts and that their collected finances would force her to 'manage domestic affairs, with an income of less (perhaps) than three hundred pounds a year'. In the past, she had told Swift 'the doctors advised [her] against marriage, as what would certainly hazard [her] life.' The question now was would she break from demanding relatives, uncongenial to Swift, and 'grow in good humour on my approach' for

> I had ever an opinion that you had a great sweetness of nature and humour, and whatever appeared to the contrary, I looked upon it only as a thing put on as necessary before a lover: but I have since observed in abundance of your letters such marks of severe indifference, that I began to think it was hardly possible for one of my few good qualities to please you.

The relationship did not prosper and Varina eventually died unmarried.

Swift's attention was still being drawn to England. He worked on editing Temple's letters and the third volume of his *Miscellanea*. In April 1701 he paid a visit to England which was the first of a series that occurred between 1701 and 1714. During this one, Stella and her older female companion, Mrs Rebecca Dingley, crossed over to Dublin where they took up lodgings in Capel Street. (Temple had left her a lease of land in Morristown, County Wicklow, Ireland and five hundred pounds; Swift added fifty pounds per year. They continued to live with a number of servants in lodgings, which they changed as necessary in order to be near Swift.) In 1702, Swift was awarded a Doctor of Divinity by Trinity College, Dublin, and in 1704 *A Tale of a Tub* was published. While he was seven months in England, the Reverend William Tisdall paid court to Stella. In addition he injudiciously showed an uninhibited letter Swift had written to him, concerning Swift's rising star in the Whig party, to the Primate, Archbishop Marsh, former provost of Trinity College, Dublin. On both counts he lost favour with Swift. Nevertheless, Swift 'spoke with all the advantages you deserve' to Stella on Tisdall's behalf regarding the match, once he knew that Tisdall had sufficient money for himself and Stella to live on. He had done this, he said, despite his own feelings about Stella 'that if my fortunes and humour served me to think of that state, I should certainly, among all persons on earth, make your choice.' Stella alone appears to have been responsible for the refusal of Tisdall.

London life: the *Journal to Stella*

In 1706 Swift was commissioned by the Archbishop of Dublin, William King, to present the case at court in England for the Irish clergy to be exempted from 'the First Fruits', fees paid to the Crown. The Church of England had been given exemption and Swift would help to argue the case for equal treatment for the Church of Ireland. As leading writers had close links with politicians, Swift's own literary gifts recommended his advocacy. At the beginning of this task, in 1707, Swift sided with the Whigs, then in power, and so formed friendships with Addison and Steele. However, the political map was redrawn over the next few years and he was won over to the Tory cause in 1710 and, as a consequence, intimacy with Pope, Gay and Arbuthnot.

In May 1709, Swift returned to Ireland, having been led on by promises to exempt the Irish clergy from the First Fruits but early on he suspected they would prove to be empty. His following visit to England in September 1710 by contrast was rapidly successful with the new Tory administration. Robert Harley (later to become first Earl of Oxford)[17] had been made Chancellor of the Exchequer in the previous month and was anxious to secure the services of the anonymous but known author of *A Tale of a Tub*. Swift was persuaded to support the Tories and from 10 November 1710 to 7 June 1711, he helped to consolidate their position by his editing and contributions to the periodical, *The Examiner*. And he also helped to turn public opinion against the Duke of Marlborough, the Whig commander of the British allies, and so secure an end to the war with France by his pamphlet, *The Conduct of the Allies*, 1711. This is discussed in the following chapter.

From 1710–1713, Swift wrote regularly to Stella and Rebecca Dingley. His letters have been collected as the *Journal to Stella* – a lively and detailed record of London court and political life. His first letter showed that Ireland had become more attractive to him, perhaps through disenchantment with London's political intrigue under the Whig regime together with the pleasure in Dublin of his recipients' company whom he addressed as 'MD' (My dears). So, on 2 September 1710, he wrote: 'I neer went to Engd with so little desire in my Life.' And even when at ease in London, having successfully secured the exemption of the First Fruits, he imaginatively remembered his own parish glebe:

> O that we were at Laracor this fine day! the willows begin to peep, and the quicks to bud. My dream's out: I was a dreaming last night that I eat ripe cherries. And now they begin to catch the pikes, and will shortly the trouts, (pox on these ministers,) and I would fain know whether the floods were ever so high as to get over the holly bank or the river walk; if so, then all my pikes are gone; but I hope not. Why don't you ask Parvisol these things, sirrahs? And then my canal, and trouts, and whether the bottom be fine and clear?
>
> (19 March 1711)

His tone towards these intimate friends is bantering and dependent on shared experiences and understanding of each other. There are running jokes such as his pretended refusal over a number of letters to assist his very good friends, Archdeacon Walls and his prolific wife: 'No truly, I will not be godfather to Goody Walls this bout.' and when Stella misinforms him of a recent death he imitates a simple man's conversational flow of jumbled worldliness and piety:

> Did the Bishop of London [Henry Compton] die in Wexford? poor gentleman! did he drink the waters? were you at his burial? was it a great funeral? so far from his friends! But he was very old: we all shall follow. And yet it was pity, if God pleased. He was a good man; not very learned; I believe he died but poor. Did he leave any charity legacies? who held up his pall? was there a great

sight of clergy? do they design a tomb for him? are you sure it was the Bishop of London? because there is an elderly gentleman here that we give the same title to.

(24 August 1711)

Hoaxes were meat and drink to him and were a fashion in court circles known as 'bites'. Swift's bite of the poet and political plenipotentiary, Matthew Prior, dramatically unfolds as it takes place in the thick of many other happenings in the *Journal* because it is a daily record. On 25 August 1711, Swift begins to suspect that Prior is on some secret war-time mission: 'They say, 'tis certain that Prior has been in France ... In my opinion, some things stand very ticklish.' 27 August: 'I should be apt to think it may foretell a peace.' 29 August, it is clear that Prior has additional private information: 'My Lord-Treasurer began a health to my lord Privy-Seal; Prior punned, and said it was so privy, he knew not who it was; but I fancy they have fixed it all, and we shall know tomorrow.' Swift learns next day that the new lord Privy-Seal is the Bishop of Bristol, Dr Robinson, but also recognises he is being left out of party secrets and concocts a revenge: 31 August. 'I will make a printer of my own sit by me one day, and I will dictate to him a formal relation of Prior's journey, with several particulars, all pure invention.' 11 September: 'This morning the printer sent me an account of Prior's Journey; it makes a twopenny pamphlet ... 'tis a formal grave lie, from the beginning to the end ... when I came in Prior showed me the pamphlet, seemed to be angry, and said, here is our English liberty: I read some of it, and said I liked it mightily, and envied the rogue the thought; for, had it come into my head, I should have certainly done it myself.' 12 September: 'It will go rarely, I believe, and is a pure bite.'

In the course of writing the *Journal to Stella* Swift mentions his visits to Mrs Vanhomrigh and her daughter Hesther whom he nicknamed 'Vanessa'. Her entanglement with him and subsequent pursuit of him in 1714 to live at Cellbridge in Ireland is examined in Chapter 4.

Archbishop King and the First Fruits

Swift's mission of securing the exemption of payment of the First Fruits brought him into close and enduring contact with the Archbishop of Dublin, William King. Until the fall of the Tories at the accession of George I on 1 August 1714, Swift was a diligent correspondent with a man who turned out to be a scheming and ungenerous ally, in a position of power above him in the church but in need of Swift's superior position in the political world. Their interlocked histories shed light on the churchmanship of the day, particularly on the practical worldliness Swift had to adopt in order to secure his own position within the church hierarchy. In their attempts to influence affairs they were both aware of great political danger and the prevalence of intrigue. On the 12 June 1708, King wrote to Swift: 'we have been terrifyed with interception of Letters at the post office,' and they adopted an art of alluding to matters, rather than spelling them out, and a discreet expression of opinions, just in case their letters might be surreptitiously opened. For example, when recounting a delicate negotiation with the Whig Lord Treasurer, John, Lord Somers, Swift omitted King's address and identity in a letter which he put inside another to his fair weather friend, the Dean of St Patrick's Cathedral, John Stearne, writing 'Direct the inclosed, and deliver it to the greatest person in your neighbourhood.'

From the outset of the First Fruits campaign, Swift's endeavours were not regarded well by fellow clerics who were envious and ready to steal credit from him. He wrote to King, 10 October 1710, 'I have since wondred what Scruple a number of Bishops could have of empowering a Clergyman to do the Church and them a service, without any Prospect or Imagination of Interest for himself.' When Ormonde was created the new Lord Lieutenant, these bishops wished ingratiatingly to solicit him to present the case for exemption from the First Fruits. They persuaded King to delay further support of Swift, which he did, gracelessly and weakly, despite his knowing that Swift had already placed a memorial with Harley. By the time he received King's letter, Swift had been privately informed that the Queen had granted the remission and he replied, 'I did not value the slighting Manner of the Bishop of *Kildare's* Letter, barely desiring Mr. *Southwell* to call on me for the Papers, without any Thing further, as if I had been wholly insignificant.' Once he knew what Swift had achieved, King tried to retrieve his position by agreeing he had 'not been treated with due regard'. Swift's retort querying their displeasure showed how Ireland in the shape of his fellow bishops was becoming distasteful: 'I should think the people of *Ireland* might rather be pleased to see one of their own Country able to find some Credit at court.' Swift still felt able to claim being 'one of their own Country' but King's patronising comment, which assumed a superior understanding of the worldliness of men, continued a process of alienation: 'It is, with submission, the silliest query I ever found made by Dr. *Swift*,' he wrote. It is probable that a man of King's temperament was unsettled by Swift's propensity to raillery[18] as an unsafe characteristic and was only too pleased to score with a stuffy superiority.

King actually was playing a dishonourable game. He had recognised in 1711 that Ormonde was not vitally concerned about the First Fruits for 'his Grace is in no haste about it'. Nevertheless he sided with the bishops to give the Duke of Ormonde the credit for the remission when he helped them to frame an address presented to him in Dublin, while no mention was made of this in another address presented to the Queen, which Swift was likely to see. Swift made it plain that those in power knew the score and would explode any further attempt to diminish what he had done: 'it is a good Jest to hear my Lord Treasurer saying often, before a deal of Company, that it was I that got the Clergy of *Ireland* their First-Fruits; and, generally, with this Addition, that it was before the Duke of *Ormond* was declared Lord Lieutenant.'

It was natural to assume that some preferment might be the reward of his successful endeavour and Swift was encouraged by the delighted King to think so. On 16 November 1710, King promised that the 'good instruments' in the affair should not be forgotten. Almost a year later he returned to the subject with a trifling reward in the shape of wise advice: 'I promised to say something as to your own affairs . . . make use of the favour and interest you have at present; after a certain age, if a man be not in a station that may be a step to a better, he seldom goes higher.' Swift dryly remarked to his friend Charles Ford, 'He was afraid, I expected something from him' and replied to King, 'But, my Lord, to ask a Man floating at Sea, what he designed to do when he gets ashore, is too hasty a Question: Let him get there first, and rest, and dry himself, and then look about him.'

Swift, whose stock was high with the ministry, himself was solicited for preferring others. Sacheverell asked politely for a position in the Custom's house and King applied for the son of a friend. When the Primate, Archbishop Marsh, died, Swift had some revenge in not suggesting King for the Primacy and added his voice to recommending Lindsay, who wrote back gratefully, 'I find myself much obliged to you for kind offices done me to Ld Treasurer by using your endeavours to promote me to a Post wch my ambition could never aim at.'

Dean and Dublin, 1715–1745

Archbishop King and Dean Swift, 1713–1729

Just before the fall of his administration, Harley secured the deanery of St Patrick's Cathedral for Swift. Swift was installed on 13 June 1713 and as a member of the chapter, through his prebend, he had been well prepared for its peculiar responsibilities. It was a situation in which the privileges and interests of the chapter and of the Archbishop were almost designedly in conflict. By his recent preferment, Swift had gained some clerical autonomy but had lost his political base and his superior was to be William King until his death in 1729. For much of this time, Swift experienced in the church what Louis Landa has described as 'unabashed political manoeuvring'.[19] He soon found that King was busy in promoting his own favourites to counterbalance Swift's influence and that he could not do much for his own friends. (In fact the opposition went deeper than Swift knew. He did not know that King, when acting as Lord Justice, 9 May 1715, had sent some intercepted letters from Ormonde addressed to Swift to the Secretary of State, since he suspected they were treasonable.)

On 17 June 1716 he complained to King that 'those who are most in your confidence make it no manner of secret, that several clergymen have lost your Grace's favour by their civilities to me. I do not say any thing of this by way of complaint, which I look upon to be an office too mean for a man of spirit and integrity, but merely to know whether it be possible to be upon any better terms with your Grace, without which I shall be able to do very little good in the small station I am placed.' Without some say in preferments his own influence within the church as Dean was reduced.

Similarly he was thwarted when he sought improvements in the living of Laracor which would strengthen the position of the church. The example of the meanness of Kilroot argued the wisdom of providing adequately for the incumbents in perpetuity and Swift had hoped to buy land with church funds increased by his success at bringing about the remission of the payment of First Fruits. The opposition to his endeavours being acknowledged forcibly reminded him of the unfair dealing of the church hierarchy.

> I am purchasing a Glebe by the Help of the Trustees [for the First Fruits], for the Vicarage of *Laracor*; and I had Vanity enough to desire it might be expressed by a Clause in the Deeds, as one Consideration, that I had been instrumental in procuring the first Fruits, which was accordingly inserted; but, Hints were given it would not pass. The then Bishops of *Ossory* and *Killaloe* had, as I am told, a Sum of Money for their Labour in that Affair, who, upon my Arrival at *London* to negociate it, were one of them gone to *Bath*, and the other to *Ireland*: But it seemeth more reasonable to give Bishops Money for doing nothing, than a private Clergyman Thanks for succeeding where Bishops have failed.

King's bland reply to this affected worldly wisdom and sententious comfort: 'ingratitude is warranted by modern & ancient custom, & 'tis more honour for a man to have it asked why he had not a suitable return for his merits, than he was overpaid.' This extraordinary self-satisfied answer fails to consider what is the morality of the payers – which include King himself – who neglect their debt.

After 1724 relations with King were smoother, since he then approved of Swift's endeavours to free Ireland from English economic imperialism. But even in 1727 when King tried to institute a new procedure of appointing a proxy for the Dean during any absence,

Swift shot back with: 'I take my Chapter to be my proxy, if I want any: It is only through them that you visit me . . . from the very moment of the Queen's death, your Grace hath thought fit to take every opportunity of giving me all sorts of uneasiness, without ever giving me, in my whole life, one single mark of favour, beyond common civilities.' King dropped the procedure.

As a clergyman, through such things as the improvements he made to Laracor, Swift strikes us as always concerned for the worldly well-being of the church as a necessary condition for its spiritual health. In his fierce defence of the dean's Chapter he was ready to protect the lower clergy from the higher. Although he spent much time away from his clerical duties, during Harley's ministry, he ensured that good curates took care of his parishioners. As the dean of St Patrick's, Swift punctiliously supervised the preaching and the good order of the services. His practical Christianity also found expression in charitable works and governing a hospital. We shall look at his religious beliefs in the following chapters as they are expressed in his writings.

The genesis of *Gulliver's Travels*

In his mid-fifties Swift felt that as a force within the community he had lost impetus and relevance. He wrote in a poem of 1721:

> The changes which faction has made in the state,
> Have put the Dean's politics quite out of date:
> Now no one regards what he utters with freedom,
> And should he write pamphlets, no great man would read 'em.

As if to reinforce this mood of depression, his friend Bishop Atterbury was impeached by the Whigs as a Jacobite[20] in 1722, his unhappy friend, Vanessa, died in 1723 and he finally fell out with the Temple family, which had contested in 1709 his accuracy in editing Temple's *Miscellanea* and then in 1729 took exception to his high-handed recommendation of a clergyman to occupy a room they owned in Trinity College, Dublin.

But the poem was wrong. In fact the work which made him celebrated in Ireland as the 'Hibernian Patriot' was yet to come. This was his successful series of pamphlets known as *The Drapier's Letters*, which were printed in 1724–1725 to resist the licence given to an ironmaster in England, William Wood, to coin copper money ('Wood's halfpence') in such quantities that according to Swift he would make an extravagant profit and the Irish currency would be debased. In addition, reflection on the experiences of his life and the need to make a significant statement in the context of the seemingly never-ending regime of the Lord Treasurer, Sir Robert Walpole (1714–1717 and 1721–1741), brought together many events imaginatively transformed in one famous work: his travels, the political power games in London, the contemporary literary and scientific dissensions, the Anglo–Irish experience in Ireland and the condition of the Gaelic Irish. This was, of course, *Gulliver's Travels*, which was published in 1726 but was in draft even at the time of the poem, when he was also reading travelogues avidly.

Choice friends

As he had done with his letters to Archbishop King, Swift used the same caution with the authorities in covering his tracks as the author of *Gulliver's Travels*, by moving the MS from place to place. His visit to England in March 1726 was partly to see it through the press but he also wanted to see Walpole in order 'to represent the affairs of *Ireland* to him in a true light, not only without any view to myself, but to any party whatsoever: and because I understood the affairs of the kingdom tolerably well, and observed the representations he had received were such as I could not agree to, my principal design was to set him right, not only for the service of *Ireland*, but likewise of *England*, and of his own administration.' Despite the good offices of the Earl of Peterborough he was not given an audience and England was even more of a foreign country to him. He wrote to his delightful companion, Thomas Sheridan, on the 8 July 1726: 'This is the first time I was ever weary of *England*, and longed to be in *Ireland*, but it is because go I must; for I do not love *Ireland* better, nor *England* as *England*, worse; in short, you all live in a dirty Dog-hole and Prison, but it is a Place good enough to die in.' The pull of both countries appears to be equal but Swift was resigned to the circumstances which age now imposed on him. In the same letter he referred to having received 'the fairest Offer . . . of a Settlement[21] here that one could imagine, which if I were ten Years younger I would gladly accept, within twelve Miles of *London*, and in the midst of my Friends. But I am too old for new Schemes, and especially such as would bridle me in my Freedoms and Liberalities.'

These friends meant a great deal to Swift and they readily and delightedly helped in finding a publisher for *Gulliver's Travels* and subsequently shared in the enjoyment of many at its success and imitations. To leave them was painful and he departed from his great friend, Alexander Pope, with the words 'I will endeavour to think of you as little as I can.' Unlike Gulliver who was prepared to view the deaths of friends as a succession of pinks or tulips, Gulliver's creator was unable and unwilling to do so. Rather, he would insulate himself from such matters. But at his age to witness the deaths of friends was also a condition of his life and his dear Stella died in 1728 and Dr Arbuthnot in 1734, after 22 years of intimate friendship. Swift imagined with wit, humour and some acerbity his own demise in

Verses on the Death of Dr Swift, 1731. In 1734 deafness from Ménière's disease ended all hopes of visiting England and again he met the unwelcome fact with a poem: *On his deafness*. Repeatedly (1726, 1727, 1739–1741) Ireland was hit by famine with one-fifth of the population dying in the last. *A Modest Proposal* (1729) was written as a savage counterblast to Anglo–Irish incompetence in addressing the famished misery of the Irish peasants. Nevertheless Swift was attended by good Irish friends and his own decline, wretched in itself, at least withdrew him from these horrors. In 1742 senility had gained such a hold that he was declared of unsound mind and memory. On 19 October 1745 he died.

The facts of his last years and death became almost immediately obscured by inventions, circulated by those who wished to damage his reputation and find some sort of retribution implicit in supposing him turned mad, bestial and exhibited by his servants for money. The success of these fictions and of other unfounded slurs on his conduct accounts for much of the repulsion felt by Samuel Johnson who was otherwise fascinated by the man and throughout his life revolved in his mind the case of Swift and his writings. For Johnson, an arbiter of taste in the later part of the eighteenth century, Swift was an example of the vanity of human wishes: a man unable to think he was only a man, who suffered a terrible fate.

And Swift expires a driveller and a show.

In pointing his moral tale with this example, Johnson demonstrated a sense of the greatness of Swift in order to represent his fall and also his power to disturb in his attempt to distance him. While some of the motives for distancing Swift related to the personal side of Johnson, much else concerned a change of social attitudes which had already begun in Swift's day and he, himself, experienced in his associations with younger intellects. Swift's older sensibility challenged eighteenth-century confidence and continues to question descendants of the Enlightenment.

Notes

1   Joseph McMinn, *Jonathan's Travels / Swift and Ireland*, Appletree Press, 1994 drawing on Harold Williams, *The Correspondence of Jonathan Swift*, v, pp. 273–4, OUP, 1965.
2   Robert Harley, Earl of Oxford. See Chapter 2.
3   See for example R.F. Foster, *Modern Ireland 1600–1972*, Penguin, 1989. Chapters 5 to 8 conveniently cover the period from Cromwell to the death of Swift. Norman Vance, *Irish Literature: A Social History*, Blackwell, 1990, p. 25, discusses the confusion of terms ('Anglo–Irish', 'old Irish', 'mixed Irish', 'old English' etc.) as a matter of the political perspective of the historian using the term.

4 This account signally leaves out the Gaelic Irish and subsequent histories have lamented the loss of the Gaelic bardic tradition and old Brehon law but, in the case of literature, Norman Vance has noted of Ireland in the sixteenth-century: 'It can be argued that the old bardic tradition was actually aesthetically moribund and that the incursion of the "new foreigners" and the collapse of traditional, aristocratic Gaelic society in a sense revitalized and eventually democratized Irish letters in Irish and in English.' Vance, *op. cit.*, p. 33 and p. 37.

5 Irvin Ehrenpreis, *Swift, the Man, his Works and the Age*, 3 vols, Oxford, 1962–1983.

6 Quoted in David Nokes, *Jonathan Swift, A Hypocrite Reversed*, OUP, 1985.

7 'Sinecures' meaning without the responsibility for the cure of souls which would require attendance within a parish as a vicar. Often prebends had very few duties. They had become a way of financing a member of a cathedral chapter.

8 Abraham Cowley, metaphysical poet (1618–1667). For most of his life Swift kept a copy of his works in his library.

9 i.e. 'a weakness for something'.

10 Louis Landa, *Swift and the Church of Ireland*, Oxford, 1954, p. 13.

11 An example of this mannered love debate may be found in John Lyly's *Euphues: the Anatomy of Wit* (1579).

12 'Proselyte', i.e. 'convert'. Swift uses the same imagery 35 years on in a letter to Gay: 'my invention & judgement are perpetually at fisty cuffs'.

13 i.e. venereal disease.

14 i.e. watered silk.

15 Grub Street was where many journalists and hack writers lived and has come to stand for them. It was located near the hospital for the insane, the Bedlam (from 'Bethlehem'), and near Moorfields, London, a low-lying area twice daily flooded by the tidal Thames.

16 Angus Ross and David Woolley (eds), *Jonathan Swift/ A Tale of a Tub and Other Works*, OUP, World's Classics, 1986, p. 198. Appendix B, pp. 192–203, covers the whole matter in this excellent edition.

17 Swift literature calls him either 'Harley' or 'Oxford'. He was created Earl on 23 May 1711 – see the short biography.

18 In earlier times Swift had taken a light tone and dared to twit King for his over-working. On 10 April 1711 he wrote 'And, I can venture to railly with your Grace, although I could not do it with many of your Clergy.'

19 Landa, *op. cit.*, p. 90.

20 Supporter of the Stuart monarchy whose descendants derived their claim to the English Crown through James II. The Latin for James is 'Jacobus'.

21 Williams is unable to identify what this was but supposes that it came from a private patron.

2   Politics and the individual

Church and monarch

In the year *Gulliver's Travels* was published, Swift exclaimed in a letter: 'I am weary of being among Ministers whom I cannot govern, who are all Rank Toryes in Government, and worse than Whigs in Church: whereas I was the first Man who taught and practiced the direct contrary Principle' (Swift to Thomas Tickell, 2 July 1726). It is a useful pointer to what lies behind the political allegory of the *Travels* and to his view of the nature of party animosities and the part he played in them during the reign of Queen Anne.

Swift believed he occupied a central role by 'governing' the ministers of state and that his political thinking was in the vanguard. Party labels, he felt, did not securely identify policy, for a person could be a Tory in one sphere and a Whig in another. And the issues that set controversy afire concerned the nature of government and of the church. We saw earlier that the concern for the 'church' revolved round the power of the 'Church of England'. Similarly the concern for 'government' revolved round the power of the English monarch. In fact both were intertwined so that the cry of 'the church in danger' which once roused Londoners to riot could be simultaneously interpreted as 'treason to the king/queen'.

Experience of the monarchy under the Restoration showed its allegiance to the Catholic cause, pushed to an extreme, threatened the power of aristocrats and squires, in the government of Great Britain and Ireland, and the treaties with other countries they supported, in order to secure peace at home and advance commercial interests abroad. The situation on the continent of Europe was one of contending powers, in which Britain tried to play off one against another, while reaping rewards for herself. But increasingly this foreign policy was manipulated by the monarchy for its own ends. The third Anglo–Dutch war had been provoked by Charles II, as the result of a secret treaty with Louis XIV in which he paid Charles a subsidy, which would enable him to act without the need for Parliament to vote him money, while Louis was able to annexe more land in Europe. James II, himself a Roman Catholic, continued more blatantly the policy of his elder brother, Charles II: a policy of winning favour for Catholics at home and acting where possible in concert with Catholic France. It had culminated in a Declaration of Indulgence (1687) which under the guise of all-round toleration restored to Catholics full liberty of worship and suspended the tests for public office. At the same time, James II dissolved Parliament to avoid opposition and, in response to that, leading public men, mainly Whig aristocrats, invited William of Orange to intervene and eventually to assume the British throne. Although William had fought against England as leader of the United Provinces in the Anglo–Dutch wars, he was nonetheless a Protestant and more acceptable than a Catholic.

This invitation was a major step towards asserting the power of the wealthy in relation to the monarchy. But it still observed the test of legitimacy to the throne through genealogical descent. William's claim on the throne (given the deposition[1] of James II) was through his marriage to Mary (Queen Mary II) who was the daughter of James II by his first wife. Queen Anne who succeeded them both was her younger sister. However, James II had a son by his second marriage, James Edward, who became known after the revolution of 1688 as the 'Old Pretender'. (The term 'pretender' was used in the sense of 'someone who lays a claim', in this case, to the British throne. He was called 'old' in order to distinguish him from a later claimant, Charles Edward Stuart, 'Bonnie Prince Charlie' or the 'Young Pretender'.) He took refuge in the France of Louis XIV and was to become a threat to the Protestant succession, when Queen Anne died in 1714, leaving no issue. Tragically for her, none of her children survived to adulthood. He kept alive the 'Jacobite' cause within the kingdom and abroad to restore a Roman Catholic Stuart. However, yet another invitation by the Whigs to take the British throne was made to a foreigner, the Elector of Hanover, who became George I. His claim had been established against 50 other possible claimants through the Act of Settlement (1701) which declared in favour of a granddaughter of King James I of Britain, the Elector's mother, Sophia, who died in 1714 only months before Queen Anne.

This set the scene for the development through the eighteenth century of a constitutional monarchy in which the throne gradually lost a struggle for power with Parliament. But already in Swift's political heyday, at the turn of the century, there was no possibility of a monarch ruling with absolute authority.

It was far otherwise in France, under Louis XIV, who reigned for an astonishing 72 years and vigorously established a centralised government, great military power and a society in which the arts and sciences flourished in an increasingly intolerant but distinctively French Roman Catholicism. Much of British foreign policy when Swift felt he was 'governing' ministers was directed at preventing, through a number of war alliances, Louis's extraordinary expansion of the boundaries of France to become the dominant power in

Europe. Swift's *Examiner* and *The Conduct of the Allies*, among other political writings, commented directly on this at the time and *Gulliver's Travels* looks back on the situation.

The War of the League of Augsburg (1689–97) grew out of a defensive league against France between Austria, Sweden, Spain and some principalities of Germany. Louis invaded the German states and also supported James II's attempt to regain his throne at the Battle of the Boyne (1690). This brought William III into the war as leader of a coalition against France. It ended with Louis ceding almost all his gains since the third Anglo–Dutch war. However, he had a more important prize in mind. Both he and Leopold of Austria had a relation (respectively a grandson and a younger son) with an equally valid claim to the throne of Spain, vacant since the death of King Charles II of Spain in 1700. These were known as the Bourbon candidate, Philip of Anjou, and the Habsburg candidate, Archduke Charles. King Charles II of Spain left the throne in his will to the Bourbon and, although Louis was prepared to partition Spain between both candidates, the Spanish and the Austrians were not. Naturally Louis was not prepared to lose all and so he declared in favour of his grandson. Although France's main enemy was Austria and William III had been prepared to uphold the will, Louis occupied fortresses in the Spanish Netherlands held by the Dutch against French expansion. William then joined the League of Augsburg making it into a Grand Alliance against Louis. The War of the Spanish Succession (1702–14) ensued, making the fortune of the successful English general, John Churchill, Duke of Marlborough, who in turn became the target of Swift's Tory satire and a focus for his onslaught on the whole war effort. This may seem surprising since only a few years before, when applying for the exemption of the First Fruits, Swift had sided with the Whigs, who held the positions of power. However, it is less so when a closer look is taken at the terms 'Whig' and 'Tory'.

Political parties and issue groups

The division of members of Parliament into groupings of 'Whig' and 'Tory' is often applied to the period of Queen Anne with the advantage of hindsight. It applies retrospectively a view of politics deriving from what occurred later in the eighteenth century. The so-called 'Whig Supremacy' from 1714–60 was largely achieved through the Whigs being identified as aristocratic supporters of the evolving constitutional monarchy, which brought over the Elector of Hanover, and as upholders of toleration of Non-conformity, which was frequently the religion of the commercial classes. The Tories were blackened as High Church, squirearchical and probably Jacobite.

This was a gross simplification but effective propaganda which enabled Whig rule for such a long period.[2] Even so it has sufficient truth to act as a focus to help us distinguish the more scattered rays of political light which preceded 1714.

Events, of which the accession of George I was one of the most crucial in developing party standpoints, and not manifestos and constitutional debates altered the direction of individual party loyalties. While we are familiar with later party leaders such as Peel, Disraeli and Blair bringing about change through manifestos discussed via well-developed party machinery, the fluctuations which made Swift and his patron Robert Harley (later known as the 1st Earl of Oxford, or 'Oxford' for short) first Whigs and then Tories did not arise in the same way. Issues encouraged groupings which dissolved and formed into new alliances as other issues became dominant.

Swift, a firm Church of England cleric, identified Toryism as the best protector of his church against Roman Catholicism and against Non-conformity but was little enchanted by any of the British monarchs who reigned after the Revolution. As he said in the letter quoted at the head of this chapter, he 'taught and practiced the . . . Principle' which was: to be a Whig in government and a Tory in church. However, his initial attempt to secure the remission of First Fruits was to pay court to the Whig lords who were in power and it was natural to secure their services by identifying with their ranks.

There was no prime minister as we understand the term today. A number of ministerial positions gave individuals the power to influence policy: Lord Treasurer, Secretaries of State (South and North), Lord President, Lord High Admiral, Lord Keeper of the Seal and Lord Privy Seal. Especially in the matter of the First Fruits the Lord Lieutenant of Ireland had great importance. The chart on pages 20–23 identifies who held these positions during the reign of Queen Anne and even so brief a span of years shows the movement of individuals jockeying for different positions in order to gain an ascendancy. During Swift's 'Whig period' a group of aristocrats known as the 'Junto' had great influence. These were: Wharton, Sunderland, Somers, Orford and Halifax, the first four of whom held one of these positions. Behind these men stood a group of powerful managers, a 'triumvir' of Godolphin, Harley and Marlborough. Marlborough was the only one of these without ministerial appointment but he was captain–general of the army, his wife was confidante of the queen and Godolphin and Sunderland were his sons-in-law.

The party system was therefore in a very early stage of development and individual personality counted for more than loyalty to a political platform. What William Temple had written was still true and was equally held by Swift as his former secretary and literary executor. '[We] are apt to ascribe the actions and councils of princes to interests and reasons of state, yet whoever can trace them to their true spring, will often be forced to derive them from the same passions and personal dispositions which govern the affairs of private lives.' And 'all great actions in the world, and revolutions of states may be truly derived, from the genius of the persons, that conduct and govern them.'

The Whigs failed Swift over the First Fruits but at the same time they were sowing the seeds of their own downfall. Their fears of the growing power of Harley led a number of them to attempt to implicate him in the trial of one of his underlings, William Greg, for being a French spy. Under pressure, especially from the Duke of Somerset and Marlborough, the queen dismissed him in 1708. However, two years later, Godolphin and the Junto put on trial a High Church priest, Dr Sacheverell, for preaching against the toleration of dissenters. The trial provoked riots in London: a well-directed campaign of destruction of Non-conformist meeting houses and dwellings, where the rioters had a free rein until they ran out of energy. One reported he 'was so tyred with what he had done before that he could not meddle with nothing but was forced to content himself with being a looker on; but he hollowed and laught with them, for there was such havock, he never saw such pastime in his life.' In London, there were cries of 'High Church and Sacheverell. God damn you, are you for the Doctor? Save the Queen's white neck' and later the spectacle of a High Church Anglican 'black-gowned bodyguard, a hundred or more strong' accompanying Sacheverell each time he went to court, while in some churches prayers were said for blessings on him, four Sundays in a row. These disturbances created a climate in which the pious and strict Anglican queen could act against Godolphin.

In the meantime, Harley had been working behind the scenes to form an opposition group and now he was appointed Chancellor of the Exchequer. Since he was not yet a peer, he could not be Lord Treasurer but in effect he controlled this position and his colleague Henry St John was appointed Secretary of State. Harley became the most powerful Tory minister from 1710–1714 and, although he had attended a Non-conformist academy and might therefore be seen as a natural Whig, he used his Tory group as the best defence for Queen Anne against Whig monied interests and Tory Jacobite extremists and was a truly moderating influence. He was extremely reluctant to oust all Whigs from power and held back root-and-branch Tories. In fact, Harley, like Swift, used the term 'Tory' as a convenient label for groupings and regroupings which he managed in order to achieve the objectives that arose in daily government.

Such management required unusual dexterity, for the political situation was turbulent and much depended on personal relationships out of which grew affectionate friendships and also self-seeking betrayals. There was no bureaucratic machine to circulate papers, arrange committees and draft proposals for further consideration. This gave an immediacy to the intimate discussions and led directly to the formulation and execution of policy. And this was in the context of the frequent alarms of the war with France and the prospect of general elections every three years. Since the passing of the Triennial Act of 1694 (which required an election at least every three years) and up to 1715 there were ten elections. In addition, the religious ferment encouraged a network of spies and informers. We have already seen that Archbishop King himself covertly reported Swift to the authorities in 1715 for possible sedition and yet a year before he appeared to be an ally, confiding to him with relish about hounding out a Presbyterian minister, William Boyse, 'yet I followed him so close, that I forced him out of his living. After this, we burned Mr. *Boyse's* book.' These precarious and disturbing situations energise the satire of *Gulliver's Travels* where Swift reflects on the stuff of politics under Queen Anne and King George I. For example, in the following passage the topics that could be guaranteed to capture the attention of politicians of the day come to life in Swift's language, carefully chosen to symbolise their unsavoury and contemptible side: plots, coded messages, trumped up accusations, stinking and foolish government, false alarms of invasion, the devastation of keeping a standing army, the greed of preying ministers, the stupidity of weak monarchs, popery, jacobitism, bribery and corruption. In Laputa:

> It is first agreed and setled among them what suspected Persons shall be accused of a Plot: then effectual Care is taken to secure all their Letters and papers, and put the Criminals in Chains. These Papers are delivered to a Set of Artists very dextrous in finding out the mysterious meanings of Words, Syllables, and Letters. For Instance, they can discover a Close-stool[3] to signify a Privy Council, a Flock of Geese a Senate, a lame Dog an Invader, a Codshead a king, the Plague a standing Army, a Buzzard a Prime Minister, the Gout a High Priest, a Gibbet a Secretary of State, a Chamberpot a Committee of Grandees, a Sieve a Court Lady, a Broom a Revolution, a Mousetrap an Employment, a bottomless Pit the Treasury, a Sink the Court, a Cap and Bells a Favourite, a broken Reed a Court of Justice, an empty Tun a General, a running Sore the Administration.

Swift's change of direction

Swift was easily plucked from the do-nothing Whigs by Harley's kindness. Harley knew of Swift's authorship of *A Tale of a Tub* and probably guessed his authorship of a squib on Godolphin, *The Virtues of Sid Hamnet the Magician's Rod,* and used all his courtesy to win over the disappointed vicar by introducing him into his family. Swift, recognising that *A Tale* had helped him to this meeting, wrote with evident pleasure about it in his *Journal* (7 October 1710): 'we sat two hours, drinking as good wine as you do, and two hours more he and I alone; where he heard me tell my business: entered into it with all kindness; asked for my powers, and read them; and read likewise a memorial I had drawn up, and put it in his pocket to show the Queen.' Although he never did introduce Swift to the queen he quickly achieved for him the remission of the payment by the Church of Ireland of First Fruits and continued to treat Swift as an intimate friend. Frequently Swift dined with him and others of his persuasion, apparently all of them giving him great licence to say and do as he wished. He became at times so confident of his position that, for example, on 8 October 1711 Swift wrote in his *Journal* about Sir John Walters who had taken exception to him on a number of occasions. On one of these Swift had given half-hearted praise to a bottle of wine and Walters expostulated 'that I abused the Queen's meat and drink'. Later, his amused friends supported him against Walters. Harley threatened Walters that he would send Swift to dine with him and 'Lord-Keeper bid him take care what he did; for, said he, Dr. Swift is not only all our favourite, but our governor.' Clearly in showing such favour Harley felt that Swift would make an important contribution to his political success.

While it may seem that mere opportunism motivated both men in Swift's changing from Whig to Tory – the achievement of remitting the First Fruits in exchange for government service – it was not a cynical move. To one onlooker it did not seem a move at all. Archbishop King, anxiously watching from Ireland for the success of his vicar's mission, asked Swift (10 February 1709) 'But pray by what artifice did you contrive to pass for a Whig?' From such a distance the nuances of party attitudes were not so easy to spot and the Whig prelate's politics narrowed down to keeping out the Pretender and holding at bay the largely Roman Catholic community surrounding Dublin. It shows the difficulty of definition that before Swift's recruitment by Harley, King considered him more of a Tory. Some of this was due to Swift's apolitical nature. Writing in *A Discourse of the Contests and Dissensions . . . in Athens and Rome,* (1701), he said, 'But there is one circumstance with relation to parties, which I take to be of all others most pernicious in a state . . . because Clodius and Curio happen to agree with me in a few singular notions, I must therefore blindly follow them in all . . . I conceive it far below the dignity both of human nature and human reason, to be engaged in any party, the most plausible soever, upon such servile conditions.' He complained to Temple's son, in 1706, 'But Whig and Tory has spoild all that was tolerable here, by mixing with private Friendship and Conversation, and ruining both.' Partisanship undermined friendship and debased intelligent political conduct.

Swift's definitions of party

In 1708 when the circumstances of Harley's implication with Greg were investigated (setting in motion events that would bring Swift into a Tory camp), Swift wrote to King, 'I never in my life saw or heard such divisions and complications of parties as there have been for some time; you sometimes see the extremes of Whig and Tory driving on the same thing. I have heard the chief of Whigs blamed by their own party for want of moderation, and I know a Whig Lord in good employment who voted with the highest Tories against the Court, and the Ministry, with whom he is nearly allied.' Soon after he published anonymously a supposed letter from a member of the House of Commons supporting the sacramental test – that candidates for public office should prove conformity to the Church of England by taking the sacrament. He argued that the greatest threat to the established church was from Non-conformists rather than Papists. King recognised his hand in this and considered this to be a Tory sentiment, since most of the Whigs were dissenters and the Tories leaned towards High Church Anglicanism, which was closer to Roman Catholicism. It is what provoked his wonder at Swift's 'passing for a Whig'.

By standing still it was possible to change sides. Writing to the Earl of Peterborough in 1711, Swift commented 'your Lordship knows that the names of Whig and Tory have quite altered their meanings'. And the Irish dimension introduced a further differentiation: 'I ought to let you know, that the Thing we called a Whig in England is a creature altogether different from those of the same denomination here, at least it was so during the reign of Her late Majesty.' (Swift, writing from Dublin, to Alexander Pope, 10 January 1721.) So, as far as Swift was concerned, the terms were slippery and he was usually careful to qualify them when applying them to himself. They had the advantage of giving him scope when dealing with correspondents who might not be wholly trusted. He told King he 'was always a Whig in Politicks' (22 December 1716) and the Countess of Suffolk 'I am a good Whig by thinking it sufficient to be a good subject, with little personal esteem for Princes, further than as their virtues deserve; and upon that score, had a most particul^r respect for the Queen Your Mistress' (27 July 1731).[4]

In such circumstances it is wiser to look at individual policies that Swift supported than to rely on labels. His letter to Pope just quoted tells us a great deal. While it may be open to the charge of rewriting history or of faulty memory, both of which accusations have been laid at his door in other cases, it looks like very good evidence of his actual opinions a decade earlier. The letter is a lengthy statement of how Swift regarded the part he played under Queen Anne. Although addressed to Pope it may not have been sent to him since when it was published by Pope in 1741, having not been included in his edition of their letters of 1740, Pope explained he 'never received' it before. But the fact that Swift wrote it in 1721 with his trusted friend in mind and ensured its publication 20 years later argues that it contained his carefully considered position.

Swift wrote about the monarchy that 'I always declared my self against a Popish Successor to the Crown, whatever Title he might have by the proximity of blood.' He believed in the right of the people to displace the monarch if this reduced their grievances, for 'the publick good will justify such Revolution; and this I took to have been the Case in the Prince of Orange's expedition, although in the consequences it produced some very bad effects, which are likely to stick long enough by us'. Believing that private pockets could easily be lined from the public purse, 'I had likewise a mortal antipathy against Standing Armies in times of Peace.' And he saw as destructive of the common good a party division, in which a rising merchant class seemed at odds with a landed community: 'I ever abominated that scheme of politicks, (now about thirty years old) of setting up a mony'd Interest in opposition to the landed.'

These sentiments are echoed in the political tracts he wrote for Harley and also find expression in *Gulliver's Travels*. For example, there is the thoroughly admirable Lord Munodi (who appears in the Voyage to Laputa), whom sponging party officials despise and ridicule for his estates: 'a most beautiful Country; Farmers Houses at small distances, neatly built, the Fields enclosed, containing Vineyards, Corngrounds and Meadows'. And later, another character, hearing about the extravagances of trading in necessities, observes 'That must needs be a miserable Country which cannot furnish Food for its own Inhabitants.'

Some of the other statements that Swift makes in the letter to Pope may owe their sharpness to the repressions of the political regime in 1721, when a recent act (the Septennial Act) allowed seven years to pass between general elections. 'As to Parliaments, I adored the wisdom of that Gothic Institution, which made them Annual: and I was confident our Liberty could never be placed upon a firm foundation till that ancient law were restored among us.' This was also a time when the act of Habeas Corpus[5] had been suspended, so that political prisoners could be imprisoned indefinitely and friends could not require that they should be brought to trial with proper legal representation. Swift attacked the casual cruelty and inhumanity of this. 'So in a plot-discovering age, I have known an innocent man seized and imprisoned, and forced to lie several months in chains, while the Ministers were not at leisure to hear his petition, till they had prosecuted and hanged the number they proposed.' Although these have a particular reference to this later period, there is no reason to contest that Swift held these beliefs in the reign of Queen Anne. This is reinforced by his distinguishing all he says of the past from what he may believe now. He shows a canniness, born of the possibility that the letter might be read by an informer, which encourages us to feel that the letter is as far as circumstances permit a true statement of his position. He warns Pope that his views in 1721 may have developed and that he certainly has no wish to wear them on his sleeve as he once did: 'what they are at present, is of little importance either to [the world] or my self; neither can I truly say I have any at all, or if I had, I dare not venture to publish them: For however orthodox they may be while I am now writing, they may become criminal enough to bring me into trouble before midsummer.' The consequence of this is that in this later period, which includes *Gulliver's Travels*, he writes a more elusive satire than the work he did for Harley.

Harley's patronage

Harley recruited Swift for his talents as a political writer and very soon the relationship became one of mutual affection. Various biographers have commented that for Swift he was a substitute father figure and evidence of this is shown in the frantic concern Swift showed when an attempt was made on Harley's life soon after he assumed power in the Treasury. His letter to King (8 March 1711) matches closely the account he wrote (with 'my heart ... almost broken') in his *Journal*, an indication of how unguarded his distress had made him. 'I write to your Grace under the greatest Disturbance of Mind for the Publick and Myself. A Gentleman came in where I dined this Afternoon and told us Mr. *Harley* was stabbed, and some confused Particulars. I immediately ran to Secretary *St. John's* hard by.' Unable to get more information from there he went in hot pursuit of news and eventually discovered that a Frenchman, the Marquis de Guiscard, had 'stabbed him just under the Breast, a little to the Right side; but, it pleased God, that the Point stopped at one of the Ribs, and broke short half an Inch'. For a few pages he pours out minute detail and then excuses himself since Harley 'hath always treated me with the Tenderness of a Parent, and never refused me any Favour I asked for a Friend.' Harley survived, was celebrated as an English hero and created First Earl of Oxford in May by the queen. And a surprising twist to the history allowed Swift to relive something like the incident in the role of protector rather than helpless onlooker, after-the-event. In November 1712 another attempt was made on Harley's life in the 'Bandbox Plot'. But Swift, seeing a glint of iron through the wrapper, took the parcel his patron had been about to open and discovered inside two primed pistols, set to go off when the lid of the box was opened. He cut the strings which had been set up to trip the triggers and all was well. Swift was delighted to have such an opportunity for demonstrating his care. And his enchantment with Harley encouraged him to identify himself in the older man. To Stella he confided (5 September 1711): 'Did I ever tell you that Lord-Treasurer hears ill with the left ear, just as I do? He always turns to the right; and his servants whisper him at that only. I dare not tell him that I am so too, for fear he should think I counterfeited, to make my court.' Much later, in *Gulliver's Travels* he made pleasant allusion to this when he describes certain servants especially employed to tap with an inflated bladder the right ear of learned Laputians to rouse them to hearing.

St John and Harley

Harley's rise to power owed much to his colleague, Henry St John, 17 years younger than him (and 11 years younger than Swift). He had a fine scholarly mind – a better classicist than Swift and fluent in the French he would use for negotiations with France. Quick thinking, vigorous to the point of recklessness, he wished to 'fill the employment of the kingdom, down to the meanest, with Tories'. And conscious of his gifts he was jealous and increasingly contemptuous of Harley. Almost as soon as Harley's administration began, St John was plotting against him by encouraging a Jacobite group within the Tories called 'The October Club' and excluding Harley from an informal club of Tories called 'The Society'. Harley noted in a memoir to the queen (1714), 'The beginning of February 1710– 11,[6] there began to be a division among those called Tories in the House, & Mr Secretary St John thought it convenient to be listing a separate party for himself.' It was an uphill struggle to turn affairs to his own advantage. The Guiscard affair which made Harley immensely popular he repackaged as a story that he was really the intended victim. Later, St John's efforts against Harley were more successful. In the meantime, he ground his teeth when Harley was created Earl on 23 May 1711 and he became only a Viscount in June 1712. (His full title, 1st Viscount Bolingbroke, gives rise to the other name by which he is known of 'Bolingbroke'.)

The Examiner

The position of Harley was the unenviable one of being threatened by the extremes of both parties. A study by W.A. Speck[7] shows that he brought Swift in as editor (October 1710) to moderate the tone of the Tory weekly journal, *The Examiner,* which had been edited by St John among others. This was a half-sheet single essay on a political theme. Number 32 on how party factions split a nation accords well with Speck's view, although it still toes a Tory line. But Swift was not aware then of the rivalry between Harley and St John and admired the brilliance of the younger man. In the following number he fell for St John's line on Guiscard's motives, even adding that as Guiscard could not get at St John he stabbed the man whom St John loved best. Another Tory writer, Mrs Manley (Mary de la Rivière), had to publish a pamphlet to set the record straight. In Number 39 Swift's emphasis coolly ignored his previous account and corrected the balance by remarking that had Guiscard's 'detestable attempt upon Mr. Harley's person' succeeded it would have been to the 'delight of *Popery* and *faction*'. In an unpublished memoir he dryly remarked that what 'Mr St John affected to say . . . [had the consequence] that Mr St John had all the merit, while Mr Harley remained with nothing but the danger and the pain.'

The driving force behind Swift's criticism of the Whigs and their ministry is that their long enjoyment of power had corrupted them with complacent belief in their own rectitude and with contempt of the people. Both Godolphin and Marlborough had held high office for eight years. Harley had four years of such office but the following two in the wilderness secured him from being joined with them in the public mind. Swift's attack therefore was fortunately not blunted since he could represent Harley as a new man. So Swift is uninhibited in picturing the corruption that comes from holding power for too long:

> But imagine a set of politicians for many years at the head of affairs, the game visibly their own, and by consequence acting with great security: may not be these sometimes tempted to forget their caution by length of time, by excess of avarice and ambition, by the insolence or violence of their nature, or perhaps by a mere contempt for their adversaries?

Godolphin fell in August 1710 and Swift turned his attention (Number 17, 23 November 1710) to Marlborough in a comparison apparently provoked by Whig supporters who had protested that the contemporary British treated their generals worse than the Romans. Ingenuously Swift asked 'Has the prince seized on his estate, and left him to starve? Has he been hooted at as he passed the streets, by an ungrateful mob?' Already Swift's readers would have known that Marlborough had been granted the huge estate at Woodstock, Oxfordshire, on which, at public expense, the magnificent palace of Blenheim was being built. But his method is to leave the reader to vent anger while he puts with restraint a selective range of detail guaranteed to make the blood boil. Whigs complain that two relatives of the general, Godolphin and Sunderland, have been sacked. 'Will the troops in Flanders refuse to fight unless they can have *their own* lord keeper, *their own* lord president of the council, *their own* chief Governor of Ireland, and *their own* Parliament?' It is a bizarre fancy that the troops on the battlefield might dictate that all the important government offices be held by members of the same family simply on the basis of their blood relationship to 'their' general. But Swift makes it almost believable that this could be what the Whigs were arguing, since he remarks that it was notorious that 'the late ministry was closely joined to the general by friendship, interest, alliance, inclination and opinion'.

Having shown that all pivots on Marlborough, Swift drops a casual menace, in his remark that Marlborough's '*real defects* (as nothing human is without them) have in a detracting age been very sparingly mentioned'. Returning to the comparison which set off the essay, Swift considers how 'A victorious general of Rome in the height of that empire having *entirely subdued his enemy*, was rewarded with a larger triumph; and perhaps a statue.' In 1710 the war still had three years to run, so Marlborough might be expected to get a smaller 'triumph' until victory was complete. Swift imagines a comic bill comparing a Roman account with a British one. 'Roman Gratitude' begins '*Imprimis* for frankincense and earthen pots to burn it in £4. 10s 0d.'[8] The smallest expense is a wreath at 2d and the largest a triumphal arch at £500. Then follows 'A bill of British Ingratitude' in which the smallest item given to Marlborough is the Rangership of Windsor Park and Pall Mall at £10 000 and the largest the palace of Blenheim at £200 000. The final totals are £994 11s 10d on the Roman side and £540 000 0s 0d on the British.

The Conduct of the Allies

In 1711 Swift was taken from *The Examiner* in order to write a pamphlet at a moment when Whig tactics posed a great danger to Harley's or, as he now was, Lord Oxford's administration. Oxford had conducted via St John secret negotiations for a peace to end the war, for after dazzling success which had made Marlborough a hero in his early victories[9] the continuation of war was costing Britain dear in life and resources and war weariness had set in. But popular opinion was not, as yet, sufficient to head off powerful opposition from the Whigs. Marlborough was strongly committed to continuing the war and securing the Spanish throne for the Habsburg candidate so that France's expansion would be severely limited. In this he was backed by the Elector of Hanover who would be the future successor to the British throne. As the queen was ailing, policy had to take account of the probable displacement of the power base at court and not alienate the next monarch. However, the moment for agreeing a peace was favourable, since a new threat appeared on the horizon to drive out the old. Joseph I, the elder son and successor of Leopold I of Austria, had died in 1711 with the result that the Archduke Charles had now become Emperor in his place and if he also inherited the crown of Spain, the allies of Great Britain would have to face the new dominating power of Austria and Spain united under one leader.

The Conduct of the Allies was timed to appear on 27 November 1711 in order to prepare Tory supporters and people in the country for the debate in the next parliamentary session, 7 December 1711. In it would be found the arguments to set the tone of the debate and the issues to provide the agenda. It was an instant success. 'My printer came this morning [29 November] to tell me he must immediately print a second edition . . . they sold a thousand in two days' reported Swift in his *Journal to Stella*. By the end of January it had run to a sixth edition totalling eleven thousand copies.

'My large pamphlet', as Swift called it, had his trademark of clear condensed writing which sets the terms of the argument and inevitably leads on to a particular conclusion. The third paragraph states a number of principles for which his following text will supply telling examples to persuade the reader that Britain has no good reason for continuing the war.

> Supposing the war to have commenced upon a just motive, the next thing to be considered is, when a prince ought in prudence to receive the overtures of peace: which I take to be either when the enemy is ready to yield the point originally contended for, or when that point is found impossible to be ever obtained; or when contending any longer, though with probability of gaining that point at last, would put such a prince and his people in a worse condition than the present loss of it. All of which considerations are of much greater force where a war is managed by an alliance of confederates, which in the variety of interests among the several parties, is liable to so many unforeseen accidents.

Part of the technique is to supply the reader with, apparently, the most up-to-date information from a source with inside knowledge. So the pamphlet contains a translation of part of one of the treaties and a summary of the progress of the war. France had already sued for peace and been rejected: 'after the battle of Ramillies the French were so discouraged with their frequent losses, and so impatient for peace that their king was resolved to comply on any reasonable terms.' A treaty of Gertrudenberg was discussed and ''Tis plain they offered many more [concessions], and much greater, than ever we thought to insist on when the war began.' But new stipulations were made by the Allies, supposedly on behalf of the British, that Louis should oppose the succession of his grandson to the crown of Spain. Louis would not go this far and the continuation of the war was ruining Great Britain for the private ends of the Allies and to line the pockets of the monied interest. They must have calculated that Louis would object. 'What could be the design of all this grimace but to amuse the people, and to raise stocks for their friends in the secret to sell to advantage?' After his analysis of Marlborough in *The Examiner*, Swift was ready for yet another case of the monied interest serving self under the pretence of contributing to public good. His tight-lipped scorn shows an inner conviction of the justice of his attack. However, for much of what he wrote he was indebted to St John.

A number of passages look like St John's interpolations and show his rivalry with Oxford gathering head. Either they were promoted by him or Swift knew that they would be particularly congenial to him. St John had tried to gain a political coup by encouraging Brigadier John Hill (a brother of Mrs Masham, who replaced the queen's confidante, the Duchess of Marlborough) in an unsuccessful expedition to take Quebec from the French, against Oxford's wishes and while he was recovering from Guiscard's attack. It had no particular reason to be included in this account of the European war except to introduce Bolingbroke's excuses for its failure: that it was caused by the 'accidents of a storm' and the 'treachery of some in that colony'. In another place St John's Jacobite leanings appear when Swift decried what the Allies could give in return for the British war effort. Great Britain did not need the Allies (foreigners all) to confirm the validity of the succession of Queen Anne (rather than the Old Pretender) to the throne: 'Otherwise we put it out of the power of our own legislature to change our succession.' Whig opponents were to seize on this passage as a veiled threat to change monarchs again and indeed restore the Pretender, denying the succession to the House of Hanover. Subsequent editions of *The Conduct of the Allies* were forced to carry a disclaimer.

More difficult to disentangle is what is due to the recklessness of St John's wish to polarise party feeling and what to Swift's own desire to support an economy based on agriculture and to root out sectarianism. Differing underlying principles may share a common outcome. This may be seen in the criticism of the Dutch. Swift had not previously attacked the memory of William III, for his regard for Temple and his Protestant credentials had much to recommend him. On the other hand, St John had no reason to support William, for his brand of religion (discussed in Chapter 3) did not require him to side with Protestant or Roman Catholic and he might have greater political power under a restored Stuart monarchy. But both Swift and St John come together on the issue that puts the Dutch in the firing line: that the nation has had to raise money to support the wars with France by a new financial system which incurs a national debt. William was to blame, for 'the true reason for embracing this expedient was the security of a new prince, not firmly settled on the throne'. This system in time has become 'a sort of artificial wealth of funds and stocks in the hands of those who for ten years before had been plundering the public' which is 'annually pawning itself'. In this we hear Swift's voice attacking the Dutch with his scorn of politicians who treat the Treasury as a 'bottomless pit' and his hatred for 'that scheme of politicks . . . of setting up a mony'd Interest in opposition to the landed'.

From this instance the hostility to the Dutch is widened and maybe St John's extremism is increasingly heard. The Treaty of Ryswick 'was concluded with great advantages to the empire and Holland but none at all to us.' The Spanish ambitions of Louis were a problem for the Dutch and 'England ought no more to have been a principal in this war than Prussia, or any other power who came afterwards into that alliance. Holland was first in danger.' And there was no moral or legal obligation to continue to support Holland. 'I can see no reason from the words of the grand alliance by which we were obliged to make those prodigious expenses we have since been at'. Worse we actually damage our own interests. 'We have conquered a noble territory for the States, that . . . will enable them to undersell us in every market of the world.' With scant regard for the tact necessary to placate the Elector of Hanover who supported the Dutch, especially in promoting the Habsburg candidate, Swift warns also against the 'rapacious German ministry'. Moderation has been thrown to the winds in the cause of promoting the peace and there is little in this line of argument to assist Oxford's bringing together both Tory and Whig views in the centre.

Oxford's moderation and distaste for party was congenial to Swift and it is tempting to see that St John has directed his hand. If so the spell of the younger man was considerable. But moderation may also call out immoderate support for itself. Swift's hatred of the hypocritical self-seeking of the monied interest posing as all concerned for the public good calls out his vigorous denial of their sham social conscience. Swift believes the continuation of the war to be a sectarian interest. It is 'a war of the *general* and the *ministry* and not the *prince* or *people*' and is related to 'that set of people who are called the *monied men*'. Its continuation is fuelled by Marlborough's 'unmeasurable love of wealth which his best friends allow to be his predominant passion'. So far the argument criticises individual practitioners but, by what we may see as a sleight of hand, the Whigs become by definition a small interest group and the Tories the true

representatives of the nation. 'The Whigs were received into employment, left to manage the Parliament, cry down the landed interest,
and worry the church.' Above party politics, the queen sees the
danger to the nation. 'The prudence, courage, and firmness of Her
Majesty in all steps of that great change, would if the particulars
were truly related make a very shining part in her story.' And she
chose Oxford and St John to avert the danger: 'Nor is her judgment
less to be admired which directed her in the choice of perhaps the
only persons who had skill, credit, and resolution enough to be
her instruments in overthrowing so many difficulties.' The partisan
nature of the Whigs is memorably fixed, as so often by Swift, with a
concrete image. 'It is the folly of too many to mistake the echo of
a London coffee-house for the voice of the kingdom. The city coffee-
houses have been for some time filled with people whose fortunes
depend upon the Bank, East India, or some other stock.'

This account of Swift's political wisdom would be unbalanced if
it left out of consideration the pressured conditions under which the
pamphlet was produced and the immediacy of the war situation.
While it may have been in prospect in August, Swift probably did
not begin work on *The Conduct of the Allies* until mid-October, having
to master opposition and government material, supplied almost daily
with information from St John and frequently meeting to agree the
thrust of his argument. At the same time events on the continent
were fluid. Phrases in the pamphlet show Swift responding to new
situations: 'the face of affairs in Christendom since the emperor's
death hath been very much changed' so that 'to have the empire
and Spanish monarchy united in the same person is a dreadful consideration.' In addition, opponents 'have not I believe cast their eye
upon a cloud gathering in the north.' Charles XII of Sweden, 'the
Swedish meteor', had cut swathes through his enemies, invading
even Russia, in extending his own domains. After a defeat at Poltava,
near Moscow, he was gathering strength again in Turkey. 'If the
King of Sweden returns and gets the better, he will think himself
under no obligation of having any regard to the interests of the
allies; but will naturally pursue, according to his own expression,
"his enemy, wherever he finds him".'

End of the ministry

The Whigs put up a stiff resistance to peace while the root-and-
branch Tories urged Oxford to concede more to France. The queen,
never possessed of a high understanding of personalities, was ailing
and had become even more dependent on her confidante, since the
death of her husband, George of Denmark, in 1708. Despite her
wish for peace she surprised the Tories by siding with the Whigs and

offering her arm to the Whig Duke of Somerset to conduct her from the debate on 7 December 1711. The *Journal to Stella* records the frantic dismay of Swift and of some of the Tories. 'Lord Dartmouth despairs, and is for giving up; Lewis is of the same mind; but Lord-Treasurer only says, Poh, poh, all will be well.' The queen's personal physician, Dr John Arbuthnot, thought it was only that she had been frightened by the debate and flattered by the attention of the Duke. Swift in his despair wrote a vigorous attack on the Duchess of Somerset called *The Windsor Prophecy*. In it he blamed her for manipulating the queen's change of heart, and recommended the queen should trust Mrs Masham. He had it published more to relieve his anxieties than to secure the dismissal of the duchess but Mrs Masham warned him that it would offend the queen. He attempted to stop it but was too late and contented himself with saying the prophecy 'was an admirable good one, and people are mad for it'. Then on the 29 December the crisis was over. The queen created 12 new peers, all Tory, and the success of her government was assured by the majority it created.

Marlborough and the Secretary for War, Robert Walpole, continued to resist and were accused of peculation with the army accounts and dismissed. Undoubtedly Swift's *The Conduct of the Allies* had proved invaluable in winning the case for peace and Oxford did what he could to redress the damage that it might have done to his credit with the House of Hanover. In January 1712 he steered through Parliament a bill to give precedence to the whole Electoral family and then presented it to the Elector's mother, Sophia, with the placatory words: 'The bulk of the nation centre in your succession, and there cannot be anything more unhappy than to have an opinion take place that your serene family were attached to any party. They are to reign over the whole nation and not to be the sovereign of a party only.'

Eventually peace was concluded by the Treaty of Utrecht, 9 April 1713. In the interim St John's machinations against Oxford began to succeed. Their disagreements over the terms of peace became acrimonious and led to factional infighting. When Oxford was ill in July 1713, St John, now Viscount Bolingbroke, attempted to juggle ministries to give his faction more power. He took the Southern department of the Secretary of State which was usually regarded as the senior of the two. He had William Wyndham appointed Chancellor of the Exchequer in order to trim the wings of the Lord Treasurer. But in a counter move, the queen appointed an Oxford supporter, George Granville (Lord Lansdowne), as Treasurer of the Household above Wyndham.

As the queen trusted Harley to the humiliating extent that she expected him to vet Bolingbroke's very able state papers in her presence, Bolingbroke set out to undermine him through Mrs, later Lady, Masham. She had supplanted the Duchess of Marlborough in 1711 as the queen's confidante. He offered to obtain for her a financial share in the *asiento*, a monopoly granted by Spain, which enabled trade in slaves between Africa and the Spanish colonies in the West Indies and, although she had been a supporter of Oxford, she switched sides. Next, Oxford (October 1713) offended the queen by asking that his son, Edward Harley, should be created Duke of Newcastle, a condition set by the widow of the Duke for Edward's marriage to her daughter. The queen either felt that Oxford had insufficient money to deserve the title or that the son was too improvident and refused. Oxford wrote a memorandum (which may not have been sent but shows his reactions) referring to himself in the third person as a man who 'seems sensible of the circumstances against him. He was always indifferent but now is more earnest to get rid of a service where his fellows cross him and his sovereign is either weary of him [and considers] him not worth or is ashamed to own him. He desires no protection from his faults.' Lady Masham now began to succeed in undermining the character of Oxford and Queen Anne dismissed him on 27 July 1714. Lady Masham's part in the *asiento* dealings then became the subject of inquiry with a possible danger to Bolingbroke but the queen prorogued Parliament before it could be pursued. Nevertheless Bolingbroke had actually shot himself in the foot by ousting Oxford because the queen died days after and there was no Tory power base to match that of the Whigs, welcoming the Elector of Hanover. Bolingbroke fled to France and threw in his lot with the Pretender hoping to get a better bargaining position, thereby enabling the smear that Tories were at heart Jacobites. Oxford remained, expecting to manipulate the political situation after the coming of the Hanoverians, but such was the rancour of party feeling and the hostility of George I that he never held ministerial position again.

Preferment: Bolingbroke and Oxford's treatment of Swift

Swift maintained that he was an independent voice in the Tory government and that he had personal hold over the ministers, possibly for his intellectual and satirical powers. To maintain his independence he refused to be paid, once hotly returning £50 sent him by Oxford and demanding an apology. And yet Oxford knew he needed money and both he and Bolingbroke were aware that Swift would not refuse an appropriate preferment in the church. Their response to this illustrates something of the value they had for him and the nature of their relationship to him.

Bolingbroke and Swift

Bolingbroke's early relationship with Swift suggests the same manipulation in his own interest that he tried to practise on Oxford. (Later it was centred on literary matters and on a more equal footing.) Even as early as the granting of remission of the First Fruits, Bolingbroke misled Swift. He assured him that the letter warranting the grant had been written when it took a further seven weeks before it was done. Since 1710 Swift had sought the post of official historian, Historiographer Royal. Bolingbroke had once written (7 January 1714) to the Duke of Shrewsbury in whose gift it was, who Swift reported 'sent Ld Bol. word, that thô he was under some Engagem^t, he would get it me'. But Bolingbroke did not press it and Swift confided 'I had thought Ld B, wd have done such a Trifle.' When Swift at the end of the Oxford ministry wrote *Some Free Thoughts on the Late Administration*, Bolingbroke without reference to him secured the proofs and corrected them to his advantage and to discredit Oxford. One of his alterations was to cut out a passage referring to what he owed Oxford in friendship and gratitude. Ford wrote to Swift, 'There is something very mean in his desiring to make alterations, when I am sure he has no reason to complain, and is at least as fairly dealt with as his competitor.' Swift wrote to another friend that 'I cannot rely on his Love for me.'

Swift had a genuine affection and respect for Bolingbroke but he was not prepared to sacrifice Oxford to his personal hatred. This was a running sore for the rest of Bolingbroke's life and almost involuntarily breaking out in successive letters to Swift. With heavy irony he referred to a 'certain great minister' (1721), maliciously called him a Jews Harp unstirred by the harmonies of heroism and 'incapable of admiring stoicism' (1722), berated Swift for writing favourably on him in a previous letter as a kind of 'Elegy upon a departed Minister' (1724), sarcastically called him 'your Hero' (1729), and accused him of hypocrisy in that he 'affected business he often hindered' (1734). Swift reminded him once that 'you taught me to love him, and often vindicated him in the beginning of your Ministry, from my Accusations.'

Bolingbroke remained in France from 1715 to 1723. Initially he supported the Old Pretender, taking the role of 'Secretary of State' in waiting, but after the failure of the Jacobite rebellion of 1715 he set about restoring his Hanoverian credentials and secretly bribed George I to allow him to return with a qualified pardon (17 May 1723). Another bribe restored his title in 1725 but he voluntarily returned to France in 1735. Here he wrote *The Idea of a Patriot King* (1740) which advocated a court tradition that Harley had done so much to support and he had done so much to undermine. During all this time he frequently corresponded with Swift, opening a new and different chapter in their relationship.

Oxford and Swift

Swift had felt in 1711 that he was 'a Man floating at Sea' and his subsequent idolising of Oxford suggests that he was looking for the older man to set him on some more stable course which would eventually arrive at a desirable port. The office of Historiographer Oxford, like Bolingbroke, had neglected to win for him. Later, in 1714, Swift wrote a letter to Oxford in which (using his own term) he 'nipped him' about hoping to write a history of the administration which 'you and somebody that shall be nameless, seem to value less than I could wish'. Swift's main hope for the more substantial reward of some clerical preferment was well known early on. In the previous ministry he had petitioned Halifax for the prebend of Westminster which 'the late King promised me' (13 June 1709). Soon after the return of Harley, Lord Peterborough wrote (18 April 1711) 'I find Mr Harley forgetts to make mention of the most important part of my Letter to him, which was to let him know that I expected immediately for one Dr Swift, a Lean Bishoprick, or a fat Deanery.' In 1712 Swift let Oxford know 'the Dean of Wells dyed' (5 February) and this was soon followed by vacancies in the deaneries at Ely and Lichfield. These were dangled in front of the aspiring vicar for almost 15 months until 13 April 1713 when they were all filled by other candidates. By then Swift had already become disheartened and plans were well advanced for him to return to Ireland with the hope of the deanery of St Patrick's, Dublin. He was sure that John Sharp, Archbishop of York, and the Duchess of Somerset had set the queen against him, probably as the author of *A Tale of a Tub* and of *The Windsor Prophecy*. But if so, Oxford did not tell him of this and probably delayed the preferments as a means of keeping Swift in England. Oxford was well known for using his patronage to secure a political outcome and would often say 'men are more apt to be influenced by hopes than rewards'. Swift may have been counting on the threat of his removal to Ireland as a means of pushing for an English preferment for, when St Patrick's was agreed between Ormonde (who had the gift of the deanery), Oxford and the queen, he wrote in the *Journal to Stella*, 'I confess, I thought the ministry would not let me go; but perhaps they can't help it.' And even in this last discussion with the queen, Oxford had argued that Swift should be made prebendary at Windsor.

A year later Oxford was disgraced. Lady Masham, anxious for the health of the queen (and her own future), passionately and vindictively accused him: 'you never did the Queen any services, nor are you capable of doing any'. The queen was reported to have said 'that he neglected all business, that he was seldom to be understood, that when he did explain himself, she could never depend upon the truth of what he said; that he never came to her at the time she appointed, that he often came drunk, that lastly to crown all he behav'd himself towards her with ill manner indecency & disrespect'. But Oxford's biographer, Brian Hill, remarks 'Oxford had not deserved the enraged Queen's wrath, and . . . we may safely discredit most of her hysterical accusations for what they were; Anne had said hardly less of Nottingham, Godolphin, and Marlborough, upon like occasions'.[10] Rehabilitation of Oxford from these slurs has come only in the latter part of this century and until then they have coloured historians' understanding of his political importance. Now they reflect on the limited intelligence of Anne and her inability to appreciate political sophistication. Such an example of royal shortcomings was not lost on Swift who had 'little personal esteem for Princes' (letter of 1731 quoted above, although in that letter he did not choose to expatiate to the Countess of Suffolk on Anne since a much worse ruler had replaced her). He remembered it when writing the character of the Empress of Lilliput in *Gulliver's Travels*. Given the anger at the palace, where Bolingbroke was riding high for a few short months, Swift would have known that his next move, to visit Oxford in his disgrace, would lose him any further credit with the high Tory government. His going to stay with him was a mark of his gratefulness to Oxford to whom he wrote none could 'make you think ill of me' and that he was a man 'sensible of the honour you did him though . . . too proud to be vain on it'.

Bolingbroke and Ormonde's flights to France (respectively in March and July) put Oxford in jeopardy, under suspicion as a Jacobite collaborator. He was imprisoned in the Tower on 16 July 1715. Whig revenge on the Tories was fuelled by the unsuccessful attempt to restore the Old Pretender in a rebellion from September 1715 to April 1716 in which the Pretender landed near Aberdeen in Scotland, where the Earl of Mar, a fervent Jacobite, had taken over most of the country except Edinburgh. Two years in the Tower broke Oxford's health. Parliament could agree no charges to prosecute him and he was released 1 July 1717, forbidden to attend court by George I, and died in retirement, 21 May 1724.

Oxford's contribution to politics

Swift's political wisdom has been seen as lacking in his attachment to Oxford. Irvin Ehrenpreis argues he left too much to be done on his behalf and tried to remain aloof from pressing for preferment while deeply resenting the failure to satisfy him. When this largely justified criticism is coupled to a judgement that Oxford was not likely to honour his promises (through indolence, deviousness and incapacity) Swift's folly becomes the greater. But Oxford was a much more skilful politician than this view presents and probably more than even Swift knew.[11] As early as 1708 Swift saw his ability to manage the political world, reporting that 'Mr Harley had been some time, with the greatest art imaginable, carrying on an intrigue to alter the Ministry, and began with no less an enterprise than that of removing the Lord Treasurer, and had nearly effected it, by the help of Mrs Masham'. Swift recognised his pragmatism which grew out of his moderating concern to maintain a plural and centrist government: 'He was saying a Thing to me some Days ago, which I believe is the great Maxim he proceedeth by; That Wisdom in publick Affairs, was not what is commonly believed, the forming of Schemes with remote Views; but the making Use of such Incidents as happen' (Swift to King, 12 July 1711). This earned him the nickname of 'Robin the Trickster' and appalled an otherwise subtle commentator, the Victorian historian Leslie Stephen, as a kind of 'hand to mouth' policy.[12] But visionary schemes may appeal less to a readership at the turn of the 21st century and working with the parliamentary grain may nowadays be seen as practical response to a duplicitous and self-seeking political community. Stephen admits that Oxford's 'reputation as a party manager was immense; and is partly justified by his quick recognition of Swift's extraordinary qualifications'.

While there is no doubt that Swift was greatly serviceable to Oxford and they had respect for each other, Stephen's judgement is overkind to Swift and less fair to Oxford. Swift did make mistakes. He had let himself be swayed by Bolingbroke in emphases he made in *The Examiner* and *The Conduct of the Allies*, not recognising the power politics being played out under his nose. In August 1711 he recorded, 'I think, they intirely love one another.' In despair he had incautiously written and published the ill-advised *Windsor Prophecy*. And he did not properly appreciate how *A Tale of a Tub* might affect a narrow-minded and dull queen (any more than he considered how Archbishop King would respond to his 'raillery').

Although Swift may seem somewhat naïve in his handling of the ins and outs of politics and sometimes appeared to succumb to a kind of death wish in his lampoons, it is easy with the advantage of hindsight and out of the heat of battle to be critical. He was wary enough in general terms to rein in his hopes of advancement when lionised. 'They call me nothing but Jonathan; and I said, I believed they would leave me Jonathan, as they found me; and that I never knew a ministry do any thing for those whom they make companions of their pleasures' (17 February 1711). He certainly miscalculated over details, as most people do, and was hurt by mistreatment and compensated for this by taking liberties in the company of friends to show his 'governorship' and to test the friendship. But he was no cipher or mere government hack. His own opinions were not to be bought in the political writings. We have seen that particularly his church views were Tory before the association with Bolingbroke. In order to write the journal and pamphlets he had to master the information and to satisfy his own conscience and judgement to provide the necessary fire. His command of the detail in *The Conduct of the Allies* demonstrates his wide understanding of the process of the war and he boasted 'I know every step of this treaty better than any man.'

Swift admired Oxford as a consummate politician. His own comment on Oxford was that 'he was the mildest, wisest and best Minister that ever served a Prince' (19 July 1714). Despite the queen's furious rejection of Oxford, Swift understood at first hand that Oxford had really served her admirably, first because he knew her well enough to discount her poor judgement. In his unpublished fragment *Memoirs relating to the change in the Queen's Ministry* (1714) he wrote 'The queen had not a stock of amity to serve above one object at a time; and farther than a bare good or ill opinion, which she soon contracted and changed, and very often upon light grounds, she could hardly be said either to love or to hate any body.' And second, he knew that Oxford honoured the queen's role in the constitution. When the bishops tried fawningly to credit Ormonde with securing remission of the First Fruits, Oxford had self-effacingly told him 'it is the Queen that did it, and she alone shall have the Merit' (15 August 1711). Preservation of a constitutional monarch as a moderating influence was regarded by Oxford as a key factor in his plural government. He wrote 'All sovereigns must of necessity have some screen between them and their people in mixed governments; the constitution places a screen between the Crown and the Commons but that is only as to the legislature. There remains to consider the person of the sovereign: and in this case it is necessary to have a personal screen' (Memorial to the queen, 10 April 1710).

Swift also meant the words 'wisest and best Minister'. He told the October Club that Oxford was the 'one great person' who could save the administration. But he believed politics did not favour men of genius and usually the dull men took charge. In a letter of 19 December 1719 he listed several instances of great men who had failed and included both Bolingbroke and Oxford, showing that it was personality and not policy that decided political fortune. 'Did you never observe one of your clerks cutting his paper with a blunt ivory knife? Did you ever know the knife to fail going the true way? Whereas, if he had used a razor, or a penknife, he had the odds against him of spoiling a whole sheet.' Lilliput, which loosely represents contemporary Britain in *Gulliver's Travels*, provides a useful gloss on this and once again shows how an understanding of the political situation can assist an intelligent and sensitive reading of Swift's satire. In a golden age, before corruption and degeneration set in, Lilliput had a government which appointed ministers with 'more regard to good Morals than great Abilities' and this was because 'Providence never intended to make the Management of publick Affairs a Mystery, to be comprehended only by a few Persons of sublime Genius'. Politics under Queen Anne belonged to an age of debased metal where subtlety and ready 'making use of such incidents that happen' was necessary to advance good government. But the duplicity and littleness of the greater number of politicians inevitably meant that weight of numbers would overwhelm the 'wisest and best Minister'. Given this human frailty, Swift held even more fast to the values of friendship, trust and community. In the golden age of Lilliput it was said that 'they look upon Fraud as a greater Crime than Theft'. A contemporary representative of Queen Anne's Britain might try to excuse fraud since 'it was only a breach of Trust'. But such a justification Swift shows to be horrific, for it struck at the root of all relationships. Swift exemplified this belief in his actions. Having given his trust to Oxford (and Bolingbroke) Swift honoured the friendships even more under adverse circumstances. We have noticed his staying with Oxford during the queen's displeasure. In the case of Bolingbroke he was prepared to visit him in France when the Whigs were in full cry, despite his preference for the politics of Oxford and his awareness of the younger man's shortcomings.

Justification for Swift's admiration of the political skill of Oxford may be found precisely in the area where Swift had most to do with government. Oxford was a pioneer in harnessing the power of the press, just as the stream of pamphlets, journals and magazines was turning into a flood. His touch was surer than Swift's, whom we have seen as sometimes rash in handling particular enemies, for he was acutely aware of the need to capture hearts and minds in order to achieve his political ends. J.A. Downie[13] has analysed his clear-sighted understanding of the importance of public opinion and vigorous use of the press to inform and persuade. In 1695 the Licensing Act expired. This released the government curb of censorship on publication, just after the passing of the Triennial Act of 1694 raised the frequency of general elections and associated political debate. This led to an enormous increase in propaganda at a time when it was a matter of immediate concern to a large section of the people. Although the right to vote was severely restricted, W.A. Speck[14] has argued that 'the electoral system was more representative in Anne's reign than it had ever been before or was to be again until well into Victoria's'. One in five adult males had a vote.[15]

Oxford funded, mainly from his own pocket, a string of writers in addition to Swift who were putting in different ways the views of his political administration: Charles Davenant, Daniel Defoe, Mrs Manley (Mary de la Rivière), Abel Roper (editor of the *Post Boy*), John Toland. Swift was unaware of Defoe's connection with Oxford, despite Defoe's prominence – he was a prolific and entertaining propagandist (in addition to being a substantial writer in his own right and generally known at least for *Robinson Crusoe*). Downie describes how Oxford orchestrated the appearance of Defoe's supporting essays in his *Review* with Swift's *The Conduct of the Allies*.[16] But Defoe was a loner which may be why Swift did not know about his closeness to Oxford. Many of the other writers were in contact with Swift. Swift had a working relationship with Abel Roper, whom Swift called his 'humble slave' and whose *Post Boy* had 5000 readers. He installed as editor of the *Gazette* first Dr William King (not the Archbishop) and then his friend Charles Ford. In addition Swift conducted most of the business of the practical production of Oxford's propaganda, particularly using the printer, John Barber. This activity helps us to understand what Swift meant about 'governing' ministers. In his *Memoirs relating to the change in the Queen's Ministry* Swift brings to the reader's attention that all sides regarded him as a political heavyweight, 'as one who was in the secret of all affairs, and without whose advice or privity nothing was done'. One cannot exonerate him from some pride in having the reputation while he is denying it. Maybe in the *Memoirs* he was cautiously downplaying his sense of his role in 1714 in the knowledge of a network of informers who might get hold of the paper he was writing. But in other senses he did govern the ministers when they accepted his rather dominating behaviour in company. And he did occupy a privileged position of having inside information of the policy-making of the government and of the personal intrigues within the administration. His claim to 'govern' is less inflated when we recall his energetic writing for the administration and the busy practicalities of his dealing with other propagandists, Defoe apart. As Downie commented 'a team of writers surrounded Swift on the Tory side, and in this sense he can be said to have organised government propaganda for the Oxford ministry.'

Notes

1   The replacement of James II with William III was not a straight-forward deposition. Although William was aware that he had a claim to the throne should it become vacant he behaved with circumspection when he invaded England with the help of a significant group of British political leaders to curb the pro French and pro Roman

Catholic policies. James II fled before the advance of William III; was returned by Kentish fishermen and fled again. William was invited to take the vacant throne.

2   The process of evolution continued. Richard Pares, *King George III and the Politicians*, OUP, 1953, p. 71, remarked 'The parties of 1760 were certainly not the same as those of 1714.' Geoffrey Holmes, *The Making of a Great Power*, Longman, 1993, Chap. 22, argues that politics from 1689–1722 was 'neither as straightforward nor as wayward as has sometimes been claimed', taking a middle way between the opposed 'Whig' and 'Namierite' interpretations of history which he explains.

3   A commode.

4   i.e. Queen Caroline, wife of George II.

5   'Habeas corpus' means 'may you have the body' – the first phrase of a formal application for bringing to public view a prisoner so that one could ensure physical safety.

6   Two calendars, Julian (Old Style) and Gregorian (New Style) were in operation, hence the two dates of year. The adoption of NS happened at different dates in different countries. Great Britain made the change in 1752. In the text of this book all dates are given in NS.

7   'The Examiner Examined: Swift's Tory Pamphleteering', *Focus: Swift*, (ed.) Claude Rawson, Sphere, 1971, 145–6.

8   The currency was given in pounds (£), shillings (s) and pence (d). Ten shillings was equivalent to 50p (half the value of a pound). Twelve old pence (d) made up one shilling, the equivalent of 5p.

9   These were Blenheim (1704), Ramillies (1706), Oudenarde (1708) and Malplaquet (1709).

10 *Robert Harley: Speaker, Secretary of State and Premier Minister*, Brian W. Hill, Yale, 1988, 222.

11 Swift shows some irritation at being left out of Oxford's conversations with Prior (*Journal to Stella*) and didn't know of his secret talks with Richard Steele, formerly a personal friend of Swift who is discussed in the following chapter.

12 *Swift*, Leslie Stephen, Macmillan, 1899, 83.

13 *Robert Harley and the Press: Propaganda and Public Opinion in the Age of Swift and Defoe*, J.A. Downie, CUP, 1979.

14 *Tory and Whig: The Struggle in the Constituencies, 1701–1715*, W.A. Speck, Macmillan, 1970.

15 *Britain after the Glorious Revolution 1689–1714*, (ed.) G. Holmes, Macmillan, 1969, 12.

16 See pages 140–1 of the book cited.

3 Swift's London and Ireland

Swift's audience

The progress of Swift's literary career seems determined by the accidents of friendships. At different times of his life he had different friends and associates and they seem to draw out different sides of his creative talent. To some extent he writes for their approval, although as time went on his choice of ideal reader/friend may have been determined by his own creative development. Whichever emphasis appears to have merit at a particular stage in his career, it is illuminating to discuss his work in the context of these friends. His genius is a social one presupposing a dialogue with readers in the know rather than the voice of an isolated artist reaching out to an ideal readership.

Working as secretary for the retired diplomat, William Temple, he felt encouraged to be the cultivated littérateur and wrote his odes on celebrated personalities and his defence of his patron in *The Battle of the Books*. He continued in this style after Temple's death in *A Discourse of the Contests and Dissensions . . .* , in his early urban pastoral poems and in editing Temple's *Memoirs*. However, Temple had also been a constraint and Swift had kept out of sight a more devastating satirical intelligence, which shows in a work which satisfied some inner need to confront circumstances that dismayed him. Temple would have disapproved of *A Tale of a Tub*, begun at university, possibly with some help from Swift's cousin, and given another boost by the disappointments and threat of Presbyterian religion at Kilroot. Its confident and ebullient satirical vein was reanimated by finding himself within the circuit of the court at St James, with the chance of making his mark, and led to eventual publication in 1704. Swift's comic side then found expression in the 'bites' or literary hoaxes, such as *The Bickerstaff Papers*. He later turned aside to the suave political pamphleteering for Oxford and Bolingbroke, where a more measured and informative tone just veiled his critical distrust of the opposition. Then, once again, he broke out into the more biting satire of *The Windsor Prophecy*, when disappointed by the momentary failure of *The Conduct of the Allies* to carry the movement for peace in the Commons. In 1715 Swift's creative flow was interrupted by his sudden return to Ireland which he felt at first as exile and the end of his literary career. But around him were Irish causes which claimed his gifts as a writer and then the letters from Bolingbroke and Pope provoked him to react to their idea of mankind, reason and the function of satire. From his responses to them and his reflection on the past he drew the issues which animate the multilayered ironies of *Gulliver's Travels*.

Of course he did not write for his friends alone. We have already noticed how Oxford capitalised on the appetite for printed information of the new reading public. Swift was a willing collaborator in this, having the same appreciation of the power of print and readiness to engage in the rough and tumble. Before meeting Oxford he had brilliantly characterised the snowstorm of pamphlets with the prefaces, introductions and digressions in *A Tale of a Tub* and drew on this understanding to give immediacy to his political writings. His ability to adopt the methods of popular journalism was more of a defining attitude than it might seem now. Alvin Kernan[1] has shown how there was still a strong feeling that it was not gentlemanly to appear in print, especially as a paid professional. Bolingbroke claimed, not too convincingly, he was not fond 'of the Name of an Author' and that it was sufficient for just a few friends to read his writings and he would 'not have the itch of making them more publick'. In varying degrees Swift and his friends paid lip service to this view while looking anxiously for public approval. On the one hand it buttresses the argument that we should examine the intimate nature of Swift's writings. And on the other that we should consider the relation of the author to the reading public, in particular the size and gender of the audience.

The reading public and literary taste

Literacy

As a preliminary, we need to assess the percentage of the populations of London and of Dublin that was literate. In one study, David Cressy argues that a conservative estimate (based on the ability to sign one's name) of **illiteracy** in London in 1720 puts it as low as 8 per cent for tradesmen and craftsmen. Particularly interesting is the observation that, for the same date, illiteracy in women in London had reduced to 44 per cent. 'This was an extraordinary emergence, a halving of illiteracy in the space of two generations . . . [it] points to an educational revolution among late Stuart and early Hanoverian women in the metropolis, a revolution which was geographically specific and to which women in less frenetic parts of the country were not exposed.'[2] In a recent study James Raven and others,[3] estimating literacy by print-runs and library holdings, stress the conservative nature of Cressy's estimate and argue that the percentage of literate readers found by his method is a 'rough minimum'. But Raven admits he can propose no 'clear-cut procedure for the measurement of functional literacy'. And in Swift's Dublin the consideration of print-runs falls foul of English legislation to prevent the existence of an Irish press. The monopoly to print all books in Ireland was held by the King's Printer, Andrew Crooke, from 1693–1732 and this was coupled with highly effective laws against the import and export of anything considered seditious or libellous. (These are facts to remember when considering Swift's Irish pamphlets.) Although there were six printers in Dublin in 1700, infringing the monopoly, Mary Pollard tells us this did not pose a significant threat to British domination: 'The very insignificance of the Dublin trade in 1700, when it lagged two centuries behind London, secured it from both the British Copyright Act and the Stamp Act of 1712.'[1] In addition there was no printed matter in Irish and books were aimed at the English-speaking Protestant ascendancy.

So while literacy in Dublin has yet to be determined, it can be argued that when Swift wrote he was conscious of a reasonably large female audience, at least in London. There is clear evidence that he had many intelligent female friends in London and valued their company and engagement in his work. And it follows that aspects of his writing which convention might consider to offend a woman, such as the scatological aspect, cannot be compartmentalised as intended only for a male ear.

In fact Swift had no wish to exclude women from his world. He was much concerned that women should have as good an education as possible to participate in all public affairs. His attempt to correct Stella's spelling in the *Journal to Stella*, which has struck some as paternalistic, has at least the merit of wishing her to fulfil her potential (see the argument in Chapter 4) and *A Letter to a Very Young Woman about to Marry* conveys much the same message in favour of reading and useful study to combat what some think to be an 'established maxim, that women are incapable of conversation'.

Maybe there was some protection to his reputation as a clergyman that his writings were not so easily available to the generality of women outside the metropolis, particularly in Ireland. And the anonymity he cultivated also cloaked his activity. This does not mean that he was ready, as it were, to foul any nest provided it were not his own. In his defence, it is a point to be considered whether he did in fact disfigure his writing with his more outspoken style and also to remember that a clergyman has a duty to less sophisticated parishioners not to act as a stumbling block. What he did in London was suited to his audience. He knew that Dublin was different and warned Pope in later years (1728) that his satirical poem, *The Dunciad*, would not be understood without notes: 'How it passes in Dublin I know not yet; but I am sure it will be a great disadvantage to the poem, that the persons and facts will not be understood, till an explanation comes out, and a very full one.'

The coffee-house

A feature of London which helped the growth of the reading public was the institution known as the coffee-house, which became available to Swift when he arrived from Dublin in 1708. Swift's mission to secure the First Fruits suddenly offered him a delicious independence. He was freed from the constraint of being sidelined from affairs of state in Dublin (as a result of the subservience of the Irish Parliament to Parliament in London) and was no longer compelled to act with the propriety demanded of a secretary to Temple, living in Horatian retirement at Moor Park. The London coffee-houses were filled with the gossiping members of this new reading public and a budding author could catch the topics of fashion and observe the reception of his writings in these haunts. Swift cheerfully wrote of this buzzing atmosphere to buoy up a friend, Robert Hunter, imprisoned in Paris after having been captured by the French, when he was sailing for Virginia as its new Lieutenant-General.

> I could send you a great deal of news from the *Republica Grubstreetaria*, which was never in greater Altitude. Though I have been of late but a small Contributor . . . The Company at St. *James's* Coffee-house is as bad as ever, but it is not quite so good. The Beauties you left are all gone off this Frost, and we have a new set for Spring . . . the best Intelligence I get of publick Affairs is from the Ladies . . . The Vogue of Operas holdeth up wonderfully, altho' we have had them a Year; but I design to set up a Party among the Wits to run them down by next Winter . . . Mademoiselle *Spanheim* is going to marry my Lord *Fitzhardinge*.
>
> (Swift to Robert Hunter, 22 March 1709)

This was when the great frost froze over the Thames, from 26 December 1708 to March 1709, so that booths could be set up on the thick ice selling gingerbread and chestnuts hot from the flaming brazier to the multitudes skating and watching sideshows. Swift says he is in immediate contact with the petty writers of the day who gained the name of 'Grub Street hacks' from the road in which many had their lodgings. He believes he belongs to a select band of wits whose superiority is tickled by the degrees of 'badness' of the rest of the frequenters of the coffee-house at St James and who can lead the fashion for what productions appear in the play-houses. He used St James as a *poste restante* and also would have met 'knots of Irish folk' there. It was only one of his haunts. In the *Journal to Stella* another coffee-house gives the stamp of authenticity to the latest foreign news, when he uses it as a byline: 'Robin's Coffee-house. We

have great news just now from Spain; Madrid taken, and Pampeluna'
(20 September 1710). Robin's coffee-house was in Exchange Alley,
just off Lombard Street near the Old Stocks Market and near the
Exchange, familiarly called the ''Change'. The wealthier citizens
and men-of-business met there and Swift knew the area well. Some
months later he joined a large party which, taking three coaches:

> all hackneys, set out at ten o'clock this morning from lord
> Shelburn's house in Picadilly to the Tower, and saw all the sights,
> lions, &c. then to the Bedlam; then dined at the Chop-house
> behind the Exchange; then to Gresham College (but the keeper
> was not at home) and concluded that night at the Puppet-Shew.
> (*Journal to Stella*, 13 December, 1710)

The Bedlam was the Bethlehem Hospital for the insane, near Grub
Street, and not far from Gresham's in Bishopsgate Street where the
Royal Society met. In his later satire, Swift placed Gulliver's home
in this vicinity in order to recall its emphasis on trade and business
affairs, the new journalism, the madhouse and the modern science.
Swift has Gulliver present a giant tooth to Gresham's, on his return
from his journey to Brobdingnag.

Pat Rogers tells us[5] that there were 3000 coffee-house establishments in London at this time and that communal reading of papers
and journals there became the rage. Addison, who was one of Swift's
early London friends, a government undersecretary and also secretary to the influential Whig, Lord Halifax, reckoned that his journal,
The Spectator, had 20 readers for each issue so that he could count
on 3000. J.A. Downie suggests the figure may be inflated but certainly many consulted the papers available to read, while drinking
the coffee or chocolate. Such places were where someone living in
a garret or an itinerant person could have an address for letters,
where jobs might be mentioned and money-business transacted, in
addition to hearing the gossip of the town. Rogers comments that
they were 'almost exclusively male preserves' but independent women
did not seem to resent this.

London illustrated (1708–1714)
Bickerstaff Papers 1708

The intimacy of the coffee-house society made possible one of Swift's
most famous 'bites'. Many would have known of the preposterous
prophecies of John Partridge's almanacs, *Merlinus Liberatus*. These
had become popular reading, which coincided with an interest encouraged by the early growth of insurance schemes. Lloyds mari-
time insurance began life in a coffee-house; fire insurance was founded
in 1680; and life insurance followed soon after. Soon such things
as cuckoldry and lying could be insured against and the fever of

the money-market was animated partly by a spirit of gambling. Bets were placed on Marlborough's battles and Parliament attempted to ban the practice. Partridge's forecasts owed their popularity to this desire to wager on the future and Swift decided to make a fool of him. Ehrenpreis accounts for Swift's exposure of Partridge as an example of his 'loathing for any saboteur of true religion, whether atheist, Dissenter, or quack' and while this is true as far as it goes, it underplays the significance of the monied interest behind Partridge's popularity. Just as a lottery might be seen as an extension of capitalistic enterprise, the taste for almanacs could be seen as an expression of those who lay out money on the future.

In the *Bickerstaff Papers*, Swift assumed various characters in a series of pamphlets. Such multiple impersonation was a natural extension of the talents Swift had shown in *A Tale of a Tub*. The first of these assumes the character of another almanac writer called Isaac Bickerstaff and he forecasts the death of Partridge. (Another was of a writer who pronounced the matter was a hoax, but Swift decided not to publish this.) Later, when the date had passed, another persona produced an account of the death of Partridge. This was followed by a broadside elegy on the death which appeared to come from an anonymous Grub Street writer – yet another Swiftian disguise. When Partridge protested, Bickerstaff came back with 'proofs' that the protester did not exist. Encouraged, no doubt as Swift intended, by this seeming controversy, other writers joined in with make-believe characters agreeing and disagreeing about the death of Partridge to the general hilarity of followers of the affair. In such a mêlée the thin protests of Partridge that he was still alive were in vain. And, by his participating at all, the spoof was complete, leaving no standards by which to distinguish Partridge's quack prophecy from Bickerstaff's phoney imitation. Swift concluded: 'If Mr Partridge . . . be again alive, long may he continue so; that does not in the least contradict my veracity; but I think I have proved, *by invincible demonstration*, that he died at furthest within half an hour of the time I foretold.'

The Tatler, 1709

The Bickerstaff affair delighted a fellow Irishman, Richard Steele, whom Swift had met with Addison. He borrowed the pen name of Isaac Bickerstaff in launching (12 April 1709) a periodical called *The Tatler* and invited Swift to contribute. In its early life the periodical probably profited from a fair amount of advice from Swift. Its medley of topics were intended to reflect the diversity of topics and interests of the London reading public and so *The Tatler* assumed the device that different numbers issued from different coffee-houses according to the nature of the establishment:

ALL Accounts of Gallantry, Pleasure *and* Entertainment, *shall be under the Article of* White's Chocolate-House; Poetry, *under that of* Will's Coffee-House; Learning, *under the Title of* Grecian; Foreign *and* Domestick News, *you will have from* St. James's Coffee-House.

This represented the profuse and varied conversation in which Swift revelled and Steele acknowledged his help when the periodical was issued in a collected edition:

> *my Acknowledgements to Dr. Swift, whose pleasant Writings, in the Name of* Bickerstaff, *created an Inclination in the Town towards any Thing that could appear in the same Disguise . . . a certain uncommon Way of Thinking, and a Turn in Conversation peculiar to that agreeable Gentleman, rendered his Company very advantageous to one whose Imagination was to be continually employed upon obvious and common Subjects*

A Description of the Morning, 1709

Swift's first major contribution to *The Tatler* was in issue number 9 for 30 April 1709. This was his poem *A Description of the Morning* which owes much of its effect to its playing with the conventions of pastoral poetry, where the reader's expectations of the usual agreeable descriptions are only partly fulfilled and are given a new turn. Such a method implies a cultivated literary reader and *The Tatler's* approach was to encourage good breeding without disturbing the reader's self-esteem. So, true to this didactic and improving style, Steele introduced the poem in the tattle of a man about town who recognises a good thing. Having descanted on the latest play by Congreve he turns to a wholly new kind of poem written by 'Mr Humphrey Wagstaff' (making allusion to the author's kinship with Bickerstaff):

> This Evening we were entertained with *The Old Batchelor* . . . The Part of *Fondlewife* is a liveley Image of the unseasonable Fondness of Age . . . an ingenious Kinsman of mine, of the Family of the *Staffs*, Mr. *Humphrey Wagstaff* by Name, has, to avoid their Strain, run into a Way perfectly new, and described Things exactly as they happen: He never forms Fields, or Nymphs, or Groves where they are not, but makes the Incidents just as they really appear. [quotes the poem]

Steele ensures his reader cannot miss the prosaic nature of the poem which turns an idealised pastoral into a more seedy urban scene. The poem's general effect is that it is written by a supremely confident insider, a townee who is wholly at ease in London. As we have seen, Swift, the clergyman on a mission from Dublin, was increasingly uneasy with his reception by the Whig grandees. So it may be that part of his motive in writing it was to pass off as socially secure but that is not apparent in the poem. Swift's arch knowingness comes over in the opening lines which seem to mark the normal signs of break of day in a town dwelling:

> Now Betty from her master's bed has flown
> And softly stole to discompose her own.

He engineers a hesitation to be sure what has happened – was Betty making the bed and running about early morning duties? – delaying the surprise of her discomposing her own bed and confirming the suspicion of her illicit love-making. It is a slight poem but Steele hailed it as a new manner of writing and its success with the reading public prepared the way for another more extended urban pastoral.

A Description of a City Shower, 1710

In *A Description of a City Shower* (1710) Swift shows even greater familiarity with London and some of the incidents are drawn from personal experience recorded in *Journal to Stella*. There he had complained of the stink coming from the channel that served as a gutter in the road outside his lodging and also he declared he would avoid if possible paying for a hackney coach by walking.

> Returning home at night you find the sink
> Strike your offended sense with double stink.
> If you be wise, then go not far to dine,
> You spend in coach-hire more than save in wine.

This is a case of private reference for friends such as Stella who would know his self-mockery in speaking of such things. He was frugal in order to be a charitable man in private and walked as much for his health as to save a fare. To other public eyes the poem might convey over-fastidiousness and meanness.

His description of a sedan chair with its occupant, possibly stranded while the chairmen have taken cover from the rain, is remarkably specific in conveying something seen and heard from first hand:

> Boxed in a chair the beau impatient sits,
> While spouts run clattering o'er the roof by fits;
> And ever and anon with frightful din
> The leather sounds; he trembles from within.
> So when Troy chairmen bore the wooden steed,
> Pregnant with Greeks, impatient to be freed;
> (Those bully Greeks, who, as the moderns do,
> Instead of paying chairmen, run them through)
> Laocoon struck the outside with his spear,
> And each imprisoned hero quaked for fear.

The enclosure of the sedan chair amplifies to the sitter inside the sound of raindrops to the din of war and then a fantastic imagination takes over the poem, shrinking the great wooden horse of Troy to a sedan chair; and wittily comparing a spear to a fop's rapier. This mimics the allegorical *procedé* of *The Battle of the Books* and looks towards the inversions of *Gulliver's Travels* where the favourite image of the wooden horse also recurs. The whole poem again conveys Swift as the Irishman at ease in London and with his friends: with shared intimacies; common judgements of social life; and an appreciation of the art of allusion which includes the mock-heroic.

Search for community: Tatlers and Scriblerians

Break with the Whigs

Soon after this, Swift's circle of friends and readers changed with his political realignment. Apart from his discontent over the lack of progress of gaining the First Fruits, Swift had other reasons for breaking with the Whig administration. His religious beliefs and his wish to advance his own career propelled him into another arena. The Whigs were keen to repeal the Act which prevented dissenters from holding public office. In the Irish House of Commons, Speaker Broderick had taken the Whig line by speaking against the Act of Occasional Conformity which required from public officials occasional acts of worship according to the rites of the Church of England, such as taking the communion. Swift was cross-questioned on this and courageously voiced his opposition. 'My Ld Sommers . . . desired my Opinion upon it, which I gave him truly, tho with all the Gentleness I could' (Letter to King, 15 April 1708). Godolphin, in veiled language, said that the granting of remission of the First Fruits depended on the Irish church making 'due Acknowlegement', or in other words taking away the religious restrictions from dissenters. Swift wrote and published round about the 24 December 1708, an anonymous *Letter . . . concerning the Sacramental Test*, which opposed the Whig religious policy and also praised Archbishop King, a fact he did not fail to bring to King's attention in an oblique manner, by pretending he had no idea who the author of the pamphlet was but that 'your Grace's Character is justly set forth: For the rest some Parts are very well, and others puerile, and some Facts, as I am informed, wrong represented' (Letter to King, 6 January 1709).

In this age of patronage, Swift knew that the art of flattery gained preferment and probably expected King to see that he was the author but he constantly refused to sacrifice principle and judgement in the praises he gave. This had the effect that, if he was playing the game, he did it gracelessly and, if he was not, he was setting himself up as a judge of his 'superiors'. So what he said fell on deaf ears. He tried several baits. He mentioned the 'deanery of Down is fallen', 10 February 1708, but this preferment needed Wharton's approval and he had already sunk his chances by opposing the Whig policy on the Test. On 9 November 1708 he wrote to Archdeacon Walls about a Reverend Thomas King's living at Swords, a prebend of St Patrick's cathedral known as 'the golden one': 'if Mr King dyes, I have desired people to tell the A.Bp that I will have the Living'. But by 8 February 1709 another relative of the Archbishop was appointed to Swords.

Swift's disaffection from his Whiggish colleagues eventually made him break from the social connections. Party politics got in the way of the friendships he so much desired. As the anonymous author of *A Description of a Shower* and of *The Virtues of Sid Hamet the Magician's Rod* he had the discomfort of hearing both being denigrated at a Whig dinner party, because they were thought to be Tory poems:

> I dined today at lady Lucy's, where they ran down my *Shower*; and said *Sid Hamet* was the silliest poem they ever read and told Prior so, whom they thought the author of it. Don't you wonder I never dined there before? But I am too busy, and they live too far off; and besides, I don't like women so much as I did. MD you must know, are not women.
>
> (*Journal to Stella*, 10 November 1710)

While Prior bore the brunt of this attack Swift could observe that friendship would not spare indiscriminate party posturing. *Sid Hamet* had attacked the Whig Godolphin, but there was nothing political about the *Shower* but its being believed to be the brainchild of a Tory. With comic ruefulness Swift advances a number of spurious excuses not to visit again – busyness, distance, not liking women – and the last for the moment encourages the illogical exemption of 'MD' (my dears) from their gender in order to allow him to banter on. Later he did indeed stop visiting Lady Lucy and also meeting *confrères* in the coffee-houses. 'I never go to a Coffeehouse' he wrote to Ford, 8 September 1711, although on 29 December 1711 he was writing his *Journal to Stella* in a coffee-house. A correction he made after this makes it clear that he meant he scarcely visited: 'I ~~frequent~~ go to no Coffee House' (26 February 1713). So he had to rely on reports from others and with some pleasurable alarm recorded that he might be targeted by the tearaway street prowlers, known as the Mohocks: 'My man tells me, that one of the lodgers heard in a coffee-house, publicly, that one design of the Mohocks was upon me, if they could catch me; and though I believe nothing of it, I forbear walking late.'

Swift breaks with Steele and Addison

While Swift was greatly concerned not to let party come in the way of friendship, his break with Richard Steele was almost inevitable as a consequence of their characters. Steele was touchy about his own claims to fame and fortune and Swift was overbearing in his desire to dominate in the friendship. In the incident which provoked the break Swift was the cooler of the two in seeing the central issue was one of honouring personal relationships and he was more desirous of continuing the friendly behaviour each had shown to the other.

The estrangement began with Steele attacking him personally in his periodical, *The Guardian*, for a piece criticising Marlborough in *The Examiner* of 11 May 1713, which he must have known was probably not by Swift. Swift had ceased to be the principal editor for the journal in June 1711, in order to concentrate on *The Conduct of the Allies*, and twice the new editor had declared Swift's non-involvement, although in fact Swift did make a rare occasional contribution afterwards but not to this number. The style of the piece was unlike Swift's. So there was enough doubt to suggest that Steele should have contacted him first.

Swift wrote to Addison asking him to intercede but he merely distanced himself and passed on Swift's letter to Steele. A short and increasingly bitter correspondence took place between the two principals in the argument. In his letter to Addison, Swift disclaimed authorship of *The Examiner* essay and told him that he had spoken in favour of Steele (which indeed he had) when the change of ministry might have lost him his government post as Commissioner of the Stamp Office. But Steele was incensed that Swift should state that he owed his position to his intercession and, as he had been seeing Harley privately in any case, would not admit that Swift had given him any of the help he needed. He answered that he doubted the sincerity of Swift's disclaimer about being the writer of the issue of *The Examiner* and he jibed that really Harley was laughing at Swift behind his back if he had made him think he had influence.

Swift replied that, if Steele thought he was the author, he should have spoken to him first privately and, as for his supposed folly in giving Harley his advice, 'if your interpretation were true, I was laughed at only for your sake; which, I think is going pretty far to serve a friend'. Becoming more pained in ensuing exchanges, Swift insisted that he had not ever attacked Steele in public but had taken care for him. Steele now justified himself that as a supporter of Marlborough he must write his opinions whatever the cost might be to himself. This did not address the issue of falsely blaming Swift and having insulted him on his wisdom in choosing Harley as a friend. Moreover, he added that Swift's criticism of him to Addison was ill usage. Swift replied that he was justified in complaining as Steele had called him, a clergyman (and a friend), an infidel. The matter had become a personal one and while they might have differences of political opinion these should not have contaminated their friendship.

Steele shifts his ground to justify himself. Even if we give him the benefit of the doubt and accept that this is a true opposition between private moralities and the duties of patriotism, such an attitude is open to question. Later in the century, Samuel Johnson coined the saying 'Patriotism is the last refuge of the scoundrel.' Defending the honour of Marlborough has a fine sound to it but cannot excuse an attack on the wrong person, a false accusation of infidelity and a dubious insinuation striking at other friendships. The break was irrevocable and, soon after, Swift published a personal attack on Steele's pamphlet *The Importance of Dunkirk Consider'd* in an essay called *The Importance of the Guardian Consider'd* (October 1713).

Unlike the fiery Steele, Addison was suave and diplomatic, in a memorable phrase of Ehrenpreis often 'pushing tact to the edge of obsequiousness'.[6] With Swift's star rising in the Harley administration, he continued to preserve an easy cordiality, writing to him on 11 April 1710 with assumed deference: 'I am forced to give my self Airs of a punctual Correspond[ce] with you in discourse with your friends at St James's Coffee-house who are always asking me Questions about you when they have a mind to pay their Court to me, if I may use so magnificent a Phrase.' Swift would have noticed the flattery contained in the idea that they pay court to Addison only as the friend of Swift and, while this would probably not have displeased him, it was not on these grounds that he continued a friend. He was not to be bought at so cheap a price. For example, when later Knightley Chetwode pursued him 'in spight of my teeth', Swift tried to shake off his fawning presence, even to the extent of his feigning being at death's door. Addison on the other hand deserved his attention for he had taken him up when he needed help with the Whigs, was a cultivated scholar and a pious moralist. Politically he was far removed, being an unquestioning supporter of the war, and of the Habsburg candidate, and an apologist for trade and the money-market which put Britain 'in the midst of a mighty affluence of all the necessaries and conveniences of life'.[7] But like Swift he was able to separate his social contacts from his political involvement. Nevertheless, as the Steele episode shows, Addison had little to offer in terms of real friendship (although the relationship remained sufficiently cordial for Swift to solicit his interest on behalf of another in 1718, the year before Addison died). Fortunately for Swift, Addison had an associate, a young genius of a poet, who would prove a more affectionate though flawed friend and also a stimulating companion as politics began to dub Swift a Tory.

The Scriblerus Club

Alexander Pope was rapidly making a name for himself with his fine poems, *An Essay on Criticism* (1711), *The Rape of the Lock* (two canto version, 1712) and *Windsor Forest* (1713). Originally he was supported by Addison at Buttons coffee-house but his friendship cooled when he discovered Addison covertly supporting the rival claims of Ambrose Phillips as landscape poet, playing off one against the other. Like Swift he learned from hard experience the bitterness of the duplicity of so-called friends and similarly he had the strong inclinations and the literary gifts that would prove every bit as capable of providing the sense of artistic community which the Irishman had sought in his urban poems, suggestive, as I have said, of shared intimacies; common judgements of social life; and an appreciation of the art of allusion.

Swift was already an established and celebrated writer when Pope, 21 years his junior, approached him in October 1713 to collaborate in a monthly burlesque called the *Works of the Unlearned*. This was the genesis of the 'Scriblerus Club' whose influence would stretch beyond the short period where actual meetings of friends took place to shape literary works that would dominate the literature of the first half of the eighteenth-century. By February 1714 the group who were going to mock false learning had narrowed down to Pope and his friend John Gay, Swift with his friend the physician to Queen Anne, Dr John Arbuthnot, whom Pope probably did not know at that time, and their mutual friend, the Irish poet and clergyman, Thomas Parnell. Later Oxford joined their company. Wit, fellowship and good spirits characterised their meetings, in which a certain amount of mutual teasing attested their intimacy. Charles Kerby-Miller tells some good stories of them.[8] Parnell heard Pope reading his *Rape of the Lock* and from memory privately translated part of it into Latin. Next day he produced the Latin and accused Pope of plagiarising a monkish manuscript. On another occasion, Parnell worried that Swift by his habit of walking rapidly would secure the best bed at Lord Bathurst's home where they were to stay. So he took a horse and rode ahead to persuade Bathurst to send a servant out saying there was smallpox in the house. Swift would not go in and instead ate a cold meal in a summer house while the others feasted inside.

With the break up of the Tory ministry, the members of the company could no longer meet so readily and it became a loose association (April 1715) leaving out Oxford and Parnell from its activities. In August, Swift departed for Ireland and the last meeting of the group as Scriblerians was in November of that year. However, their association gave rise to a number of important works each with Scriblerian colour. The matrix from which they sprang was the

Memoirs of Martinus Scriblerus which was largely composed in 1714, with all the group contributing to some extent. In 1716–18 a smaller group of the Scriblerians, consisting just of Pope, Arbuthnot and Gay, met and Arbuthnot provided most of the supplementary ideas with Pope polishing them. Some further additions were made in 1726–29 including a chapter in which Martinus promises to tell elsewhere of his travels in terms which suggest those of Swift's Gulliver. The *Memoirs* trace the unfortunate adventures of a misguided virtuoso who is unable to discriminate between true and false learning. Although it was not published until 1751, this guiding pseudo-biography lies behind other notable works of the Club: Pope's *Key to The Lock* (1715) which gives a burlesque scholarly annotation to Pope's poem; Gay's one-act play, *The What D'ye Call It* (1715), a burlesque tragedy; Pope and Arbuthnot's *Peri Bathous, or the Art of Sinking in Poetry* (begun 1715, published 1728), a mock primer undermining pretentious critics who dogmatically apply the rules of rhetoric to the appreciation of poetry; Swift's *Gulliver's Travels* (1726); and Pope's *The Dunciad* (three-book version, 1729). In an early draft this was originally called 'The Progress of Dulness' and Swift who read it in manuscript on a visit to Pope prevented him from throwing it in the fire, thereby preserving the core of what became one of Pope's most admired satires. Pope generously credited Swift with helping to stimulate the poem and it clearly consummates their common attack on Scriblerian mediocrity, with its central history of an identifiable rabble of nit-wits taking over the metropolis, the seats of learning and the whole country and with its accompaniment of a huge apparatus of pseudo-notes from crazed commentators.

Swift's friends: Gay and Arbuthnot

While Pope and Swift were the major literary figures among the Scriblerians, the other members extended the sense of activity into something more representative than a clique or coterie and, as Swift wrote to Gay, nourished 'the best and greatest part of my life . . . there I made my friendship and there I left my desires' (8 January 1723). Writing became a communal enterprise. He had suggested in a letter to Pope that someone should write a 'Newgate pastoral' and this was the germ of the idea for Gay's *Beggars' Opera* (1729). The opera took London by storm with its representation of the criminal world of the highwayman, Macheath, presided over by the Newgate jailer, Peacham, and mirroring the social distinctions of the fashionable world in the low life of rascals, interspersing songs to well-known English airs as a kind of riposte to the arias of Italian operas in vogue. Like *Peri Bathous* it reflected by implication on highflown taste and subverted the watchwords of the Whig political regime by placing them in the mouths of rogues. Lavinia Fenton, the 19-year old actress who played Polly Peacham, became a celebrity, eloped, had her 'sayings' collected and printed and was painted in the dungeon scene from the opera by Hogarth. Swift with some pride delicately alluded to his contribution in a friendly letter to Gay (1731) about discovering 'scheames for writing' when 'it is possible, that sometimes a friend may give you a lucky one just suited to your imagination'.

The letters between Swift and Gay and between Swift and Arbuthnot provided a lifeline for the exile in Dublin. Arbuthnot's dependable friendship, no matter how long the gap in contact, comes over in such warm greetings as these: 'I can not help imagining some of our old club mett together like Mariners after a Storm', 'Your deafness is so necessary a thing, that I allmost begin to think it is an affectation', 'I have not had the pleasure of a line from you these two years; I wrote one about your health, to which I had no answer.' We have seen Swift's refusal to damage his friendship with Oxford under pressure from Bolingbroke and can infer how greatly he must have appreciated being himself on the receiving end of such loyalty (ready to resume contact after unexplained gaps) and good humour. Aware of his great pleasure in Arbuthnot, Swift comically wrote to Pope how he kept his feet on the ground and gave praise with discrimination by discovering he has a fault. But it turns out to be such a fault as makes no difference and becomes a characteristic aspect of Arbuthnot's familiar figure: 'Our Doctor has every Quality and virtue that can make a man amiable or usefull, but alas he hath a sort of Slouch in his Walk.' Arbuthnot had done much the same to Swift in thinking his deafness 'so necessary a thing'.

Part of the value of the close friendship of the Scriblerians was in the disagreements it provoked. Critical faculties remained sharp and, given the difference in generations, there might be unresolvable difference of opinion, despite very cordial feelings. It was Arbuthnot, born in the same year as Swift, who could share Swift's scepticism regarding the optimism of the younger Scriblerians, Pope and Bolingbroke. Swift could rely on him to take for granted his cordial friendship towards them, when he wrote that the simple pleasures of retirement which Pope and Bolingbroke affected in comfortable circumstances[9] cut no ice with him. 'You and I could not live with My L^d Bo – or Mr Pope; they are both too temperate and too wise for me, and too profound, and too poor' (Swift to Arbuthnot, November 1734). And Arbuthnot's sympathetic understanding of Swift made him mention the recent death of Gay with the kind of sardonic humour that would encourage Swift not to dwell too much on his sadness but to gird his loins to beat off an ever-present Grub Street enemy, 'Curle (who is one of the new terrors of Death) has been writing Letters to every body for memoirs of [Gay's] life' (Arbuthnot to Swift, 13 January 1733). When Arbuthnot died two years later, Swift wrote to Pope that 'The Death of M[r] Gay & the Doctor hath been terrible wounds near my heart' (12 May 1735).

The uses of exile

Given the bonds of friendship and cultural identity with those in England, it is small wonder that Swift felt the bitterness of separation in making Ireland his permanent home after 1715. With hindsight we can see that it gave him opportunities for reflection and to exercise self-discipline to adjust to new circumstances which led to some of his greatest satire, such as *The Drapier's Letters*, *Gulliver's Travels* and *A Modest Proposal*. It is also the beginning of the period in which he wrote most of his poems with their specific reference and conversational tone, one of which (*In Sickness*) begins:

> Tis true – then why should I repine,
> To see my life so fast decline?
> But, why obscurely here alone?
> Where I am neither loved or known.
> My state of health none care to learn;
> My life is here no soul's concern.
> And, those with whom I now converse,
> Without a tear will tend my hearse.
> Removed from kind Arbuthnot's aid,
> Who knows his art but not his trade;
> Preferring his regard for me
> Before his credit or his fee.

This tone of lament should not be taken as the result of a simple antipathy to Ireland. In the first place Swift had no love for nationhood of any sort, English, Irish or Scottish. (He wrote to Pope, 'I have ever hated all Nations', 29 September 1725.) His public spirit turned on a concern for individuals and shared humanity. In the second place, Ireland's identity was crushed under a narrow and illiberal policy, stemming from Poyning's Law of 1494 which disabled the Irish Parliament from legislating without prior approval from the English Parliament (see p. 28). Swift was as much complaining about the conditions which had been imposed by English policy, the results of which he was suffering from too. As he wrote to Pope, Ireland was sidelined from the mainstream of political decision-making, all of which occurred in London. 'I have continued ever since in the greatest privacy, and utter ignorance of the events which are most commonly talked of in the world; I neither know the Names nor Number of the Family which now reigns, further than the Prayer-book informs me. I cannot tell who is Chancellor, who are Secretaries, nor with what Nations we are in peace or war' (10 January 1721). Apart from the personal check to his career and the sense of mortality that it brought, there seemed little scope for his talents in Dublin under the restrictive nepotism of Archbishop King so that 'I was three years reconciling myself to the Scene and the Business to which fortune hath condemned me, and Stupidity [i.e. 'insensibility'] was what I had recourse to' (to Gay, 8 January 1723). The remoteness of London inspired the image in *Gulliver's Travels* of a flying island which could only be reached by a petitioner sending a paper to be threaded on a kite string and blown upwards by the wind to somewhere near its destination. On the eve of the publication of this momentous work Swift doubted he would be heard: 'my voice is so weak that I doubt [Fortune] will never hear me' (to Pope 29 September 1725).

Home thoughts from Ireland

It is unlikely that such an individual as Swift would have been content in any country but his remarks over a period show a genuine interest in and sympathy for Ireland. It certainly exercised a strong attraction when he imagined in the *Journal to Stella* being 'plaguy busy at Laracor cutting down willows' and dreamed of his cherries, trouts and canal. After the success of his pro-Irish pamphlets and of *Gulliver's Travels* had, as it were, validated his own self-worth in this new situation, he wrote with equal condemnation of both countries.

> God forbid I should condemn you to Ireland (*Quanquam O!*) and for England I despair; and indeed a change of affairs would come too late in my season of life and might probably produce nothing on my behalf . . . Except absence from friends, I confess freely that I have no discontent at living here; besides what arises from a silly spirit of Liberty, which as it neither sowers my drink, nor hurts my meat, nor spoils my stomach farther than in imagination, so I resolve to throw it off.
>
> (to Pope 10 May 1728)

He would not accept Pope's view of him having a national role and said for 'your kind opinion of me as a Patriot . . . I do not deserve; because what I do is owing to perfect rage and resentment, and the mortifying sight of slavery, folly, and baseness about me, among which I am forced to live' (to Pope 1 June 1728). At the same time he reflected on circumstances in national terms.

> As to this country, there have been three terrible years dearth of corn, and every place strowed with beggars, but dearths are common in better climates, and our evils here lie much deeper.

93

Imagine a nation the two-thirds of whose revenues are spent out of it, and who are not permitted to trade with the other third, and where the pride of women will not suffer them to wear their own manufactures even where they excel what come from abroad.[10]

(to Pope 11 August 1729)

And the ordinary folk were in no doubt whose side he was on, even if they did not appreciate the finer points which qualified Swift's defence of their rights. When he returned to Dublin, 8 October 1729, Williams[11] notes that he 'was received with general rejoicing from the populace, the ringing of bells, bonfires, and illuminations'.

Eventually Bolingbroke found him the living of Burghfield, near Reading, England, and wrote, 'I suppose it will not be hard to persuade them that, it is better for them you should be a private parish Preist in an English county, than a dean in the metropolis of Ireland, where I know they have felt, y^r authority and influence' (18 July 1732). Swift replied that it paid less than he was getting in Dublin, for it was 'just too short by 300 ll a year . . . I want to be Minister of Amesbury, Dawly, Twitenham, Riskins and Prebendary of Westminster, else I will not stir a step.' Apart from his unpreparedness to lower his standard of living and his standing, we can see that his choice of parish names includes all the locations where his friends were plus what he considered he was promised by King William **in 1692**, the prebendary of Westminster. So he wanted more freedom to be with friends than seemed possible and a restitution for past neglect. He told Gay 'I would rather be a freeman among slaves than a slave among freemen. The dignity of my present Station damps the pertness of inferior puppyes & Squires' (3 October 1732) and he boasted to Pope, 'I walk the streets in peace, without being justled, nor ever without a thousand blessings from my friends the Vulgar. I am Lord Mayor of 120 houses, I am absolute Lord[12] of the greatest Cathedral in the Kingdom: am at peace with the neighbouring Princes, the Lord Mayor of the City, and the A. Bp. of Dublin' (8 July 1733). At the same time it rankled that he no longer inhabited the corridors of power and rubbed shoulders with the powerful:

I walk the streets, and so do my lower friends, from whom and from whom alone, I have a thousand hats and blessings upon old scores, which those we call the gentry have forgot. But I have not the love, or hardly the civility, of any one man in power . . . nor am able to do the least good office to the most deserving man . . . What hath sunk my spirits . . . is reflecting on the most execrable Corruptions that run through every branch of publick management.

(Swift to Pope, 9 February 1737)

Ireland's claim

A Proposal for the Universal Use of Irish Manufacture, 1720

Despite Swift's hatred for nations, political events stirred him to write from a viewpoint that was increasingly pro-Irish. In 1719 the Irish House of Lords had appealed directly to the king of England, George I, to assert his authority against the English House of Lords. A dispute over the property of Maurice Annesley in County Kildare had raised the question of what was the highest legal authority for Irish matters. Annesley had owed money to a widow, Hester Sherlock, and she was awarded possession of some of his lands by the Parliament of Ireland 'until she should Receive thereout a certain Sum of Money to her Decreed to be Due and Chargeable on the said Lands'. Annesley appealed to the English House of Lords; regained his lands; and the High Sheriff of Kildare, who had carried out the order to seize the lands, was fined, demonstrating the subservience of Irish law to English law. The Irish House of Lords petitioned the king, asserting the status of Ireland as an independent member of the kingdom, owing direct allegiance to the king rather than through an English Parliament. Part of the pamphlet is reproduced on plate 7. In response, the English passed a Declaratory Act in 1720, asserting 'full power and authority to make laws . . . to bind the kingdom and people of Ireland'. In a letter to Ford (4 April 1720), Swift contrasted the better terms that Scotland had been given. It had a separate policy-making Parliament up to the Act of Union 1707, and afterwards had strong representation in Parliament at London, sending 16 peers to the House of Lords and 45 MPs to the House of Commons. Swift argued that the lack of freedom crippled Irish abilities for self-government: 'the Question is whether People ought to be Slaves or no . . . fetter a Man seven years, then let him loose to shew his Skill in dancing, and because he does it awkwardly, you say he ought to be fettered for Life'. Despite their 'having been the most loyall submissive complying Subjects that ever Prince had' Irish folk, including Non-conformist settlers, now said 'no Subjects were ever so ill treated'.

At the same time as this outrage, England moved to pass a Bill which protected its own manufacture of wool and silk. Swift countered with (May 1720) *A Proposal for the Universal Use of Irish Manufacture,* as a riposte 'to persuade the wretched people to wear their own Manufactures instead of those from England' (letter to Pope, 10 January 1721). In this letter Swift attacked the Cromwellian settlers who left the mark of their conquering zeal on the demolished tower of Ormonde's castle in Kilkenny. He recalled speaking to 'a certain

Minister', possibly Oxford, about 'that Whiggish or fanatical Genius so prevalent among the English of this kingdom: his Lordship accounted for it by that number of Cromwell's soldiers, adventurers establish'd here, who were all of the sourest Leven, and the meanest birth, and whose posterity are now in possession of their lands and their principles'. The dispossession of the native Irish and the merely subordinate positions available to them clearly troubled him. He could make common cause, for as he wrote on 28 April 1739: 'My Grandfather was so persecuted and plundered two and fifty Times by the Barbarity of Cromwell's Hellish Crew . . . that the poor old Gentleman was forced to sell half of his Estate to support his Family'.

The pamphlet was extremely popular and the printer, Edward Waters, was prosecuted. Seditious material was treated as matter of common law and the jury were merely required to 'decide on the facts of a publication – whether or not that publication was libel was a decision that was made by a judge'.[13] The trial jury refused to convict and nine times Lord Chief Justice Whitshed sent them out to reconsider. After 11 hours they recorded a 'special verdict' which left Waters to the mercy of the ambitious judge. Swift, however, negotiated to have the matter quashed, using his contacts with Sir Thomas Hanmer, stepfather of the new Lord Lieutenant of Ireland, Charles Fitzroy, 2nd Duke of Grafton.

The Drapier's Letters, 1724, and Lord Lieutenant Carteret

Soon after, in July 1722, another English event brought Swift into Irish ranks protesting against unfair treatment. An ironmaster, William Wood, bribed the Duchess of Kendal, mistress of King George I, and had gained a patent in the crown prerogative to mint small copper coins for use in Ireland. The Irish immediately expressed hostility on several grounds. They feared that he would flood the market (which might sustain an influx of no more than £20 000) in order to make the considerable profits he boasted were there. They believed that the coin would be debased by being very much below the value he was permitted to rate them at and by being easily forged. They argued that the matter had been agreed without consultation with the Irish Parliament. Indeed it was a lax arrangement. Initially there were no checks to be made on Wood's mint in Bristol and the rate of coins was set at 30 pence to the pound weight of pure copper rather than the 23 usual in England. Eventually Wood agreed to reduce the quantity of coin from £100 000 to £50 000 and his coins were assayed by Sir Isaac Newton. But this did not calm the situation. The profit had to come from somewhere and Newton's assay[14] of the copper that Wood provided left doubts concerning Wood's ability, let alone his wish, to control the quality of his coin. While the assay showed that each piece was above the face value, the coins were still of unequal weight. Perhaps these had been selected and others would be under weight. In addition, they were 'all manufactured after March 25, 1723' whereas the coins sent to Ireland were minted in 1722.

Swift took part in the considerable protest by writing five letters in the character of a draper, the first coming out in March 1724 and the last in December of that year. Although Swift was not unique in his arguments, his pamphlets have a special effectiveness. The draper speaks in the accent of the common working man but there are hints enough for the enjoyment of Dubliners that Swift is in fact the author, confident of his ability to handle a prosecution. He released each letter with a particular thrust at crucial points in the development of the political argument. As Wood protested and counter-attacked with 'evidence' that the Irish wanted the coin and that those who opposed were Jacobites and papists, Swift met each blow with another that raised the stakes.

In the first letter, the draper's connection with the woollen trade makes it natural for him to connect this affair with events which Swift described in his *Proposal* of 1720:

> About three Years ago, a little Book was written, to advise all People to wear the *Manufactures of this our own Dear Country*: It had no other Design, said nothing against the *King* or *Parliament*, or *any Man*, yet the POOR PRINTER was prosecuted two Years, with the utmost Violence, and even some WEAVERS themselves, for whose Sake it was written, being upon the JURY, FOUND HIM GUILTY.

The draper and Swift are thus seen as allies and a radical view emerges from their agreement. Both events show how the English dominate Irish affairs and that it is necessary to rise above party attitude to embrace 'our own Dear Country'. Swift warns the Irish that they may not see where their best interests are and ventures on to revolutionary ground. According to Ehrenpreis the Drapier's initials, 'MB', may stand for Marcus Brutus, the republican Roman who struck down Julius Caesar whom he believed to be a tyrant.

The Duke of Grafton found the matter too hot to handle and Walpole sent in his stead as Lord Lieutenant of Ireland, John 2nd Lord Carteret, as a useful way of sidelining this rival Whig MP and possibly compromising him. Swift had a high regard for him, a younger man (born 1690), and despite his belonging to the other party. He set to to involve him in the Drapier's cause. In a number of private letters between them Carteret met Swift's courtly grace and indirection with diplomatic guile and charm.

In a welcome-to-Ireland letter, Swift enclosed the first of the published Drapier's letters as though it were a curiosity he had happpened to come across. When there was no reply he sent a second letter. Belatedly Carteret, who had probably guessed the authorship, confessed he was in the wrong and acknowledged the courteousness of Swift's reminder: 'If a months silence has been turn'd to my disadvantage in Yr esteem, it has at least had this good effect, that I am convinced by the kindness of yr reproaches, as well as by the goodness of yr advice that You still retain some part of yr former friendship for me' (Carteret to Swift, 20 June 1724). Swift then apologised for his own bullying tone, remarking that as an inferior he must be allowed to write the last letter (since it would need no reply). Carteret wrote again refusing to see him as an inferior and amusingly imagined Swift's reaction: 'Methinks I see you throw this letter upon Yr table in the height of spleen because it may have interupted some of Yr more agreable thoughts' but, he continued, 'I am not altogether insensible of the Genius, wch has outshone most of this age, & when You will display it again can convince us that its Lustre & strength are still the same' (4 August 1724).

Behind all this was Swift's attempt to coax support and Carteret's wish to oblige, without being ensnared in an open alliance which would give Walpole the excuse to sack him. So his strategy was to delay and appear in public to oppose illegal attacks on the government, until the weight of Irish opposition should make it necessary and politically wise to yield. It was for Swift to manage the manner and pace of persuasion.

In the Drapier's fourth letter Swift decided to tempt the hand of officialdom. He picked up the phrases from the petition of the Irish House of Lords to George I and met head on the decision that it was subordinate to the English Parliament, characterising such a view as narrowly English and tantamount to slave-owning. Irish folk who accepted these conditions were 'weak', an ambiguous phrase which could mean either weak in the head or too cowardly to resist.

> Those who come over hither to us from *England*, and some *Weak* People among our selves, whenever in a Discourse we make mention *of Liberty* and *Property*, shake their Heads, and tell us, that *Ireland* is a *Depending Kingdom*, as if they would seem by this Phrase, to intend that the People of *Ireland* is in some State of Slavery or Dependance different from those of England.

As M.B. Drapier, Swift loses all his Anglo–Irish identity and adopts a purely Irish stance.

Intending to force a confrontation of the authorities and himself, rather like the Sacheverell trial, he followed this with another, *A Letter to the Lord Chancellor Middleton*, in which he revealed that the author, M.B. Drapier, was none other than Jonathan Swift. But Archbishop King, now much reconciled to his dean, received a veiled warning from Carteret that even if M.B. Drapier were found to be Dr Swift he would be imprisoned without bail until 'his Majesty's pleasure shall be further signified to me'. Swift could not count on a confrontation in Ireland which would expose the greater injustice behind Wood's patent which had been given full support by Walpole. So he did not publish the letter and achieved his objective in the same manner as his *Proposal* with a repeat of the prosecution of his printer. Swift had a different printer from Edward Waters and this time it was the turn of a man called John Harding who could plead ignorance of the identity of the author and unawareness of the seditious content.

However, this prosecution was diverted by another tactic of Swift. Writing anonymously he produced a short *Seasonable Advice* to the grand jury of 23 men who had been assembled to decide on the case of Harding. He pointed out that three of the Drapier's letters had occasioned no offical action and that the fourth in the main repeated the same arguments. If Harding were convicted it would be tantamount to approving Wood. Carteret directed Lord Chief Justice William Whitshed to present the *Seasonable Advice* to the jury to consider whether it constituted interference with the course of law but they refused to condemn it. Whitshed dismissed them and impanelled another jury, delaying the question until the last days of the term for the court to sit. But they presented a document penned by Swift which declared against all who would impose Wood's halfpence on Ireland and asserted loyalty to King George I.

Carteret was now able to advise Walpole privately against continuing with the patent. Not knowing this, Swift had the Drapier publish on 14 December 1724: *A Letter To the Right Honourable the Lord Viscount Molesworth* in which the tradesman tactically confesses that he went too far and desires clarification of how Ireland's dependency may be understood. Although the pamphlet is interesting for seeing the development of Swift's political thought, the Drapier had already succeeded. Wood withdrew from the patent; Walpole secretly awarded him a munificent pension of £24 000 over eight years – to be drawn on the Irish exchequer. In April 1725 Swift was made a freeman of the city of Dublin.

Gulliver's Travels, 1726

The Irish political pamphlets not only restored Swift to an active role as writer. Consideration of the corruption and intolerance of the Walpole regime must have animated memories of the moderating politics of Oxford as Swift returned to the Scriblerian project of chronicling the travels of a virtuoso among the unlearned. Already, as the case of Wood's halfpence was drawing to a close, he had completed a first draft of *Gulliver's Travels*. He wrote to Ford, 19 January 1724, 'I have left the Country of Horses, and am in the flying Island, where I shall not stay long, and my two last Journyes will soon be over.' It was also natural that this work, more wide-ranging and reflective than the pamphlets, should also absorb the three-cornered debate that he was enjoying by letter with Bolingbroke and Pope.

Bolingbroke as a formative influence

After restoring his fortunes with the Whig government, Bolingbroke assumed the role of elder statesman in writing to Swift, telling him 'I am no longer the Bubble you knew me' (12 September 1724). With Oxford out of the way he felt able to purloin his political theory in *The Idea of a Patriot King* and advised Pope on the theological content of his *Essay on Man*, verging perilously on a deistic religion which did not require the revelation of Christianity as set out in the Bible but looked at the evidence of regulated nature for evidence of the existence of a Supreme Being.

It has been suggested that Swift was so enchanted by the brilliant and younger politician that he was uncritical of his arguments. But we have seen Swift's refusal to join in his vilification of Oxford and he cannot have been unaware of the self-serving flexibility of the man who cast off his first wife, his allegiance to the Protestant constitutional monarch, and then his espousal of the Papist Pretender, finally to assume the political garments of the man he did so much to undermine. It is more likely that Swift had a more sceptical view of human nature, as a man born in the Restoration, and was prepared to entertain relationships in which the flaws of personality were a matter to negotiate. Certainly it seems that Bolingbroke's animadversions on the nature of mankind in these letters acted as a stimulus to Swift's considered disagreement, especially in the latter books of *Gulliver's Travels*.

There is a gap in the correspondence between 1719 and 1721 when Bolingbroke responded to a letter of Swift's now lost. Swift had published his *Proposal* and Waters had been ineffectually prosecuted. Bolingbroke decided to lecture him on his over-optimistic idea of Man and the stupidity of talking sense or doing good to the rabble:

> is it possible that one of yr age & profession should be ignorant that this monstrous Beast has passions to be mov'd, but no reason to be appeal'd to, and that plain truth will influence half a score men att most in a Nation, or an age, while Mystery will lead millions by the nose? ... leave off instructing the Citizens of

Dublin. believe me there is more pleasure and more merit too, in cultivating friendship, than in taking care of the State. fools & knaves are generally best fitted for the last.

(28 July 1721)

Swift's *Drapier's Letters* (1724) showed his refusal to adopt this advice and so does *Gulliver's Travels*. For soon after this letter Swift was imagining the voyage to the country of the Houyhnhnms in which the bestial man-like Yahoos are contrasted with the rational horses who rule over them. One of the strands of this satire is to represent the Irish citizens of Dublin as Yahoos, on whose side stood the Drapier. The horse-like rulers in this interpretation would be the English. As they were the rational beings, they could be expected to include the 'half a score of men' whom Bolingbroke thought should be better advised to cultivate friendship than introduce political reform. In the views of the Houyhnhnms, Yahoos are unteachable and, even among their own kind, they confine friendship to the few of a particular high caste. But as will be seen in Chapter 5, *Gulliver's Travels* does not endorse the Houyhnhnms' arrogant dismissal of fallible humanity. In fact the whole of this voyage is devoted to a careful examination of the implications of such a view as Bolingbroke espouses.

Bolingbroke ascribed his low opinion of the generality of mankind and his high opinion of his own small circle to his religious orthodoxy. This appears in another letter written while Swift was revising *Gulliver's Travels*. The occasion for this is his objection to Swift considering that he was in any way a free-thinker (a sceptic in religion):

I must on this occasion set you right as to an opinion which I should be very sorry to have you entertain concerning me. The term Esprit Fort, in English free thinker, is according to my observation, usually apply'd to men whom I look upon to be the Pests of Society, because their endeavours are directed to losen the bands of it, & to take at least one curb out of the mouth of that wild Beast Man.

(12 September 1724)

Bolingbroke sees religion like the horse's curb, as an appropriate restraint for man just at the time when Swift had written his tale juxtaposing horse to Yahoo. The established church is a useful bogey to the unreasonable beast but Bolingbroke excepts a select few from its terrors, such as the man who 'searches after truth wth out passion, or prejudice, & adheres inviolably to it . . . a wise & honest Man, and such an one as I labour to be'. Despite his modest phrase, 'labour to be', most of what he says surrounding this suggests that he thinks he is an untainted witness, able to instruct a dean and a poet in religious and moral truth. He leaves little middle

ground for the fallible conjecturing thinker who is less confident of
what is truth and so less able to 'adhere inviolably to it'. Bolingbroke's
stark opposition Swift appeared to produce between the perfect
reasoning horse and the degenerate Yahoo. In choosing a horse to
stand for perfection maybe Swift combined a memory of two things.
The first was Narcissus Marsh's logic (see Chapter 1) that 'Man is
a rational animal. No horse is rational. Only rational animals are
capable of discipline.' The second was that when he returned to
Ireland to become dean he once named his horse 'Bolingbroke'.
The appropriateness of this is one we may conjecture. Swift knew
that Bolingbroke was headstrong, high mettled and sexually ramp-
ant – all of which terms may apply to a horse. And maybe Bolingbroke's professed beliefs of dispassionate rationality conjured up the
image of his true nature represented by the horse. Certainly, when
he invented the unemotional reasoning horses, Swift's fantasy was
extreme for it reversed the norm[15] in which it comes naturally to see
the horse as a figure of animal passion needing to be broken-in and
the control of a curb (see also plate 9). In this a warning is implicit.

Bolingbroke believed that reason, especially his reason, could
arrive unaided and secure at the nature of truth. 'Reveal'd religion,'
he continued, 'is a lofty & pompous structure erected close to the
humble & plain building of Natural Religion.' While Bolingbroke
makes obeisance to the loftiness and splendour of Christianity based
on the revelation of the Bible and of church history ('reveal'd religion') he shows that he believes that religion based on conclusions
drawn from the evidence of nature alone ('natural religion') is so
close to Christianity that only externals distinguish the two and both
sets of believers have a neighbourly similarity. He argues that a
free-thinker, bent on 'pulling down yr house about yr Ears . . . would
destroy the other for being so near it'. This is an odd sense of
priority for a professed Christian, that he should hate the *esprit fort*
because his attacks on the Church might damage irreparably the
structure of natural religion. In addition he pays scant attention to
elements of Christian doctrine which go beyond the 'science' of the
evidence of nature. These are such things as the gift of faith, the
power of liturgy and worship, the mystery of the sacraments and of
theological statements (such as the meaning of the Trinity), and the
nature of a progressive revelation. Without these elements Christians would argue that all a natural religion might do is encourage
a belief in a god made in a human image, sometimes referred to as
'the Supreme Being'. And that would be deism not Christianity.

In fact this was just what Bolingbroke was foisting on his friend,
the Catholic Alexander Pope. Pope wrote to Swift that he was plan-
ning a book which would enable the reader to 'look upon this life
with comfort and pleasure' and would put 'morality in good humour'

(19 June 1730). Proud of his part in this which would become *The Essay on Man* Bolingbroke wrote 'does Pope talk to you of the noble work which, att my instigation, he has begun, in such a manner that He must be convinced by this time I judged better of his tallents than He did?' (2 August 1730). Later he referred to his philosophy as resting on 'irrefrageable reasons' (2 August 1731). Subsequently Pope had a time trying to defend the deistical quality of the thought of his poem and the easy optimism of its 'whatever is, is right'.

Swift's view was that free-thinkers undermined Christianity. He argued vigorously against John Toland who published the seminal tract for free-thinkers, *Christianity not Mysterious*, in 1696. Although Toland was Irish and later, as a protégé of Molesworth, wrote against the Declaratory Act, Swift did not change his opposition to him. In 1708 he noticed 'the trumpery lately written by Asgil, Tindal, Toland, Coward and forty more' in *An Argument . . . [against] Abolishing Christianity*[16] and argued that if Toland had not ridden on the back of Christianity 'who would ever have suspected . . . Toland for a philosopher . . . Toland, the great oracle of the anti-Christians, is an Irish priest, the son of an Irish priest'. Four years before the time Bolingbroke asserted he was not an *esprit fort* but one who admired the buildings of religion, Swift had commented adversely on the libertinism of free-thinkers, especially those who think of religion as a building, in *A Letter to a Young Clergyman* (1720):

> for what use is freedom of thought if it will not produce freedom of action? which is the sole end, how remote soever in appearance, of all objections against Christianity; and therefore the freethinkers consider it as a sort of edifice, wherein all the parts have such a mutual dependence on each other, that if you pull out one single nail, the whole fabric must fall to the ground.

He rejected the arguments for natural religion, although good morality might be learned from the ancients, for nothing could substitute for 'the absolute necessity of divine revelation to make the knowledge of the true God'.

Pope and the elucidation of Gulliver's Travels

It is unfortunate that much of the correspondence between Bolingbroke and Swift of the period of *Gulliver's Travels* is lost, for it is likely that this contained a number of references to the work in progress. On 1 January 1722 Bolingbroke wrote 'I long to see yr travels' showing that he was familiar with the idea of Swift's new satire and later, before its publication on 28 October 1726, refers to the 'travels into those Countrys of Giants & Pigmeys' (24 July 1725). Pope was also in the secret: 'Your Travels I hear much of' (14 September 1725). So the argument about reason and the bestiality of man was conducted in the context of all three knowing about *Gulliver's Travels*. And we can infer that Swift was nettled by Bolingbroke and sceptical of his views. He must have called him an '*esprit fort*' for Bolingbroke to attempt to dissociate himself from deism or atheism. We know Swift scorned 'you pretenders to retirement' (20 September 1723) and infer from another occasion some months later that Swift criticised Bolingbroke still for not giving him preferment in the past. It seems Swift had written that it was 'either not in the power or will of the ministry to place [me] in England' and Bolingbroke wished this to be changed to reflect on Oxford alone as not having the will to do so. In the same letter Bolingbroke continued with an assault on Swift's concern for the people of Ireland 'as you describe your publick spirit, it seems to me to be a disease' (25 December 1723).

On 29 September 1725, Swift wrote to Pope a letter which is much quoted for its bearing on *Gulliver's Travels*. To be properly understood it should be seen as part of a sequence of remarks rather than as a summary and it should be placed in the context of Bolingbroke's advice to cultivate friendship instead of imagining one could change human behaviour. This letter to Pope is as much directed towards Bolingbroke (to whose correspondence he refers) who, since 1723, had been free to return to England; was sometimes with Pope; and would write a joint letter with him. Seen as part of a series of interchanges between them it shows how important a community of writers was for sharpening Swift's art, for at the same time he was reshaping *Gulliver's Travels*. Some time after the first draft of *Gulliver's Travels* Swift had switched the position of the third and fourth travels, possibly because the argument with Bolingbroke assumed a greater importance in his mind. It seems likely that Bolingbroke's easy and self-satisfied belief in the powers of reason (within his small circle of 'half a score of men') struck Swift as typical of the drift of religious belief into free-thinking in the second decade of the century. This would fit with Swift's later representation of another totally reasonable and inhuman being, the projector in *A Modest Proposal* (1729). And he made other changes, for he wrote, 'I have employed my time (besides ditching) in finishing correcting, amending, and Transcribing my Travells, in four parts Compleat newly **Augmented**, and intended for the press' (my emphasis). In this letter to Pope, he remembered Bolingbroke's scoffing at his 'publick spirit' and wished to exculpate himself from being seen as a charitable optimist for 'I have ever hated all Nations professions and Communities and all my love is towards individualls.' And then he took up the matter of who or what possessed reason, wishing to expose the 'falsity of that Definition [of man as] *animal rationale*; and to show it should be only *rationis capax*. Upon this great foundation of Misanthropy (though not Timon's manner) The whole building of my Travells is erected.' Although our interest has centred on the land of the Houyhnhnms we should notice that now Swift felt that the whole work, newly augmented, was based on this distinction. His view is that man aspires to reason and that he cannot love man for being 'noble in reason'. On the other hand, unlike Shakespeare's Timon who cursed the world for its unreason and made no converts, Swift's manner was to 'vex' his readers (as he explained earlier in the letter). 'Vex' means to irritate in the sense of disturb complacent thinking, so that Swift intended his writing to reform.

Pope wrote back enthusiastically with a Biblical reference, a hope that Swift would 'make them *Eat your Book*' (15 October 1725). In this he refers to the apocalypse of *Revelations* x. 9 where, after the breaking of the seventh seal, an angel gives the gift of prophecy in the shape of a book which when eaten is sweet in the mouth but bitter in the belly. While Pope conflates this with the avenging angel pouring out a vial of wrath in a later chapter of *Revelations*, it is clear that he sees the morality of *Gulliver's Travels* as having a religious foundation. At the same time he combined this sentiment with the enlightened utilitarianism of 'I really enter as fully as you can desire, into your Principle of Love of Individuals: And I think the way to have a Publick Spirit, is first to have a Private one.'

On 26 November 1725, Swift followed this up closely, picking up his expressions one by one and showing how keenly he read and considered the letters he received. Much concerns Arbuthnot and Gay. Then he picks up Pope's wish to 'meet like the Righteous in the Millenium, quite in peace' and refuses to accept the satisfaction of having fought for true religion. He scoffs: 'to hear Boys like you talk of Millimums and Tranquillity I am older by thirty years. Lord Bol – by Twenty and you by but Ten'. This reveals his sense of not only being older but, through his exaggeration of adding both age differentials together, of belonging to another time. They are merely 'boys', representatives of an age which believes in an easy benevolence founded on small intimate friendships, good nature and reason. His scepticism comes from being born during a period of religious wars and experienced in the corruption of the world. And yet he has more faith in fallible humanity than their clique-ish superiority gives them.

> I tell you after all that I do not hate Mankind, it is vous autres who hate them because you would have them reasonable Animals, and are Angry for being disappointed. I have always rejected that Definition and made another of my own. I am no more angry with [Walpole] Then I was with the Kite that last week flew away with one of my Chickins and yet I was pleas'd when one of my Servants Shot him two days after.

While Swift was pleased to say since 'the Twenty First to the f[if]ty eighth year of my Life' he had been constant in his view of the world, he also recognised that imperceptible change may happen. Despite the temptation to score points in the battle (Bolingbroke had once written 'I found means to have the last word, which in disputes you know is the capital point' – 25 December 1723) Swift was ready to re-examine long-held opinions. He objected to Pope writing against the seventeenth-century French moralist and wit, Rochefoucauld, 'because I found my whole character in him, however I will read him again because it is possible I may have since undergone some alterations'. But in this interchange on the nature of reason we can feel a growing conviction of his position even though time had moved on.

Bolingbroke then penned what he felt was a devastating addendum to another of Pope's letters:

> Pope and you are very great wits, and I think very indifferent Philosophers, if you dispise the world as much as you pretend . . . I should blush alike to be discover'd fond of the world or piqu'd at it. Your Definition of Animal [capax] Rationis instead of the Common one Animal Rationale, will not bear examination. define but Reason, and you will see why your distinction is no better than that of the Pontiffe Cotta between mala Ratio and bona Ratio.
>
> (14 December 1725)

He denies he has any concern ('fond' or 'piqu'd') for humanity and he likens Swift's arguments to old-fashioned ways of thinking. He refers to those of 'Pontiffe Cotta'. This is a humorously disparaging reference to a character in a dialogue written by Cicero. Cotta says: 'Then again, what lust, or avarice, or crime is either embarqued upon without the exercise of forethought, or accomplished without the mental activity and reflection which constitute reason? For every belief is a manifestation of reason, of right reason, we may add, if it is true, and of wrong if it is false.'[17] Such a distinction Bolingbroke dismisses, since he takes the view that man is rational but may either abuse or use his reason well. Once again the generation gap opens between him and Swift. The idea that there were several types of reason was current in the seventeenth century to which Swift's Christianity belongs and Swift accepted that much of religion was a mystery, impenetrable to reason. The function of reason was subservient: to show God. Luther had distinguished between the reason of the noble savage (which dimly shows truth) and that of Christianity which (guided by the selective teachings of the Bible and of the Church) was the handmaid of God. Woolton had seen right reason as that which selects from the evidence of nature all that conduces to true belief. Selection like this denied the free play of reason on experience that Bolingbroke proposed.

Philosophy versus satire

The difference of religious viewpoint becomes marked in an interchange between Pope and Swift, where Pope assumes more and more the attitude of the religious thinker and affords Swift that of the satirist. In his homage to Swift in *The Dunciad* he presented Swift as the true descendant of his favourite authors, Cervantes, the author of *Don Quixote*, a burlesque of chivalric romance, and Rabelais, the author of *Gargantua* and *Pantagruel*, exuberant mockeries of formal academic learning. In the draft he balanced the licence of this with an image of him as a grave minister of religion:

> Whether you chuse Cervantes' serious air,
> Or laugh and shake in Rablais' easy chair,
> Or in the graver Gown instruct mankind,
> Or silent, let thy morals tell thy mind.

However, the printed version substituted for the last two lines the author of *Gulliver's Travels* and *The Drapier's Letters*

> Or praise the Court, or magnify Mankind,
> Or thy griev'd Country's copper chains unbind.

The gain in specific reference is at the expense of almost de-frocking the clergyman.

Swift did not fall out with his comrades despite a growing difference of outlook. He still needed their stimulation and wrote 'I look upon my Lord Bolingbroke and us two, as a peculiar Triumvirate, who have nothing to expect, or to fear; and so far fittest to converse with one another' but still he felt more keenly the wickedness of the world, refusing to be called a patriot 'because what I do is owing to perfect rage and resentment, and the mortifying sight of slavery, folly, and baseness about me, among which I am forced to live'. Generously he accorded them finer feelings for 'you despise the follies, and hate the vices of mankind, without the least ill effect on your temper; and with regard to particular men, you are inclined always rather to think the better, whereas with me it is always directly contrary' (1 June 1728). When this is tied in with his statement that it is 'vous autres hate mankind' and remembrance of his involvement in *The Drapier's Letters* the anomalies can only be accounted for by a difference of mind-set – between a seventeenth-century clergyman, profoundly believing that no man was free of the taint of original sin, and an eighteenth-century moralist, believing in the perfectability of man. When man failed to live up to high expectations, hatred and despising was the reaction of the latter. But the clergyman, while angered by actions of folly and baseness, was merely confirmed in his low expectations.

Pope felt that times had changed the needs of society. Politics and religion would not speak so well as before.

> Let Philosophy be ever so vain, it is less vain now than Politicks, and not quite so vain at present as Divinity: I know nothing that moves strongly but Satire . . . I fancy if we three were together but for three years, some good might be done even upon this Age; or at least some punishment made effective, toward the Example of posterity, between History, Philosophy, and Poetry or the Devil's in it.
>
> (Pope, jointly with Bolingbroke, to Swift, March 1732)

and continued on 20 April 1733:

> I have not the courage however to be such a Satyrist as you, but I would be as much, or more, a Philospher. You call your satires, Libels; I would rather call my satires, Epistles: They will consist more of morality than wit, and grow graver, which you will call duller.

It is likely that Swift did not welcome his position as religious teacher usurped by a Catholic moralist but this is a serious debate in which the candour and sincerity of both make it possible for each to sympathise with a sharing of ideals even though there seems to be a blindness to root beliefs. It is less easy to appreciate the cocksure interventions of Bolingbroke who promised 'to write a pretty large volume . . . which must . . . render all your Metaphysical Theology both ridiculous and abominable' (March 1732) and preened himself on its probable success: 'about Posterity one may flatter oneself'. He mentions *The Essay on Man* with a proprietary air of one who has given Pope the good ideas and fishes for a compliment by asking 'you have seen I doubt not the Ethic Epistles' (12 April 1734). Ehrenpreis quotes an Austrian observer[18] who said of him:

> He investigates everything, takes everything in, and can always be relied upon to make a formal statement. Neither his rank, his credit, capacity, or steadiness make one believe him . . . Besides this, he is given to the bottle and debauchery to the point almost of making a virtue out of his open affectation that public affairs are a bagatelle to him, and that his own capacity is on so high a level that he has no need to give up his pleasures in the slightest degree for any cause.

Swift's tolerance of Bolingbroke may have some element of being starved of intelligent company but more importantly attests his belief in the fallen nature of humanity. Aware of Bolingbroke's faults and special pleading (decrying Oxford, propagating free-thinking), Swift would not compromise his own views but was happy to continue as a friend. This is worth remembering when trying to judge the satirical thrust of his writing.

The published correspondence with Pope

Even his beloved Pope was not free from behaviour which betrayed their friendship, particularly when it came to his desire to publish their correspondence as a record of the success of the Scriblerian enterprise. The evidence suggests that Swift knew in broad terms of his underhand dealings relating to this but did not cast him off. He had tolerated before a slander on his thrift, representing him as a miser, in one of Pope's Horatian Epistles. Swift is imagined as one who is appalled at wasting money on building a house:

> Pray heav'n it last! (cries Swift) as you go on;
> I wish to God this house had been your own:
> Pity! to build, without a son or wife:
> Why you'll enjoy it only all your life.

Pope gives himself the part of offering the worldly wisdom that property cannot be held by the family or even the good for ever:

> What's *Property?* dear Swift! you see it alter
> From you to me, from me to Peter Walter

The representation had hurt Swift so that he had protested

> I desire to be represented as a man of thrift onely as it produceth liberty and Independence, without any thoughts of hoarding; and as one who bestowes every year at least one third of his income; though sunk a third by the misery of the Country.
>
> (1 May 1733)

Although Swift was careful with his money and thrifty, he gave much to charities; he put aside money for benefactions in his will; and even his loans were set at a low interest, just sufficient to cover the employment of someone to oversee his accounts. Nor was he devoted to possessing money, showing little concern when he lost nearly £400 through the bankruptcy of a friend in 1712 and again, in 1725, when he was in danger of losing £1200 (more than a year's wages) through the maladministration of another friend. But Pope neglected to change the lines and yet their intercourse continued.

Their closeness was such that Swift could joke, without doing harm, about Pope's diseased crippledom and his religious belief by calling him an 'ill Catholic and a worse Geographer' when he called Ireland a paradise. (The multiple puns here, such as 'ill' meaning 'sick' and 'ill Catholic' meaning 'bad Catholic theologian', are typical.) So great was his regard that the best he wished was to be celebrated in Pope's poems: 'I pleased you once with a passage in

one of Cicero's letters to a Friend: *Orna me* (i.e. 'give me honour' –
Swift to Pope, 12 May 1735, repeating the sentiment on 3 September 1735). Time and again he professed his affection as 'one who
esteems and loves you about half as much as you deserve. I mean as
much as he can' (29 September 1725). When separated from him
he wrote that in order to reduce the pain 'I will endeavour to think
of you as little as I can' (1 August 1726). While Swift had visited
England in 1726 and 1727, once the political danger was over
(signalised by Bolingbroke's return from exile in France in 1723 and
his own celebrity after the success of the Drapier in 1725), his visits
were not reciprocated, despite pressing invitations. Pope on a number
of occasions, from 1723 to 1733, tantalised him with the prospect.
Swift eventually realised that he would never do so and Pope's half-
promises abraded the wound of his exile. In fact sea-sickness would
have put at risk Pope's frail constitution which he finally admitted.
Swift did not lose his longing to see him or his affection for him. And
as he grew older and lost more friends he said 'I cannot properly call
you my best friend, because I have not another left who deserves the
name, such a havock have Time, Death, Exile and Oblivion made'
(9 February 1737).

Pope was anxious for their letters, suitably edited by him, to be
published during his lifetime. But it had to be done as though he
had nothing to do with it and for them to appear to a reader as
though eavesdropping on the very best conversation. He may even
have had the project in mind during his writing to Swift, judging by
the placing of some modestly disclaiming sentiments in a number of
letters. In asking for his own letters back he elaborately represented
it as an innocent amusement, purely for his private pleasure and to
prevent them from falling into hostile hands. Swift teased him that
the letters were quite safe for 'Executors . . . have strict orders to
burn every letter left behind me. Neither did our letters contain any
Turns of Wit, or Fancy, or Politicks, or Satire, but mere innocent
friendship; yet I am loth that any letters, from you and a very few
other friends, should die before me.' But he knew the value of letters
as speaking the character of the correspondent, for he had written to
Lady Betty Germain:

> But, as to letters I receive from your Ladyship, I neither ever did
> or ever will burn any of them, take it as you please: For I never
> burn a letter that is entertaining, and consequently will give me
> new pleasure when it is forgotten. It is true, I have kept some
> letters merely out of friendship, although they sometimes wanted
> true spelling and good sense, and some others whose writers are
> dead.

> (8 June 1735)

Once the letters were published in a supposed 'pirated' text in Dublin (1740) Pope sent up a smokescreen which falsely implicated others in the doing of it: the 2nd Earl of Oxford, Swift and his carer and relative, Mrs Martha Whiteway. Swift dragged his feet over the publication, while Pope pretended to Robert Nugent, an Irish poetaster mutually acquainted with Pope and Swift, that the letters had been hastily published by Swift's vanity: 'the greatest of Genius's . . . may have nothing left them at last but their Vanity. No Decay of the Body is half so miserable! . . . I despair of stopping what is already no doubt in many hands . . . I have pressd him to secure me from this Very thing.' Similarly to Ralph Allen, a rich worthy living in Bath, he wrote he had been 'trying all the Means to *retard* it; for it is past preventing, by his having (without my Consent or so much as letting me see the book) printed most of it . . . The excessive Earnestness the Dean has been in for publishing them' and he represented Swift's affectionate supporters as self-serving profiteers: 'the Deans People, the Women & the Bookseller . . . finding his Weakness increase, they have at last made *Him* the Instrument himself for their private profit' (3 October 1740). During the same time, Mrs Whiteway was writing to Pope with simple dignity and trust in his friendship for the ailing dean.

A Modest Proposal, 1729

To go back in time to 1729, having marked the tendency of even his closest friends to betray friendship at some juncture, allows us to appreciate the justice of Swift's view of the corrupt heart. *A Modest Proposal* chills many readers, especially during a first reading when the enormity of the proposal to banish hunger and overpopulation in Ireland by eating their babies breaks in on them, after the measured and reasonable presentation with its supposed social concern for the starving peasants of Ireland. The reaction between form and content is violent, sometimes leading to the thought that Swift is sick in the head. But when read from the point of view of being convinced of human failing, in the painful knowledge of devastating famine and with a dismayed sense of almost universal rationalistic optimism, its effect seems well judged to attack all three. It is a logical step from the coldly reasoning Houyhnhnms to the scientific projector, a Gulliver whose madness seems totally sane, and it is another emotional step towards increased sympathy for the Irish poor.[19]

Notes

1   *Printing Technology, Letters & Samuel Johnson*, Alvin Kernan, Princeton, 1987.

2 *Literacy and the Social Order: Reading and Writing in Tudor and Stuart England*, David Cressy, CUP, 1980, 147.
3 *The Practice and Representation of Reading in England*, (eds) James Raven, Helen Small and Naomi Tadmor, Cambridge, 1996, 10.
4 *Dublin's Trade in Books 1550–1800*, M. Pollard, Oxford, 1989, 31.
5 *The Eighteenth Century*, (ed.) Pat Rogers, Methuen, 1978, 46.
6 Ehrenpreis, ii, 233–4.
7 Addison wrote this in his pamphlet, *The Present State of the War*, 1707.
8 Charles Kerby-Miller (ed.) *The Memoirs of the Extraordinary Life, Works, and Discoveries of Martinus Scriblerus*, OUP, 1988.
9 Bolingbroke at Marcilly was enjoying the attentions of the Marquise de Villette.
10 In 1729 he wrote the *Proposal that All the Ladies and Women of Ireland should Appear Constantly in Irish Manufactures* but this was not published until 1765.
11 Harold Williams (ed.) *The Correspondence of Jonathan Swift*, 5 vols, OUP, 1963–65, iii, 353.
12 As dean he had jurisdiction over the liberty of St Patrick's which was about $5\frac{1}{2}$ acres.
13 M. Pollard, *op. cit.*, 17.
14 Herbert Davies (ed.) *The Drapier's Letters to the People of Ireland . . .* , OUP, 1935, 234.
15 This can be traced back to Plato's *Phaedrus*, written in the fourth century B.C. Hans Baldung Grien, one of whose paintings is discussed later, engraved (1534) three representations of horses as figures of base animality: teeth bared and sexually roused, ejaculating and kicking.
16 The full title is *An Argument to prove that the Abolishing of Christianity in England may, as things now stand, be attended with some Inconveniencies, and perhaps not produce those Many Good Effects proposed thereby*.
17 Cicero, *De Natura Deorum*, (ed.) Francis Brooks, Methuen, 1896, iii, XXVII.
18 Ehrenpreis, ii, 456.
19 *A Modest Proposal* is further examined in the Critical Survey of Chapter 6.

4 Women and the body

Swift's relationships with women

Much recent literary criticism has considered Swift's attitude to women over a range of issues. Does what we know from his biography reveal unacceptable male dominance, particularly with regard to Stella? Do his writings represent women in patriarchal or misogynist fashion? Some see Swift as imprisoning and others as liberating.[1] Complicating the debate are aesthetic concerns such as how relevant is the biography to textual analysis; how valid is the biographical interpretation; what is an appropriate rendering of femininity. In addition, Swift's writings include material that is scatological, often in relation to representation of the female body. The link between excrement and sex is therefore another issue, given human physiology. For example, Yeats, writing in 1931, has Crazy Jane argue with a bishop, who represents religion and respectability, that there is the necessity of 'fair and foul' consorting together for

> Love has pitched his mansion in
> The place of excrement.

While this suggests the topic has a modern relevance, it cannot escape our notice that in our case it is a dean, who supports the established (though minority) church in Ireland, who is addressing such material and not an inspired or mad woman who is an outsider.

Our surprise comes from having a modern mental set of attitudes which in looking at Swift's writings encounter a cultural shift in relation to religion, respectability and the position of women. Approval or disapproval, if that is the object of the reader, should be suspended until we have a good idea of the nature of Swift's literary enterprise. For this book is written from the point of view that a knowledge of biography and context may illuminate an understanding of an author's text. Whether the application of this knowledge does or not depends on the tact and suppleness of the reader. As a ready and self-contained example of what the use of context means, readers may have had a similar experience of mental shift when brought up with a jolt in Milton's agonised and longing sonnet on his dead wife, his 'late espousèd saint', whom he sees in a vision 'washed from the spot of child-bed taint'. To understand the movement of the poet's mind we need to know that he imagines her purified state in terms of the Hebraic law which considered that any woman who had recently given birth was unclean. In Swift's case issues are not usually so clear-cut and may challenge attitudes which we hold dear.

In addition we may not readily know where 'he' stands in relation to the challenge, while at the same time being quite sure that the challenge is intended, often as result of catching undertones. We read the surface meaning and at the same time carry on an internalised commentary of varying agreement and disagreement until a particular word fuses both readings. Two examples illustrate this. Gulliver is 'at much pains' to make his Houyhnhnm master understand 'every one' of a list of terms such as 'Begging, Robbing, Stealing, Pimping, Forswearing, Flattering' and so on, which show the worst aspects of humanity. This comes after pages of description of the violence and viciousness of warring human beings. We could wish he would spare us the detail and while Gulliver uses the word 'pains' to indicate the particular care he takes to draw out the meaning, the reader is mortified by the 'pains' of being identified with the baseness so expertly described. In *A Modest Proposal*, when a beggar child of the 'poor people of Ireland' is represented as 'just dropp'd from its Dam', the terms of animal husbandry reduce its nature as a human being to no more than that of a domesticated beast. The reader rejects this in a movement of sympathy towards the child and the phrase 'poor people of Ireland' which originally conveyed, in almost a technical fashion, their poverty now holds the sympathetic idea of pity for their unfortunate plight as well. Both these examples indulge an imagined enormity which the readers form in their mind while carrying on an internal evaluation. Then comes a word which brings both strands together, rather like a Freudian slip, which exposes the undercurrent of detailed disagreement. As Swift is such a master of controlled expression in these contexts, it is reasonable to consider whether there is a similar artistic wholeness in 'his' comments on women and bodily functions.

Domination and friendship

Despite the many attractive qualities of Swift as a friend, there are others which set him at a little distance, suggesting an otherness which prevents familiarity. Loyal and industrious in promoting the careers of contemporary and younger friends, he nevertheless stood apart as though not entirely convinced of the bond. Sir Walter Scott printed a list of friends, now lost, which Swift had made, classifying them as 'grateful, ungrateful, indifferent, doubtful'. The document is too ambiguous to be conclusive, since names do not always securely identify and the adjectives have other meanings – 'grateful' might mean 'pleasing' and so on. But still it is a reckoning or stock-taking of whom he could count on. And this was a habit shown earlier in the *Journal to Stella* when at the age of 44 he wrote: 'I was at Court at noon, and saw fifty acquaintances I had not met this long time: that is the advantage of a Court, and I fancy I am better known than any man that goes there' (25 November 1711).

Also he devised tests of friends before admitting them fully to his confidence. He quarrelled with Oxford about being treated like a hired hand when he sent £50 to help Swift in his necessity and he angrily warned Bolingbroke 'never appear cold to me, for I would not be treated like a school-boy', remembering how once Sir William Temple had made him feel small. Both men continued to show him affection and respect and Swift felt assured of their genuineness. In another case, later in life (1718), he showed his younger friend Sheridan that there were bounds to the liberties that might be taken with him. Both had exchanged a vigorous and rapid flurry of rid-dling poems, sometimes written instantaneously on receipt and each vying to outdo the other until their own personalities become part of the subject matter. Sheridan wrote a long poem, now lost, on the funeral of Swift's muse since he pretended that Swift's poems had lost their life. Swift had called him a 'goose' so in another poem Sheridan imagined outliving him:

> Though you call me a goose, you pitiful slave,
> I'll feed on the grass that grows on your grave.

Swift felt that Sheridan had gone too far with this and, while he wrote a defence in *Mary the Cook-Maid's Letter to Dr Sheridan*, with typical indirection he wrote another poem on the proper nature of wit in the form of a letter to another mutual friend but intended for Sheridan to see. This was called *To Mr Delany* and argued that wit at another's expense should be

> That irony which turns to praise.

(When he had called Sheridan a goose he had added that all his swans were geese.) Like the raillery he had commended to King (see Chapter 2) Swift saw his own wit could easily be misunderstood for criticism:

> And fools would fancy he intends
> A satire where he most commends.

But Sheridan's wit had reproached him for 'those defects he cannot mend' and so he applied the rules of raillery to what he saw as the character of Sheridan:

> Some part of what I here design
> Regards a friend of yours and mine,
> Who full of humour, fire and wit,
> Not allways judges what is fit;
> But loves to take prodigious rounds,
> And sometimes walks beyond his bounds.

As with Steele, Swift turned to a second friend, as one who knew the offender better, to act as an arbitrator:

> If he be guilty, you must mend him,
> If he be innocent, defend him.

Delany showed Swift's poem to Sheridan who is said to have burned the copy in a fit of mortification. His conduct with Swift afterwards was more circumspect and he grew closer in his confidence.

Swift's fear of betrayal and his manipulativeness in his correspondence show his concern to control the extent of his relations. This was irrespective of gender. His friendships with women operated on much the same terms as those he had with men. In a letter to the Reverend John Kendall (11 February 1692), when Swift was 25, he wrote defending himself against suggestions that he was running after women. This was for others, either 'young, raw & ignorant Scholars, who for want of knowing company, believe every silk petticoat includes an angell' or those who were gnawed by the 'maggot' of passion. As for him 'a thousand Household thoughts . . . drive matrimony out of my mind'. And he saw himself as 'naturaly temperate'. It may be argued that Swift might be playing down his true nature, as he would wish to cool any suspicions of behaviour that might jeopardise his MA at Hart Hall and probable career dependent on patronage in the church. However, there is evidence that he was not sexually passionate, but friendship with either sex occupied a central role which stimulated his genius and nourished his intelligence and concern.

We have little of his wooing of Jane Waring, 'Varina', except where Swift has experienced rejection. Nevertheless the terms are cool in his last letter to her which asks her whether she is ready to throw in her lot with him through thick and thin:

> These are questions I have always resolved to propose to her with whom I meant to pass my life; and when you can heartily answer them in the affirmative, I shall be blessed to have you in my arms, without regarding whether your person be beautiful, or your fortune large. Cleanliness in the first, and competency in the other, is all I look for.
>
> (4 May 1700)

At the age of 32 he jotted down some resolutions *When I come to be old* which included 'Not to hearken to Flatteryes, nor conceive I can be beloved by a young woman. Et eos qui hereditatem captant, odisse ac vitare. (To hate and avoid those who try to gain an inheritance.)' Distrust is the keynote to which is added an ambition that he might, when old, be worth befriending for his money. And self-mockery is latent in this ambition, too, surfacing in the final resolution 'Not to set up for observing all these rules, for fear I should observe none.' However, subsequent history accorded with his distancing himself from younger women. Two women who probably contemplated marrying him, Stella and Vanessa (Esther Johnson and Esther Vanhomrigh), were both younger. Vanessa died reproaching him for not reciprocating her passion. Stella maintained contact with him in Ireland in a very cordial relationship but they lived in different houses and there is no firm evidence that they married.[2]

On 28 January 1728, the day Stella died, Swift began a memoir of her which showed a deep bond and respect for her that honours her independence and worth as an individual. She was 'the truest, most virtuous, and valuable friend, that I, or perhaps any other person was blessed with'. The piece is openly subjective (written 'for my own satisfaction'), anecdotal and reflective, soberly assessing her faults and foibles as well as her wonderful strengths. 'I cannot call to mind that I ever once heard her make a wrong judgment of persons, books or affairs . . . Never was so happy a conjunction of civility, freedom, easiness and sincerity.' Written over a number of days with difficulty from emotion and sickness, the obituary has all the positive features of genuine memories captured from mental turmoil on the page, whereas a more polished performance might conceal by elegance of expression. Several times, as he returns to the force of her character, he mentions her ability to silence a coxcomb but 'She never mistook the understanding of others; nor ever said a severe word, but where a much severer was deserved.' Vivid images of her arise, as when she 'put on a black hood to prevent her being seen' and took a pistol to the window to fire at armed rogues who were attempting to break into her house.

Pains of friendship

The sense of loss evident in his memoir attests Swift's capacity for deep pain. His letters from two years before her death are particularly revealing. He was in London negotiating the publication of *Gulliver's Travels* when a false alarm that she was sinking reached him and he immediately feared the worst.

> What you tell me of Mrs J – I have long expected with great Oppression & Heavyness of Heart We have been perfect friends these 35 Years. Upon my Advice they both came to Ireld . . . I am of Opinion that there is not a greater Folly than to contract too great and intimate a Friendship, which must leave the Survivor miserable.
>
> (to Worrall, 15 July 1726)

Believing this was the end he had to unload his grief on other correspondents, enlarging on the vulnerability of someone who loves a friend and loses a companion by which:

> a man must be absolutely miserable; but especially at an age when it is too late to engage in a new friendship. Besides this was a person of my own rearing and instructing, from childhood, who excelled in every good quality that can possibly accomplish a human creature . . . Dear Jim, I know not what I am saying; but believe me that violent friendship is much more lasting, and as much engaging, as violent love.
>
> (to Stopford, 20 July 1726)

He could not trust himself to go to her bedside, 'Nay if I were near her, I would not see her; I could not behave myself tolerably, and should redouble her Sorrow' (to Sheridan, 27 July 1726). He comforted himself that good friends less involved would be of more service but shrank from facing the detail of death even by report. A year later, after another alarm, he begged Sheridan to 'tell me no Particulars, but the Event in general' (29 August 1727). When, indeed, the time came, during her last four months he frequented her bedside and prayed with her. After her death, writing to his remaining best friend, Pope, he expressed a hope which he knew could not be fulfilled: 'I do not only wish as you ask me, that I was unacquainted with any deserving person, but almost, that I never had a friend' (13 February 1729).

Female friends

Despite the impulse towards solitude as a defence against the sorrows of death, Swift had many female friends in addition to the male Scriblerians discussed in the previous chapter. His relationships with them vary according to character. We have seen how he kept Lady Betty Germain's letters to read again in order to renew the original pleasure of hearing from her. She and her companion, Biddy Floyd, went back to his London years and he had celebrated both in different poems at the time. Lady Betty's letters rattle on, violating grammar and spelling, but exhibiting energy and worldliness. She would recall the pleasure of this past by using the odd phrase from his poem about her, *Mrs Harris's Petition*, such as her garrulous servant's talk of 'the time of Gooseberrys'. She connected him with court and possible influence and had sufficient standing to disagree with him over his low opinion of the character of the Countess of Suffolk, playfully reducing his clerical status to parson but also dropping any pretension to grandeur herself when telling him 'tho you are a proud parson (yet give you, Devil, your due) your a sincere, good natured, honest one . . . Adieu my ever honourd old friend, and dont let me see any more respects or Ladyships from you –' (1 May 1733). He could be equally frank to her. His last known letter to her (for many are lost) makes testy rebuke of her indolent and anti-Irish heir, the Duke of Dorset, Lord Lieutenant of Ireland, but does not suggest that his friendship with her lost its savour.

The Duchess of Queensberry, patroness of Gay and a noted beauty, conducts a correspondence in quite a different key and one in which she shows wit, intelligence, charm and understanding of the foibles of an ageing man. Swift is arch, gallant and bantering but also demanding. Conscious of the physical look of the written page, Swift begins an address to the Duchess at the foot of a letter written to Gay: 'Madam, – My beginning thus low is meant as a mark of respect, like receiving your Grace at the bottom of the Stairs' (19 November 1730). Then he stands on his dignity sanctioned, he says, by a law in England which says it is a duty 'that the first advances have been constantly made me by all Ladyes who aspired to My Acquaintance'. Gay, the Duchess and Swift enjoy a fertile interchange of badinerie and, when the Duchess writes alternate lines with Gay, Swift detects it and replies 'Lo here comes in the Dutchess again (I know her by her dd's)' (28 August 1731). She retaliates with an obscure saying worthy of Partridge 'Poll manu sub linus darque dds' which may be cod Latin meaning 'the dark dd's by Poll's hand under the line'. Swift became so attached to her contributions that he chided her for not writing when Gay was away and then candidly admitted this was his testiness which made it 'my misfortune to quarrell with all my acquaintance' (10 July 1732). When Gay died, Swift feared the correspondence would cease as he could no longer be useful to her and telling this to Pope said 'she seems a lady of excellent sense'. Her reply must have touched his heart. Pope had shown her the letter and she said that after the death of Gay she was 'more inclind to write to you' but what did he mean that she only *seemed* such a lady of excellent sense? Battle recommenced with Swift justifying himself with the remark that letters might be 'false copies of your mind' to which she gave the perfect return:

> my letters are never false copies of my mind, they are often I believe imperfect ones of an imperfect mind . . . whatever I write is at that instant true, I would rather tell a lie than write it down for words are wind (tis said) but the making of a memorandum of ones own false heart would stare one in the face immediately.
> (12 April 1733)

As a third example of his female friends, his cousin, Martha Whiteway, ministered to his old age in ways which we have already seen as having genuine affection and simple dignity. She cheered his declining years and there is a pleasant example of their friendly repartee. On this occasion she wrote on his behalf, when he was 73, a letter of congratulations to William Richardson on his marriage to a woman whom she had heard was 15 years old but whom the dean would say was 50 (implying that Swift was so crusty). Swift added a postscript saying that his failing memory had been prompted by this 'beggarly cousin of mine' to which she immediately added the words that he made 'no contrast' with her when it came to beggarliness. Picking up the pen from this 'Teaser at my Elbow' he consented to her view of the worthiness of the young wife and hoped they would both come 'where Mrs Precipitate (alias Whiteway) says, I will give you a Scandalous Dinner' (13 May 1740).

The last example is of a woman who was a doughty opponent of Swift and ready to accuse him of treating women as second class. The Countess of Suffolk, whom Lady Betty defended, was a woman of strong character and high position at court, like Mrs Masham (whom Swift called that 'dangerous adventurer'). Formerly Henrietta Howard, she was the mistress of the future George II and friendly with the future Queen Caroline. Swift met her through Pope and Bolingbroke in 1726 and cultivated her friendship as an intelligent woman, who suffered deafness as he did, and wrongly thinking that, like Mrs Masham, she also had great influence and might help his friend Gay. Early on they indulged in witty repartee and Swift in the guise of Gulliver sent her a small crown from the tiny kingdom of Lilliput. However, the accession of George II did nothing to secure Gay in the way he had hoped and he blamed Walpole and the Countess for this. Walpole had wrongly thought Gay had satirised him and Swift believed 'the trite old Maxim of a Minister never forgiving those he hath injured' had caused him to do nothing. (There is nothing trite in Swift's twist of the more common maxim that you never forgive those who injure you into the psychological truth that guilt at injuring others makes you never forgive them for making you feel guilty.) As for the Countess, she had never intended to assist Gay, exhibiting 'the insincerityes of those who would be thought best Friends' (23 November 1727). He upbraided her and she replied 'You seem to think you have a Natural Right to Abuse me because I am a Woman and a Courtier.' She felt 'great resentment; and a determin'd resolution of Revenge' but casting about could find only one example of his imprudence to use against him. 'I expect to hear if peace shall ensue, or war continue between us, if I know little of the art of war, yet you see I do not want Courage' (25 September 1731). Swift replied circumspectly and forcefully, 'Your Ladyship's letter made me a little grave, and in going to answer it, I was in grave danger of leaning on my elbow, (I mean my left elbow) to consider what I should write, which posture I never used except when I was under necessity of writing to Fools, or Lawyers, or Ministers of State.' He rebutted the specific charge of imprudence. 'And now Madam I utterly acquit Your Ladyship of all things that may regard me, except your good opinion, and that very little share I can pretend to in your memory, I never knew a Lady who had so many qualityes to beget esteem, but how you act as a friend, is out of my way to judge' (26 October 1731).

The bounds of decency

Swift's 'failure' to marry Stella is often adduced to support an argument about his sexuality. Ehrenpreis says that 'Women's bodies, the pleasures of lovemaking, the comforts of marriage, scared him.'[3] However, Carol Houlihan Flynn sees him as only too attracted to sexual activity. She speaks of Swift's love of exercise, which he said he took to try to offset Ménière's disease, as sexual sublimation: 'To chastise his unruly desire, Swift mortifies his body, working always to "stay lean".'[4] His celibacy was 'self protective, his way of defending himself and those he loves against the body that will always betray. But he still insists throughout his life and letters upon calling up a sexuality he is bent on denying.' In his private writings, such as the daily letters to Esther Johnson collected under the title of the *Journal to Stella*, Swift enjoys *double entendres* and intimacies which raise questions about propriety and sexual power politics. Although these are worth considering to help understand some of his public writing, the amount is not great and it is in the context of a daily history which exhibits a great variation of mood: exhilaration at political success, anger at Irish bishops, anxiety about his future, heartache over the stabbing of Harley, pain from medical problems.

Female schooling

Esther Johnson was born in 1681 and just 20 when Swift wrote his journal to her. He had been her tutor when she was eight and the childish language he sometimes adopts refers back to that time. As more than half the *Journal to Stella* is an editorial transcript[5] which excises or adapts many of these usages, we have an imperfect record but there is enough to catch a particular tone of condescension often turned on himself, pet name contractions based on the sound of consonants run together, such as 'Ppt, pdfr, MD' ('poppet, poor dear fellow, My Dear') and scraps such as this: 'when I am writing in our language I make up my mouth just as if I was speaking it' indicating the origin of phrases in childish substitutions for 'l' and 'r' like 'ourrichar Gangridge' ('our little language') and 'good mallows, little sollahs' ('good morrow, little sirrahs'). This waggishness merges into other wordplay when he mock-accuses Stella and Mrs Dingley of being drinkers, then falls into the 'r/l' substitutions and puns on 'boozing' at the same time as admitting he's making fun of them. 'O Rold, I must go no further fear of aboozing fine Radyes' (11 October 1712). This 'nursery talk' has no private association for us, in contrast to what Stella may have remembered, say of Moor Park. So it may not greatly appeal to us. Private intimacies and lovers' 'baby talk', read cold, are often embarassing and without knowing Stella's side of the matter we cannot say how much she appreciated it and to what degree it was merely a game. It seems likely that Swift himself would have removed such detail had he prepared the *Journal to Stella* for publication. The journal was kept because he valued the record of events and in the letters which survive in his own handwriting there are scratchings out suggesting that he had made a preliminary editing out of such matter. The intimate talk belongs with school-room word games such as : 'He gave me al bsadnuk lboinlpl dfaonr ufainfbtoy dpionufnad.' The code is easily cracked by taking alternate letters and so poses no great intellectual puzzle, but it is not a negligible side of Swift's personality, being part of a continuum that leads through the riddling poems with Sheridan to the inventive codes of *Gulliver's Travels*. We may value it as characteristic of the writer while to Stella, who had known him in her childhood, it presents what would have been endearingly familiar.

However, other phrases play on the tutor/child relationship while recognising that she is now a grown woman. As such it has drawn criticism even though we do not know what Stella herself felt about it. Readers have observed that as the tutored girl she is subservient. Sometimes the roles are reversed to make her a governess but this occurs at the whim of Swift, who for his own pleasure does it and retains control. Ehrenpreis regards it as a device to keep her 'dependent while he remained free'.[6] Flynn sees it as having titillation both ways and quotes from the journal for 14 December 1710 where he feigns submission and then threatens to whip her –. Put like that it sounds damaging until the whole passage is read:

> Ah, why don't you go down to Clogher nautinautinautidear girls; I dare not say nauti without dear; O faith you govern me. But, seriously, I'm sorry you don't go, as far as I can judge at this distance.
> [Gives instructions to make Parvisol his servant sell her horse and then picks up her raillery about Esther Johnson being latinised as Jonsonibus:]
> Faith, if I was near you, I would whip your – to some tune, for your grave saucy answer about the dean and Jonsonibus; I would, young women.

Then the flexibility of tone becomes apparent and qualifies the reader's responses. The passage begins with affectionate upbraiding, pretending the writer is fearful of the women. 'But, seriously' stops the fooling and is followed by direct concern and practical advice. However, in her previous letter, Stella had outsmarted Swift in a pun on her own name. Vexed and delighted by her wit and teasing he had no witty retort to give her. So he would whip the 'young women' (the elder chaperoning Dingley is included) to make them dance to another tune. While this removes the imagined incident from a sadistic sexual scenario it may still seem distasteful in treating them as small children to be smacked.[7] There is no doubt that Swift feels he is going beyond the bounds, hence his insistence: 'I would'. But he also knows he would not do so, since the presence of Dingley in his invention, if nothing else, acts as a disapproving monitor. Swift's language is mock bluster. The experience seems to endorse the comment of Angus Ross and David Woolley[8] that in the *Journal to Stella* 'enjoyment . . . comes from his informality of language . . . It is speculative, but not too far-fetched, to say that this is an "Irish" feeling for English, ironical, aware of social complexities of discourse, enjoying anarchy and discontinuity in conversation and communication.' It should also be added that some of Swift's comments in the role of tutor are nothing more than tutoring. He had a responsibility for Stella's education, her capitalising on her property by moving to Ireland and her appearing not at a disadvantage when he could assist. So on 20 October 1711 he wrote in the *Journal to Stella*: 'Stella has made twenty false spellings[9] in her writing; I'll send them to you all back again on the other side of this letter, to mend them; I won't miss one.'

Sexual intimacy

Swift's intimate tone with Stella has also been considered to have a sexual nature, indulging fantasies at a safe distance. Sometimes he writes as though she were in his bedroom. 'Smoake [i.e. 'smoke out' in the sense of 'discover'] how I widen the margin by lying in bed when I write. My bed lies on the wrong side for me, so I am forced often to write when I am up' (26 September 1710). 'Oh, silly, how I prate and can't get away from MD in a morning. Go, get you gone, dear naughty girls, and let me rise' (13 December 1710). However in both cases the main point is that Stella is not there so that, in the first, he has to explain how his bed is situated and, in the second, the jocularity would lose its effect if she were there. Certainly he wishes her to appreciate and share vicariously the effort he has in writing, lying on the wrong side (making his writing off-centre on the page), and also to know that her letter keeps entering into his mind so that he is prevented from going about everyday business, comically transforming this into an elaborate sense of decorum. Similarly, in another example, the pun on sheets (papers or bedclothes) is lost if we consider the apostrophe to Stella's letter to be first and foremost that it is occupying a place in his bed. 'Come out, letter, come out from between the sheets: here it is underneath, and it won't come out' (1 January 1711). In fact he enjoyed endowing the written page with a life of its own (perhaps a tribute to lively writing or the mysterious way papers disappear when you want them) and this is in a context where he changes MD into comrades rather than attractive members of the opposite sex: 'And now, boys, for your letter, I mean the first, N. 21. Let's see; come out, little letter' (20 October 1711).

There is nevertheless a value in seeing his tone as having a sexual *double entendre* and being more than prattle. It is to note that Swift does not have an inhibition a more correct person might have when writing to his intimates. This provides a clue to the indecencies and scatological passages in the works he wished to be published, if we consider the freedom he shows to his intimates and remember that his published writing often has a personal meaning directed at some of his circle. In rattling on excitedly about his first and highly significant meeting with Oxford he became entangled by a *double entendre*. He said he did not intend to do this but also he did not bother to strike it out. Probably this was because he knew his witty reader would 'smoake' the mistake, laugh at him and not take offence. In addition his preserving the error was being true to the immediacy of feeling, which he is at pains to convey in all the examples quoted in the preceding paragraph and which runs through the entire journal.

> And, to-day, I was brought privately to Mr. Harley … he has appointed me an hour on Saturday at four, afternoon, when I will open my business to him; which expression I would not use if I were a woman. I know you smoakt it; but I did not till I writ it.
> (4 October 1710)

He knew well enough the decorum usual between a man and a woman but this relationship would not suffer from small breaches of convention. So he smudged but did not obliterate 'clap' (meaning venereal disease) when speaking of the sexual perils of a lone woman in London: 'I know nothing of his Wife being here. It may cost her a Clap. (I don't care to write that Word plain.)' (21 March 1712).

This unreserve is not confined to sexual matters. He details Arbuthnot's symptoms of bloody urine and the progress of his own 'spots full of corruption' (later diagnosed as *herpes miliaris*):

> I was not able to go to church or court to-day for my shoulder. The pain has left my shoulder, and crept to my neck and collarbone. It makes me think of poor Ppt's blade bone. Urge, urge,

urge; dogs gnawing. [30 March 1712] The spots increased every day, and bred red little pimples, which are now grown white, and full of corruption, though small. The red still continues too, and most prodigious hot and inflamed. The disease is the shingles. [31 March 1712] . . . they were not properly shingles, but *herpes miliaris*, and twenty other hard names.

(10 May 1712)

The distaste which may arise from reading the full account should be tempered by considering the context and the psychology. If it had been a report to Arbuthnot, the gifted doctor of the Queen, the description of symptoms would be appropriate and helpful for diagnosis. But medical science then was less exact than now and other opinion, particularly from a loving friend, might give aid. Also, Swift needed sympathy in addition to medicine. His own body had been confronting him with a perplexing progressive illness since 1708. We now know this as Ménière's disease, but Swift did not have that advantage and considered wrongly that eating fruit, which he adored, had caused it and that exercise would ameliorate it. Williams tells us[10] that Swift's giddiness and deafness 'had a common origin in the left ear, a trouble designated Ménière's disease or *labyrinthine vertigo*. As the years passed the malady would have had an increasingly depressing physical and mental effect.' With the benefit of hindsight we may underplay the terrors of the progress of what he called in his first written reference a 'cruel distemper'. He kept watchful guard on it, by frequently recording its attacks in his account books, and the *Journal to Stella* shows now and then the concern he has of it gaining hold and worsening:

I dined with Lord Anglesea to-day, but did not go to the House of Commons about the yarn; my head was not well enough. I know not what's the matter; it has never been thus before: two days together giddy from morning till night, but not with any violence or pain; and I totter a little, but can make shift to walk.

(18 April 1711)

From his own experience, Swift was always conscious of pain and disease. 'I can never be sick like other people, but always something out of the common way; and as for your notion of its coming without pain, it neither came, nor staid, nor went without pain, and the most pain I ever bore in my life.' This gave urgency to his sense of mortality, particularly his own. 'I was 47 Years old when I began to think of death; and the reflections upon it now begin when I wake in the Morning, and end when I am going to Sleep' (letter to Pope, 31 October 1729). It is significant he chooses when he was aged 47, for it was the year Queen Anne and his hopes of preferment in

England died. Ménière's disease had become increasingly debilitating; one of his best friends, Pope, was stunted by the crippling Pott's disease (Pope referred to himself as having a 'jade of a body'); England was in the thrall of corrupt ministers and he was too early wrenched from a promising and useful career in London to languish under an Archbishop, busy in hedging him round with favourite appointees and ready to undermine him. Already sensitive to reversal (bearing in mind his testing of friends and his resentment of Temple's coldness), he must have felt bitterly the shortness and physical decay of life. From 1714 onwards he speaks of himself as marked by illness even though others who visited him noted his good health. Having been not able to write for a month in which one spell of giddiness lasted five hours, he told Charles Ford, 'You healthy People cannot judge of the sickly' (4 April 1720). Recurrent haemorrhoids added to the pain. 'I fell into a cruell Disorder that kept me in Torture for a Week' and the symptoms and treatment required 'more of a Stoick than I am Master of, to support it' (2 April 1724). Psychologically he felt tortured by his body and he claimed kinship with Pope as 'a man subject like us to bodily infirmities' (10 May 1728). Out of this experience came the imaginative creation of the Struldbruggs in *Gulliver's Travels*, human beings condemned to live for ever while their bodies and minds decayed.

Poems to Stella

The group of birthday poems to Stella have a strongly biographical content which draws on these considerations of unreserve. Each was written in particular circumstances and stands alone but an overview of some characteristics of a selection helps to define their peculiar intimacy and candour.

To Stella, Visiting me in my Sickness, 1720?

Swift shows in this poem that he is keenly aware of the demanding nature of his revelations of sickness and the impositions they make on Stella, who did not have a robust constitution. She herself suffered from a weak stomach and about 1723 began the decline that led to her early death. The climax of the poem is his praise of her service to him as representing the type of true honour:

> Then Stella ran to my relief
> With cheerful face, and inward grief
> And, though by heaven's severe decree
> She suffers hourly more than me

All that goes before builds up to this, with first a description of the debased and cheapskate standards that are taken for honour in worldly society – in swear-words, duels, processional carriages, betting with cheats and prostitution. In such a context other standards must raise our values:

> . . . lest we should for honour take
> The drunken quarrels of a rake;
> Or think it seated in a scar,
> Or on a proud triumphal car,
> Or in the payment of a debt
> We lose with sharpers at piquet;
> Or, when a whore in her vocation,
> Keeps punctual to an assignation

Stella's actions are recalled in anecdotes that specifically relate to actual incidents such as when she bravely took action against the armed burglars.

> Nor calls up all the house at night,
> And swears she saw a thing in white

The sum of all her parts is that she represents true honour to such a degree that she causes him to rethink its being a masculine quality. It is more perfectly expressed in a woman where it had its origin:

> Say, Stella, was Prometheus blind,
> And forming you, mistook your kind?
> No: 'twas for you alone he stole
> The fire that forms the manly soul;
> Then to complete it every way,
> He moulded it with female clay

To Stella, Who Collected and Transcribed his poems, 1720?

As if to counter such unconditional praise, Swift wrote another poem which strikes as cruel in its severity. It begins with no hint of the cruelty to come by celebrating the virtues of their shared friendship which is above passion. The rejection of passion recalls, for us, his words to Kendall that he was 'naturaly temperate':

> Thou, Stella wert no longer young,
> When first for thee my harp I strung:
> Without one word of Cupid's darts,
> Of killing eyes, or bleeding hearts:
> With friendship and esteem possessed,
> I ne'er admitted love a guest

Their mutual esteem is founded not on externals which the good fortune of inherited beauty, or the possession of money and youth confer.

> Your virtues safely I commend,
> They on no accidents depend

Then comes the turn which tries to give credence to his praise by salting it with criticism. We saw before, when overjoyed by Arbuthnot, he pretended to criticise him for having a kind of a slouch. Here, to our surprise, his criticism is not one which encourages us to dismiss it and esteem even more the object of his praise. Instead he adopts the voice of a stern clerical authority, as though set apart from the partial judging of a partner involved in the issues:

> Resolved to mortify your pride,
> I'll here expose your weaker side

The fault he perceives (but he is judge and jury) is that she lets her spite override her good qualities.

> Truth, judgement, wit, give place to spite,
> Regardless both of wrong and right

And as a last cruel twist he taunts her that as she has copied out for him all his poems to her she will have to do so with this:

> Say Stella, when you copy next,
> Will you keep strictly to the text?

The copying which she does out of friendship and esteem for him now is something like a schoolroom punishment and requires her complete submission to his point of view. It seems that Swift wrestled to be sincere in his poems to her and that he would at all costs avoid the puffing up of romantic adoration but has fallen into the trap of censure, which makes us reflect on the quality of his disinterestedness. We don't know whether Stella merits the praise or the blame but that is not the issue. The movement of the poem, with Swift manipulating the response to Stella, calls in question what kind of esteem tunes the 'harp I sung'. At the same time, he may have felt he had gone too far in his censure, for several other poems try to qualify the judgement and to reduce the status of the poems. In *Stella's Birthday* (1723) he confesses that the writing is more for his showing well than accurate representation:

> Nor do I ask for Stella's sake;
> 'Tis my own credit lies at stake

This swings too far the other way in self-criticism, suggesting a purely selfish motive for writing. We may feel from the evidence of *Stella at Woodpark* (1723) that this is because she had let him have a taste of her anger which he now felt was justified and therefore reined in his sallies at her expense because he 'feared' that she would think him 'too severe':

> Thus far in jest. Though now I fear
> You think my jesting too severe:
> But poets when a hint is new
> Regard not whether false or true:
> Yet raillery gives no offence,
> Where truth has not the least pretence;
> Nor can be more securely placed
> Than on a nymph of Stella's taste

Certainly he could see that he was oversevere, for after her death in 1732 he reflected on his bad treatment of friends in his confession to the Duchess of Queensberry that it was 'my misfortune to quarrell with all my acquaintance'. And in his last poem to Stella (1727) before her death he asks her to take his tribute seriously:

> From not the gravest of divines,
> Accept for once some serious lines

The poems to Stella, part party turns and part attempts to do justice without overstating or undervaluing the relationship, are an important indication of the nature of his attachment. Swift wrote (1725) that he at the age of 56 and she at the age of 43 were too old for love lyrics but the bond between them was strong, once again expressed in terms of 'esteem and friendship':

> Adieu bright wit, and radiant eyes;
> You must be grave, and I be wise.
> Our fate in vain we would oppose,
> But I'll still be your friend in prose:
> Esteem and friendship to express,
> Will not require poetic dress

Another poem about Mrs Elizabeth Cope, *The First of April*, written at the same time, indicates that the household thoughts which had driven Swift in his youth from marriage now had an attraction. Swift may have felt affinities between her tender mothering of children and Stella's care for a charity child. The attentions of the woman and the plight of the child Swift renders with great sensitivity and good humour, seeing the mother:

> Softening with songs to son or daughter,
> The persecution of cold water.
> Still pleased with the good-natured noise,
> And harmless frolic of her boys

The wholesome normality and charm reminds us Swift was also an attractively observant and sympathetic man as well as a severe critic and difficult friend.

Vanessa at arm's length

Despite the strong attachment of Swift to Stella (the 'violent friend-ship') which made the final separation almost unbearable he ex-pressed his feelings with reservations, qualifications and sometimes censure. These are the specific qualities that define what he meant by a relationship without 'Cupid's darts' even though by 'friendship and esteem possessed'. It is not necessary to look for concealed or sublimated passion in his heterosexual contacts if full credit is given to this aspect of his personality that he repeatedly stresses. Although he might be self-deceived or rewriting his history it is at least worth seeing where accepting his self-valuation might lead us. Early he spoke of himself as 'naturaly temperate' and his language to Varina does not sigh with unrequited ardour. But that does not make him into an unfeeling being. There are plenty of instances to suggest his emotional capacity. The misery of bereavement, the care given to Stella, the suggestion of being held captive ('possessed') by the feel-ings of 'esteem and friendship' point to the sensitivity that impelled him to speak vigorously on behalf of the poor and oppressed in Ireland. A man of feeling who enjoyed intimacy with intelligent women but did not want sexual contact could easily be an enigma. And it seems to be as such that he inspired the romantic passion of Esther Vanhomrigh.

The references to Vanessa in the *Journal to Stella* are discreet and do not convey the urgency of her feeling for him or the great inter-est he took in her to the extent that when he moved lodgings he circled round the home of the Vanhomrighs near St James Square. This may be seen on the map on Plate 3. His lodgings included suc-cessively Bury Street (mistakenly rendered as 'Berry Street' on the map), Suffolk Street, Leicester Fields and Little Rider Street. How-ever, the vicinity of these addresses any aspiring political figure would also have found convenient for the court at St James. Twenty-eight letters of Swift and 17 of Vanessa's drafts exist and they offer no conclusive evidence of a physical sexual relationship. Vanessa with wit, intelligence and emotional blackmail entangles Swift in making a contact which he finds he is not willing flatly to resist. Apart from the obvious flattery to his self-esteem to have a woman whom he could admire make a set at him there was also a pleasure in raillery where the risks were high.

In his *Hints towards an Essay on Conversation*, about 1710, he writes 'Raillery is the finest part of conversation' and defines it as to 'say something that at first appeared a reproach or reflection, but, by some turn of wit, unexpected and surprising, ended always in a compliment, and to the advantage of the person it was addressed to'. When Swift practised this on Archbishop King he miscalculated. It is evident that such speaking at first discomforts the object of its praise and that what follows may not be waited for by a person who stands on dignity or be thought adequate for the pain of being fooled. In addition such behaviour leaves Swift wholly in charge of the exchange which in itself may irk. King did not warm to him and for some years tried to undermine him. In the case of Sheridan he found a non-passive 'victim' whose replies went into areas he found discomposing to his own dignity. But Vanessa at first seemed to be prepared to play the game of compliment without wishing to turn it into a declaration of passion where physical responses would be the forfeits.

Swift in his depression needed the lively commentary of Vanessa when he withdrew from the crumbling government in June 1714 to Letcombe Basset on the Berkshire Downs and so she was the first person he wrote to. She needed his advice in handling the debts of her mother, recently deceased in July of the same year. However, she appears to have visited him unchaperoned and he wrote with some desperate asperity, 'You should not have come to Wantage for a thousand Pound. You used to brag you were very discreet; where is it gone?' (12 August 1714). His letter continued with an emphasis on the 'perfect Esteem and Friendship I have for you' in an attempt to keep the relationship on a sober footing and tantalisingly for the romantic detective said he would 'not answer your Questions for a Million; nor can I think of them with any Ease of Mind'. This letter gives clear evidence of Swift's wish for caution in their contact and enough to suggest that this caution was not merely a device to avoid discovery by spies opening his letters, although that was a worry, while acting as a cover for pursuing more ardently a clandestine alliance. Esteem and friendship were not the responses Vanessa was looking for. And if, as many critics believe, *Cadenus and Vanessa* was written in the autumn of 1713 (with later revisions), he had been for some time trying to cool her ardour. For in that poem he is Cadenus, an anagram of 'decanus' (Latin for 'dean'), and like the Stella poems it attempts to establish the standing of their relationship as one also without Cupid's darts in which:

> His want of passion will redeem,
> With gratitude, respect, esteem:
> With that devotion we bestow,
> When goddesses appear below.

He gave her a copy as a way of setting the rules of their conduct towards each other and we shall return to this poem after considering further evidence from the letters.

In Dublin he professed it went 'to my Soul not to see you oftener' but firmly gave his role as giving 'you the best Advise, Countenance & Assistance I can' (? end of 1714). She pleaded the extremity of

131

her case in trying to handle her mother's 'importunate creditors' in this 'disagreable place amongst strange prying deacitful people' and that it was 'a very great punishment you fly me' (? December 1714). When he accused her of causing the servants to tittle tattle about them she answered 'I am sure I could have bore the Rack much better than those killing, killing, words of yours.'

Although the record is patchy, a letter of December 1716 from Swift indicates that the dangerous game of contrived meetings continued over the next two years. She had got a certain Provost Pratt out of the way by pretending she was returning from Dublin to Cellbridge on the day Swift was to arrive. Swift wrote anxiously, 'If he comes, you must piece it up as you can, else he will think it was on purpose to meet me; and I hate any thing that looks like a Secret' (? December 1716). Some time in 1720 Vanessa is confident enough of her allure to write to Swift 'I know tis as impossible for you to burn my letters, without reading them, as tis for me to avoid reproving you when you behave wrong.' And she warns him she will stop at nothing: 'I have determined to try all manner of humain artes to reclaim you.' Swift tried to turn this into high raillery but also with a lightly stressed threat: 'If you write as you do, I shall come seldomer on purpose to be pleased with your Letters.' On 4 August 1720 he wrote with more determination to bottle the genie he had released in his earlier days. 'One would imagine you were in love by dating your Lett^r Aug. 29th by which means I received it a month before it was written.' And he asked her to use a dash to expunge endearments 'a Stroak thus – signifies every thing that may be said to Cad [i.e. Cadenus]'. Subsequent letters from Vanessa turned this prohibition to her advantage for she wrote with a frenzy of urgent dashes for which the reader could supply the most intimate endearments and in the same year made her declaration 'I was born with violent passions which terminate all in one that unexpressible passion I have for you.'

In February 1721 Vanessa's sister Mary ('Molkin') died, probably from consumption, leaving Vanessa without a chaperone. In April Swift went on extended travels to friends in the north of Ireland. Five weeks out, at Clogher, he wrote, 'Remembr I still enjoyn you Reading and Exercise for the Improvement of your Mind and Health of your Body, and grow less Romantick, and talk and act like a Man of the World' (1 June 1722). (Once again he endows a female friend with a male gender.) He did not return until October. Vanessa's reply to Swift's letter shows that she had been reading parts of *Gulliver's Travels* in draft, since she makes allusion to an incident in Chapter 5 of the 'Voyage to Brobdingnag' and probably to the Yahoos in the 'Voyage to the Country of the Houyhnhnms'. So Swift included her in the very small number of friends privileged to know of his work in progress and this gives substance to his injunction to turn from her passionate involvement to reading in which she could still share and encourage the fruits of friendship and esteem. But like her sister she too fell ill, at the end of 1722, and died on 2 June 1723 at the age of 35.

After Vanessa's death, manuscript versions of the poem *Cadenus and Vanessa* found in her papers began to circulate and finally it was published in 1726. David Nokes sees this as evidence of a break between her and Swift. He believes that her bequest to Berkeley, whose opinions were not those of Swift, and the failure to mention Swift showed 'a strong whiff of spite'; credits the story of Sheridan's son that Vanessa challenged Stella that she had married Swift – which Stella affirmed; and also gives Sheridan's story that Vanessa ordered her executors to publish the poem and her letters.[11] Ehrenpreis argues that the younger Sheridan had no first-hand knowledge of the case and is unreliable; there is no evidence for the marriage; and the bequest is not surprising as Swift probably preferred not to be named; that he spoke of Berkeley 'with tenderness and admiration' (more will be said of Berkeley in Chapter 5); and that some legatees may have been recommended by Swift, for four were on 'excellent terms' with him.[12] This study sides with Ehrenpreis on the issue and, even if there had been a final break, for most of the tantalising relationship Vanessa's threats of exposure were not carried out but used as devices to win more contact from Swift. She knew that his displeasure and the loss of his company would be the consequence of such exposure.

When the busybody Chetwode, whom Swift accepted on sufferance as a companion, hinted that the manuscripts of *Cadenus and Vanessa* were likely to be printed, Swift replied:

> I am very indifferent what is done with it, for printing cannot make it more common than it is; and for my own part, I forget what is in it, but believe it to be only a cavalier business ... Neither do I believe the gravest character is answerable for a private humoursome thing, which, by an accident inevitable, and the baseness of particular malice, is made public.
>
> (to Chetwode 19 April 1726)

Granting that Swift would not be entirely open to this correspondent and that his affectation not to remember the poem is damage limitation, he still makes a good case that the publication does not harm him. To call it 'a cavalier business' links the work with the genre of courtly compliment that flourished at the beginning of the seventeenth century. (Swift's definition of 'raillery' could equally be applied to this tradition.) The art of these poems relied on elaboration and valued artifice above realism. This did not necessarily mean that the poem seemed unreal but more that it created its own world. Shakespeare wrote that 'the truest poetry is the most feigning' and John Donne claimed that in his own poems: 'I wrote best when least in truth.' In addition, Swift distinguished between public and private verse. In another letter (to Tickell on 7 July 1726), unwilling to give the poem's title he says 'The Thing you mention which no Friend would publish . . . ought to caution men to Keep the Key of their Cabinets.' While we notice the hurt and sense of betrayal in his phrases concerning 'the baseness of particular malice' and material 'which no Friend would publish' Swift does not specifically name the individual responsible and his feelings seem justified when we consider that *Cadenus and Vanessa* was an intimate communication, intended to honour the lover but tactfully steer her towards friendship. The conception of a private verse is a matter to return to when looking at other poems that offend public taste.

Cadenus and Vanessa turns on a debate before Venus on whether women can truly love in an age where they seem more interested in 'fans and flounces, and brocades'. (Swift alludes to the situation in *The Rape of the Lock*.) Venus turns to the classical poets and to the seventeenth-century love poets, Cowley and Waller, to support her claim that females are intelligent. But it is in vain, for they denigrate all other women but their own. (Finding the mistresses of other poets lacking is a frequent device of a cavalier poet who bestows special regard on his own mistress. Swift's poem conforms to this tradition and we know that he had copies of Cowley and Waller in his library.) By her arts she bestows graces on a female baby which she names 'Vanessa' and tricks Pallas Athene into giving the infant qualities

> For manly bosoms chiefly fit,
> The seeds of knowledge, judgement, wit.

Much later, when Vanessa has grown into a young woman, some of the fops prattle foolishly on fashionable matters and Vanessa says

> . . . she valued nothing less
> Than titles, figure, shape and dress;
> That merit should be chiefly placed
> In judgement, knowledge, wit and taste

In justifying this

> Through nature, and through art she ranged,
> And gracefully her subjects changed

but the fops are unimpressed by a woman with a mind and

> Their judgement was upon the whole,
> 'That lady is the dullest soul –

Such a woman requires the companionship of a man who also has a mind, so Cupid singles out Cadenus

> Grown old in politics and wit;
> Caressed by ministers of state,
> Of half mankind the dread and hate.

By this mythological framework, Swift establishes the uncommonness of their qualities which draw them together and shifts the responsibility for their attachment to the gods, as a matter of fate. The compliment flatters and soothes Vanessa (the reader) in preparation for a more direct statement of how the matter has got out of hand. Cadenus had agreed to be her tutor and, while neither was to blame for what happened next, he was surprised by her ardour.

> She wished her tutor were her lover;
> Resolved she would her flame discover:
> And when Cadenus would expound
> Some notion subtle or profound,
> The nymph would gently press his hand,
> As if she seemed to understand;

In comic fashion Swift projects himself as an other-worldly and antiquated Cadenus running through a variety of emotions as he worries about the sincerity of her passion, the culpability of his behaviour, the tongue-wagging of gossips. Despite the allegory, identifiable features of Esther Vanhomrigh keep the application of the story in mind, such as her inheritance of £5000 and her raillery. Swift's own temperateness is represented there, too, in Cadenus's 'want of passion', as is his value for friendship based on 'respect, esteem'. The poem does not resolve the clash of wills and draws a veil over the outcome:

> But what success Vanessa met,
> Is to the world a secret yet:

Venus grows tired of the encounter and dismisses the debate on love, realising that she needed to reform men as well as women. The upshot of this is that passionate love in the world, as it is, seems doomed to folly in general terms and in the particular case of Cadenus and Vanessa, the difference of age and temperament produces an impasse.

In the light of *Cadenus and Vanessa* Swift's poem to *To Stella, Visiting me in my Sickness* reads like an amends. Like Vanessa, Stella is singled out by the goddesses to stand out among her sex. She is gifted with a sense of honour by Pallas Athene who recognises her wit is more than usual for women. Like Vanessa she has been offered Swift's ideal relationship of 'friendship and esteem' and unlike her has accepted. There is no explicit link between the poems but it is reasonable to suppose that Swift had the poem to Vanessa in mind while framing the one to Stella and that it helped him to define his pleasure and satisfaction in Stella's company.

The question of morbidity and scatological coarseness

The sensibility Swift reveals in his behaviour towards women as shown in his letters and poems is one that does not fit a romantic norm. While he has a genuine affection for women he does not profess a deep sexual love, being 'naturaly temperate'. At the same time he claims an intimacy which allows him to dominate and to express himself in terms of physicality ranging from the sexual to the medical. It is the same sensibility that animates his poems which encompass descriptions of bodily decay and defecation. Critical response to these poems is often one which reflects the horror expressed by some contemporaries and soon after by Samuel Johnson in his *Life of Swift*. Writing, probably in August of 1780, he asked 'by what depravity of intellect [Swift] took delight in revolving ideas, from which almost every other mind shrinks in disgust . . . what has disease, deformity and filth, upon which the thoughts can be allured to dwell?'

Johnson was a robust man acquainted with living in poverty on the streets of London and unsqueamish about crude sleeping arrangements in the Highlands of Scotland and yet he identifies this as a moral failing not just a matter of taste. What turns the tastelessness to 'depravity of intellect' seems to lie in the 'delight' and allurement he believes Swift has with these subjects. Johnson, himself, in his private diaries did record with some anxiety his own bowel actions with the letter 'M' as a code for the Latin 'merda' ('excrement'). And this makes the point of taste that such matters are for private eyes only and to be disguised from common view. But taste changes and what one age sees as indecent another may tolerate. For example, later, James Joyce in *Ulysses* (1922) portrayed Leopold Bloom in the privy 'seated calm above his own rising smell'. Seen as grossly indecent when first published, this episode now raises less adverse criticism.

On this matter of taste there has been considerable comment both for and against the value of such writing. An approach which seems more interesting than a dismissal of poor taste or loss of moral direction is to consider what relationship Swift's dwelling on 'disease, deformity and filth' has to his art. Johnson links all three together and this seems to spring from the sense that the human body is corruptible and contains an inner corruption. From Swift's dilating on Ménière's disease and haemorrhoids (illness with death hovering

136

somewhere in the wings) is a short step to writing of excretion (internal corruption) and to cosmetic covering of the body now seen as corrupt. Swift was fascinated by such matters but his interest also exhibited fastidiousness. In the *Journal to Stella* on 21 October 1711 he recorded, 'I was to see Lady –, who is just up after lying-in; and the ugliest sight I have seen, pale, dead, old, and yellow, for want of paint. She has turned my stomach. But she will soon be painted, and a beauty again.'

Swift's presentation of gross physicality is part of the continuum of the character he projects in his writing. We noted Angus Ross's comment that he had 'an "Irish" feeling for English, ironical, aware of social complexities of discourse, enjoying anarchy' and the disgust that Swift raised may be seen as a part of his Irish unreserve. To go against the social norms and to appear anarchic in venturing on to subjects not mentioned in polite company squares with the harum scarum digressiveness of such writings as those of the supposed author of *A Tale of a Tub*. And as we know that work offended the queen, damaging Swift's chances of preferment – a matter he alluded to in *Gulliver's Travels* allegorically and indecently when he had Gulliver urinating on the palace of the tiny Lilliputians in order to put out a fire, just as the tract had hoped to dampen the flames of religious enthusiasm. There was no guarantee that the stiff dignity of authority would unbend to his iconoclasm any more than it did in his attempts to engage Archbishop King in raillery. Similarly *A Windsor Prophecy* was ill judged if he hoped to ingratiate himself.

Not all his readers were so offended. Pope certainly had his own vigorous line of scatological imagery, particularly in *The Dunciad* where a parody of ancient Greek funeral games has his heroes competing at pissing the highest and diving into the sewage of the Thames whose female denizens are ambiguously described as 'nutbrown maids'.[13] And those who did not indulge in such writing might still appreciate descriptions of physical decay even when they were the butt of the joke. Lady Acheson, who is one of the characters described in *Death and Daphne* discussed below, reportedly kept a copy of the poem and had pleasure in showing it to visitors such as Lord Orrery.

One defence that is made for Swift is that most of the poems with this subject matter were private but that does not account for all of them or for the passages in *Gulliver's Travels*, especially those that describe the gross bodies of the female giants, the decayed frames of the ageing Struldbruggs who can never die but continue to deteriorate, and the excreting ape-like but human Yahoos. But the issue of what was private writing is a live one if we ask what was meant by public writing. We have already found it necessary to modify our view of the public nature of writing a book in Swift's time in the discussion of the intimacy authors still felt with their readers (see Chapter 3). Bolingbroke had said he was not fond 'of the Name of an Author' and that his writings were only for friends since he did 'not have the itch of making them more publick'. Kernan's study related this to the idea that for many writers making a book was an amateur affair mainly directed at friends even though concerned to make money. Many of Pope's footnotes to his *Dunciad* are concerned to retail the minor conflicts of a group of writers in a way which is of interest to the relatively small number of readers who have a stake in the gossip of the town. Book production was also an intimate matter. Bookseller and publisher were often the same person and dealt directly with the author rather than through agents and editors. So it was possible to write a book as though for your Scriblerian friends who would not jib at the scatological elements. Literature had not assumed a quasi-religious status of public exhortation and high seriousness.

One consequence of this blurring of the distinction between private and public was the temptation to convey private meanings which might pass by the general reader. An example from *Gulliver's Travels* which illustrates this also bears on Swift's scatology and shows the ingenuity required of the reader to tease out its meaning. Swift's friends knew he exercised to keep healthy and that he was liable to come out with some physically gross remark. Accordingly, for their amusement, he allegorises himself for the moment as Gulliver when, in the land of the giants, he takes his exercise by trying to leap a giant cowpat and lands in the middle. Swift may even be making a concession to friendly critics by suggesting he does make mistakes of taste ending up in grossness and looking ridiculous. But so multi-layered is his writing the implied meanings may not stop there and he may also refer to his tussling in verse with Sheridan which ended up in ribaldry. For he used similar language to describe this in an earlier private poem. In *A Left Handed Letter* (20 September 1718) he wrote of their verbal wrestling as an employment in which 'we both act the part of the clown and the cow-dung'. And there may be a sting in the tail. For the clown in this poem is Antaeus, a giant, whose strength was drawn from the earth. Hercules could only defeat him by holding him head high and throttling him. If Sheridan is Antaeus, whose dead body is eventually cast on the ground (among the cow dung), then Swift is Hercules. In this instance the private references do not matter all that much to the general understanding of *Gulliver's Travels* and the episode may be simply enjoyed as a comic invention of the perils of living in a land of giants. But we should remember the cast of mind that such writing exhibits when confronted with some especially slippery satire as it may help us to avoid losing our own ground.

Swift's fascination with physical deformity and grossness is fuelled by his sense of his own bodily infirmities and his painful aware- ness of human mortality. The improvements to the microscope by people such as Robert Hooke of the Royal Society and its wider use on the wave of scientific enthusiasm had brought a closer look at the human body. In the *Journal to Stella* Swift records buying for Stella one of them since, he said, she was a 'virtuoso', a term used mock- ingly of the scientists of the Royal Society: ''Tis not the great bulky ones, nor the common little ones, to impale a louse (saving your presence) upon a needle's point; but of a more exact sort, and clearer to the sight' (15 November 1710). It is characteristic of Swift's sense of the vulnerability of the body that he should mention the louse and he remembered this when Gulliver looks at the giants as though seeing humans through a microscope. They are crawling with lice and he watches 'their Snouts with which they rooted like Swine' and 'There was a Woman with a Cancer in her Breast, swelled to a monstrous size, full of Holes in two or three of which I could have easily crept.' Compassion for the human condition is behind the disgust at the inflictions of disease on the body which hastened the onset of death. What he saw in others he felt keenly in himself. As we have seen his sense of his own demise was sharpened by the loss of his role in England. It was something that he feared before then. In the *Journal to Stella*, 3 January 1713, he wrote indignantly of the death of Lady Ashburnham while her contemptible husband ('her lord's a puppy') lived on. 'I hate life when I think it exposed to such accidents; and to see so many thousand wretches burdening the earth, while such as her die, makes me think God did never intend life for a blessing. Farewell.' Later he wrote to Pope (13 February 1729) of a physician, Dr Helsham, who cared little when a friend died for 'it is no more than poor Tom! he gets another, or takes up with the rest, and is no more moved than at the loss of a cat'. He half hoped he could be like Helsham, free from the pain of parting from friends, but he honoured Lady Acheson who 'hates him mor- tally by my character'.

For a clergyman to think in this way is to ally him to a tradition which was less in evidence during the eighteenth century than it had been in the seventeenth. The presence of death behind the view of the body as corruptible flesh is a part of Christian thinking in the Elizabethan and Jacobean period. John Donne (1572–1631) preached in a sermon[14] that flesh was a mud wall wasting fast with corruption and that scents to disguise its smell were but a living embalmment: 'Dissolution and putrefaction is gone over thee alive.' In this he was sounding a traditional Christian sentiment of the flesh being an encumbrance to the soul. One of the early Christian fathers, St Jerome (*c*. 340–420), had written 'Inter faeces et urinas nascimur'

('We are born between excrement and urine'), thereby stressing our closeness to the natural processes of decay. In the midst of life we are in the presence of death. 'Memento mori' ('remember to die'), the phrase uttered to remind Roman emperors that their triumphs were short-lived, found expression in sombre poems, paintings and engravings. A favourite topic was a skeletal death confronting a naked woman (beautiful but also defenceless). Sometimes, a third naked woman appears with her flesh rotting from her body, representing the pass to which ageing before death will bring the young woman. An example of this tradition is illustrated later in this book. Hans Baldung-Grien's painting, Plate 10, shows death as a grim lover, one foot rotted and his lips fallen from his teeth, bared in a love bite on the neck of a woman. When Swift draws from these images of corruption, it is sometimes an attempt to exorcise his deep-rooted horror of death by playing games with his fears but the sombre reality is seldom far away. On his birthdays, he would read from Chapter 3 of the *Book of Job*: 'Let the day perish wherein I was born, and the night in which it was said, There is a man child conceived.'

Swift's scatological writing relates to his sense of mortality and also belongs to an earlier generation. We have already seen his kinship to this earlier period for he had defended *Cadenus and Vanessa* as a 'cavalier business' linking himself to the poets of the early seventeenth century. A number of those who mattered to Swift mingled scatological elements in their writing. Swift was in some ways a rival of his older cousin, John Dryden (1631–1700), who was a considerable poet, prolific and for some time Poet Laureate. Dryden's satirical poem *MacFlecknoe* has been seen as a prototype for Pope's *Dunciad* and freely descends into the scatological, seeing a poetaster's neglected sheets of poems put to other uses as food wrappers and toilet paper, 'Martyrs of Pies and Reliques of the Bum'. Swift owned a folio edition of the works of and quoted with pleasure from the great court poet and rival to Shakespeare, Ben Jonson (1572–1637). His poems include *On the Famous Voyage*, a mock heroic journey down an open sewer, the river Fleet leading to the Thames, to the 'croaking sound . . . of frogs? No, guts wind-bound Over your heads'. And going further back in time, Rabelais (1494?–1553) was also important to Swift as the author of the adventures and travels of the giants Gargantua and Pantagruel. It was his favourite reading-matter throughout his life and was available in a seventeenth-century English translation from the French. Like the Scriblerian project it was directed at satirising false learning and promoting humanist values. Incidental to the rambling plot are episodes of uninhibited coarseness and ribaldry, such as a chapter on the best bum wipes for a baby giant. In *A Tale of a Tub* Swift matches the coarse humour of these authors but elsewhere he has a darker mood of disgust.

The morbid poems

Death and Daphne

During the years 1728–1730, Swift made three long visits as a welcome guest at Market Hill, the home of Sir Arthur Acheson and his wife, the former Anne Savage, who eventually separated from her husband about 1732. For the amusement of the family he wrote a number of private poems, now called the Market Hill poems. One of these was *Death and Daphne* (1730). Stella had been dead only two years when Swift wrote this poem on a woman threatened with marriage to a macabre skeletal being. But the poem presents the matter as comedy, centering on the device that Pluto, King of Hades, had found the death rate had slowed, reducing the population growth of his domain. Part of Swift's pleasure in writing this, no doubt, came from his own success in promoting the peace at the Treaty of Utrecht (simply called 'the Peace' in the poem) and in seeing similarities between Pluto the death-monger and a Whig grandee sitting in committee. Pluto summoned Death to present his performance indicators:

> The phantom, having humbly kissed
> His grisly monarch's sooty fist,
> Presented him the weekly bills
> Of doctors, fevers, plagues, and pills.
> Pluto observing, since the Peace,
> The burial article decrease;
> And, vexed to see affairs miscarry,
> Declared in council, Death must marry.

The object of this is to propagate 'deathlings' who will help prosecute their sire's business and increase the throughput of recruits for burial. But Death must be marketed as a handsome beau and hellish coquettes deck him out with grotesque parodies of the accoutrements of a lordly fop, which Swift describes in comic detail that exhibits clever parallels, beginning with

> A periwig of twisted snakes;
> Which in the nicest fashion curled

and including an ebon snuff box 'Of shin-bones rotted by the pox'. Death makes an entrance in the upper world and catches the attention of Lady Daphne (a caricature of Lady Acheson) who being

> Charmed with his eyes and chin and snout,
> Her pocket-glass drew slily out;

She is implicated in being attracted to the grotesquely revolting by seeing his nose as a snout and also later by considering death the counterpart of her image. The allusion is sharp since she was thin and unhealthy, probably consumptive, for she died young. (Sheridan, writing to Pope, alluded to her as 'Skinnybonia'.) Her deathly image frightens away the amorous Death and Swift, like a *deus ex machina*, pronounces her doom, which is a complete reversal of the usual fate of star-crossed lovers who vainly ask that death should not come near and yet it is similar in thwarting their desires.

> Cease haughty nymph; the fates decree
> Death must not be a spouse for thee:
> For, when by chance the meagre shade
> Upon thy hand his finger laid;
> Thy hand as dry and cold as lead,
> His matrimonial spirit fled,

Although Lady Acheson approved the poem and it is a comic *tour de force*, the elements of Swift's discomfiture are also there to see in the rough treatment of an admired woman and playing with the fearful decay of the body under sentence of death.

A Beautiful Young Nymph Going to Bed

This process is taken a step further in *A Beautiful Nymph Going to Bed* (1731). We return to the London of *A Description of a City Shower* where the seamy side of the town is explored. Here an attractive woman prepares for bed and in the removal of cosmetics and beauty aids reveals the raddled body beneath.

> Now, picking out a crystal eye,
> She wipes it clean, and lays it by . . .
> Now dextrously her plumpers draws,
> That serve to fill her hollow jaws.
> Untwists a wire; and from her gums
> A set of teeth completely comes.

This recalls the Hans Baldung Grien in its time-lapse presentation of the process of bodily decay. Every detail undoes the conventional beauty of a cavalier love poem where an eye may be hyperbolically described as crystal in lustre and is now real glass. In a vicious twist, the following morning she cannot restore even her false beauty:

> The crystal eye, alas, was missed;
> And Puss had on her plumpers pissed.

While it is apparent that the woman is a prostitute (syphilis has rotted her teeth) and that there may be a sort of justice in her downfall, rather like the popular engravings of William Hogarth, *The Harlot's Progress*, the animus which drives the poem comes from the revulsion of uncleanliness and the fear of death. It is localised in the fate of the nymph but in *Gulliver's Travels* the decaying Struldbruggs show that all of us, not just prostitutes, are doomed to come to this pass.

The scatological poems

The presence of urination and diseased sexual intercourse in this poem of physical decay justifies Johnson's grouping of 'disease, deformity and filth' as allied in their fascination for Swift. It is not clear, however, where Swift feels he goes over the boundary of 'good taste'. In another Market Hill poem, *A Panegyric on the Dean* (*c.* 1730), he has Lady Acheson praising him for building, as he actually did, two privies, 'Two temples of magnific size'.[15] Again he uses the mock-heroic parody of pastoral that had been so successful in *A Description of the Morning*. But part of his subject is to describe the urine and excremental piles which are 'offered' in these temples as though they were the bushes and trees of an idyllic landscape:

> Whose offerings placed in golden ranks,
> Adorn our crystal river's banks;
> Nor seldom grace the flowery downs,
> With spiral tops, and copple crowns:

Little other than that it is ingenious may be said in its favour. But it should be observed that distaste is scarcely energised and a contrast will be apparent when noting three poems in which women excreting is the object of horror.

The Lady's Dressing room, 1732

The situation of this poem is that Strephon idealises his 'haughty Celia' and invades her dressing room to find with increasing distress evidence in her discarded, filthy clothes and in her commode of her bodily functions: dandruff, earwax, sweat, worms and faeces. The effect is to make him see her even when appearing clean and well-appointed as irremediably tainted by the gross evidences he found:

> By vicious fancy coupled fast,
> And still appearing in contrast

Again a moral voice intervenes requiring Strephon (and others similar to him) to accept the uncleanliness of the human and rejoice in what it can become:

> He soon would learn to think like me,
> And bless his ravished eyes to see
> Such order from confusion sprung,
> Such gaudy *tulips* raised from *dung.*

The poem arouses vigorous debate. Whose fancy is 'vicious': Strephon's or that of the poet who conceived the situation? Feminist

143

criticism sees it as a male soiling of the female or actually liberating women from being idealised sex-objects (subverting 'the
phallocentric').[16] Swift himself referred to it as a parody of the robing
of Belinda in Pope's *Rape of the Lock* to which it makes reference by
echoes in its opening lines. However, the fact that he returns to the
subject in the other poems gives grounds for supposing that his
interest is more deeply rooted than a *jeu d'esprit*.

Strephon and Chloe, 1731?

Strephon appears again in the role of discoverer of his mistress's
natural functions. This time it is Chloe and he does not react with
squeamish horror. Her example gives licence to their mutual indecency, vying at wind-breaking. But this leads to a further and more
surprising outcome. Swift, as narrator, draws a moral with familiar
elements from the Vanessa and Stella poems. If those poems represented a diptych of contrasted rarefied states of unrequited passion
and fulfilled friendship, *Strephon and Chloe* transforms it into a triptych
with a middle panel of grotesque and unenlightened baseness. The
message is not to rely on passion's idealising or on passion at all:

> On sense and wit your passion found,
> By decency cemented round;
> Let prudence with good nature strive,
> To keep esteem and love alive.

Prudence is a strange substitution for passion but as the timorous
may say that discretion is the better part of valour, so prudence is
the lot of the 'naturaly temperate'. While Swift dwells far longer on
the details of excretion than may be necessary for the moral point of
his acceptance of the baseness of the human condition, he guards
against such criticism by distancing himself from those who indulge
the habit:

> Some call it witty to reflect
> On every natural defect;

Swift's point that the greater value is to be found in 'esteem' and
good 'sense' in the context of what might otherwise be regarded as
a frivolous poem has support from the Vanessa and Stella poems as
a conviction deeply held.

His poem *Cassinus and Peter* (1731?) which is generally considered
among the scatological poems is mainly a rewriting of *Strephon and
Chloe* with the moral sanity assigned to Peter whose queries of Cassinus
elicit the idealising folly of his amour. Cassinus complains in traditional guise of the wounded lover, dying for his passion, as so often
described in seventeenth-century love poetry:

> Here Cassy lies, by Celia slain,
> And dying, never told his pain.

But it is not the brilliance of her beauty and shafts of light from her eyes that staggers him to his limp collapse. The closing couplet with its epigrammatic concision and the inevitability of the couplet rhyme leads the reader on through three mellifluous repetitions (sibilant and labial) of 'Celia' to a brutal monosyllable

> Nor, wonder how I lost my wits;
> Oh! Celia, Celia, Celia shits.

D.H. Lawrence, deeply offended by the poem, wrote that of course she did. Swift would have agreed that Cassy shows the folly of an exquisite but the poem remains open to the charge that undue emphasis is given to the process of defecation.

Mary the Cook-Maid's Letter to Dr Sheridan, 1718

A problem of categorising and grouping such as this discussion of the scatological is to over-emphasise the trait in Swift. Swift did not invariably represent women as goddesses with base natural functions and much other poetry would be left if such poems were avoided. While it is instructive to consider them as shedding light on his fears and disturbing a cosy familiarity with a uniquely gifted man, other emphases should be made. He was just as capable of presenting a portrait of a woman with insight, sympathy and convincing presence. We have noticed his poem on Elizabeth Cope, in which he acts as an approving bystander, honouring the domestic goodness of a personal friend. He is equally at home, below stairs, imagining the wholesomeness of one of his servants. In the quarrel with Sheridan which ended in Delany's intervention he wrote a defence of himself as though from Mary who was the maid for his cook. She is offended on his behalf for Sheridan calling Swift a knave:

Knave in your teeth, Mr Sheridan, 'tis both a shame and a sin,
And the Dean my master is an honester man than you and all
    your kin:
He has more goodness in his little finger, than you have in your
    whole body,
My master is a parsonable man, and not a spindle-shanked hoddy-
    doddy.

The characterisation is of a generous, spirited, and well-intentioned woman, but not to be taken too seriously given the limited education shown by the language. Swift demonstrates a good ear for the rhythm of speech in tumbling extra syllables and accentual emphasis, for the colloquial phrase 'hoddy-doddy', and for the comic misprision of 'personable'. Her morality seems very sane with its sense of social responsibility even though (an unsentimental touch by Swift) she ends with a trivial and self-interested criticism.

> I am but a poor servant,
>> but I think gentlefolks should be civil.
> Besides, you found fault with our victuals
>> one day that you was here,

Of course she is the mouthpiece of Swift and the poem is not being praised for being an authentic portrait of a living individual. Rather, it exists as a convincing creation which Swift uses for defusing the silly quarrel of 'gentlefolks' and finding a medium through which to show his affection for Sheridan, even though Mary and Saunders the man might take up their master's cudgels:

> 'My master is so fond of that minister that keeps the school;
> I thought my master a wise man,
>> but that man makes him a fool.'
> 'Saunders' said I, 'I would rather than a quart of ale,
> He would come into our kitchen,
>> and I would pin a dishclout to his tail.'

Notes

1   A useful summary from one of the contenders in this argument is in Ellen Pollack's, 'Swift among the Feminists' in *Critical Approaches to Teaching Swift*, (ed.) Peter J. Schakel, AMS Press, 1992, 65–75.

2   He wrote to Chetwode that 'those who have been married may form juster ideas of that state than I can pretend to' (12 February 1730).

3   Ehrenpreis, iii, 191.

4   Carol Houlihan Flynn, *The Body in Swift and Defoe*, CUP, 1990, 96.

5   Twenty-five letters in Swift's hand (holographs) have survived and the 40 others are dependent on the printed version edited by a relative, Deane Swift.

6   Ehrenpreis, ii, 659.

7   Compare the Old Woman who lived in a shoe who 'whipped them all soundly and sent them to bed'.

8   Angus Ross and David Woolley (eds), *Jonathan Swift*, OUP, 1989 (revd), xxi.

9   Flynn writes (p. 120) that these were misspellings of 'philosophically knotty words' but they are quite ordinary and indicate the inequality of male/female literacy that Cressy speaks. Rather than showing the triumph of Swift's abstruse learning it shows his tutor's concern for her not to lose face in everyday correspondence: 'You must not be angry, for I will have you spell right, let the world go how it will.'

10   *Correspondence*, v, 226.

11   Nokes, 263–4.

12 Ehrenpreis, iii, 389–90.
13 The emphasis on dung is not a simple downgrading of a noble original. In Homer's account of the games Ulysses wins the race when Ajax slips on the dung and gore of animals slaughtered for the funeral pyre of Patroclus.
14 Sermons, II, xx.
15 Swift's enjoyment of the joke that privies may be seen as temples is caught up in *Gulliver's Travels* where the first residence of Gulliver in Lilliput is in a 'polluted' temple where he answers a call of nature and emerges 'having occasion for fresh Air'.
16 Pollack in *Critical Approaches to Teaching Swift*, (ed.) Peter J. Schakel, AMS Press, 1992, 68.

5 Swift and contemporary ideas

Swift was an avid reader not only of books with classical status, the so-called 'Ancients' in *The Battle of Books*, but also of the 'Moderns'. Ehrenpreis reports that Swift visited the Sheridans at Quilca and 'When Swift ran out of new books to read there, he re-read old ones.' Sheridan's library was twice the size of Swift's. It included contemporary plays and popular fiction, and Swift wrote much of *Gulliver's Travels* there and mentioned particularly Sheridan's 'Books, his Mathematicks' to Thomas Tickell (letter 18 September 1725). The energy of his reading matches the prolific writing of his correspondence and pamphleteering and informs much of his comment and satire.

Gulliver's Travels clearly derives part of its popularity from the taste of many contemporary readers for travel compilations and the records of journeys and voyages. Swift himself owned Hakluyt's *Principal Navigations, Purchas His Pilgrims*, and Dampier's *New Voyage Round the World*. While he seldom reports titles of what he is reading we know that he enjoyed travelogues and that in 1720 he read Herbert's *A Description of the Persian Monarchy now beinge: the Oriental Indyes Iles and other parts of the Greater Asia and Afrik*. In the character of Gulliver, Swift specifically refers to 'my cousin Dampier' and closely imitates the style of Sturmy's *Mariners' Magazine* in the description of the storm in Book II. Although he makes fun of the outlandish, exaggerated or arrogant claims of travellers, Swift has much in common with the sensibility of the explorer and navigator. His own life was one of frequent travel, either across the Irish Sea or up and down Ireland which, as Joseph McMinn tells us, required 'stamina and patience' to negotiate its largely 'primitive and unpredictable' roads.[1]

Swift's interest in travel-writers inevitably engaged him with contemporary scientific and philosophic thought and so *Gulliver's Travels* is a fine test case for considering his attitude to them. The division between science and philosophy was less emphatic in his time and thinkers encouraged active commerce across a wide range of what are now seen as specialisms. Navigation depended on scientific discoveries and exploration would reveal new peoples, leading to reflection on the origin and nature of society. In choosing the form of a travelogue, Swift had a natural medium for considering the endeavours of the Royal Society's natural philosophers and the writings of John Locke on government and human understanding. At the same time he could draw on the fantasy and allegorical meaning of other writers of travels such as Rabelais and Cervantes.

148

The Royal Society

The Royal Society began in 1645 through informal meetings in London of men with interests and expertise in experimental science. (In the first decades of the eighteenth century this included medicine, natural history, mechanics, mathematics, optics and astronomy.) It received its first royal charter in 1662 and from 30 November 1703 until his death in 1727 Sir[2] Isaac Newton was its president. Much of its importance was commercial. Its concern for the discovery of new sea routes and improved means of navigation was very significant for the nation's trade. One of its purposes was to 'Deliver the Anxious *Seamen* from the *Fatal Accidents* that frequently attend their *Mistaken Longitude*' and at that time astronomy was considered the art that would 'discover' the longitude. (Gulliver ranked this along with the discovery of perpetual motion and of the philosopher's stone as impossible unless given the immortal energy he supposed the Struldbruggs to possess.) Greenwich Observatory had been built in 1675 to counter the French Observatory built in 1671 and it was placed in the sole charge of the Royal Society in 1710. The presidential status of Newton was a key factor in determining the society's acceptance of the astronomical and mathematical principles necessary for accurate computation. His *Principia* was published in 1686 and again in 1714 with the addition of his commentary, the *General Scholium*. On mathematical principles he accounted for the motion of bodies in the heavens and propounded the theory of universal gravity, adding in the later version that the discovery of first causes (such as signs of a divine creator) 'have no place in experimental philosophy'.

John Locke (1632–1704), the leading philosopher of the day, became acquainted with Newton and read some of his manuscripts in personal communications. Mathematics appeared to him to be the queen of sciences. In his posthumously published (1706) essay, *Of the Conduct of the Understanding*, he expressed most succinctly the belief that underpinned most of his writing:

> I have mentioned mathematics as a way to settle in the mind a habit of reasoning closely and in train; not that I think it necessary that all men should be deep mathematicians, but that having got the way of reasoning, which that study necessarily brings the mind to, they might be able to transfer it to other parts of knowledge as they shall have occasion.

He saw a necessary interconnection between all branches of knowledge and in the same essay spoke against a partial approach to enquiry.

But the contempt of all other knowledge, as if it were nothing in comparison of law or physic, of astronomy or chemistry, or perhaps some yet meaner part of knowledge wherein I have got a smattering or am somewhat advanced, is not only the mark of a vain or little mind, but does this prejudice in the conduct of the understanding, that it coops it up within narrow bounds and hinders it from looking abroad into other provinces of the intellectual world, more beautiful possibly and more fruitful than that it had laboured in; wherein it might find, besides new knowledge, ways or hints whereby it might be enabled to cultivate its own.

His magnum opus, *An Essay Concerning Human Understanding* (1689), which we consider later, also proposes to use the mathematics of Newton as a model for discussing what is knowledge and how do humans acquire it. In paragraph 194 he says 'the incomparable Mr *Newton*, has shewn, how far Mathematicks applied to some Parts of Nature, may, upon Principles that Matter of Fact justifie, carry us in the knowledge of some, as I may so call them, particular Provinces of the Incomprehensible Universe'. And he concedes that not many are mathematically proficient.

And though there are very few, that have Mathematicks enough to understand his Demonstrations, yet the most accurate Mathematicians, who have examin'd them, allowing them to be such, his Book wil deserve to be read, and give no small light and pleasure to those, who, willing to understand the Motions, Properties, and Operations of the great masses of Matter, in this our Solar System, will but carefully mind his Conclusions, which may be depended on as Propositions well proved.

Since the conclusions of Newton, if not the methods, have become part of our own familiar mental equipment, Locke's concession reminds us that what he was proposing was highly innovative. Newton's mathematics were so new and controversial that they were contested by other mathematicians of considerable stature, such as Hooke and Leibnitz. And there is evidence that Locke himself did not understand except in general terms Newton's reasoning. His recourse was to take their accuracy on trust based on a community's assent – that of 'the most accurate Mathematicians'. For Swift these aspects of innovation and the submission to the authority merely of other natural philosophers were to be key features in how he responded to Locke's approach.

As time has moved on, the purblind and hangers-on in this scientific endeavour have become obscured and only the worthy disputants are given a place in most histories. In the thick of things it was less easy to see who was worthy. During the period of Oxford's ministry, Swift had actual contact with the zealous and off-beat proselytes of Newtonian mathematics. On 29 March 1712 he wrote to Archbishop King: 'A Projector [i.e. scientist] hath lately applied to me to recommend him to the Ministry, about an Invention for finding out the Longitude . . . I understand nothing of the Mathematicks, but I am told it is a Thing as improbable as the Philosopher's Stone, or perpetual Motion.' Almost these very words, which were stock-phrases,[3] he used again in the passage where Gulliver imagines the glories of being a Struldbrugg. Like Locke, Swift had to consult others more mathematically adept than he was to be sure of the improbability of the reasoning and there was no guarantee they would be right. Even Newton had dismissed on practical grounds the approach that actually succeeded. The discovery of an exact method of fixing the longitude had to wait for official recognition until 1764 when Harrison's chronometer and not this 'Projector's' so-called solution won the day. This man's name was Whiston and he was a good example of the confusing enthusiasts who, by hanging on to the coat-tails of better scholars, made it difficult to perceive what the significant developments were.

William Whiston (1667–1752) was vicar of Lowestoft-with-Kisingland, Suffolk, who combined interests in mathematics, theology, history and prophecy. So far he conformed to Locke's recommendation of 'looking abroad into other provinces of the intellectual world'. Unfortunately this did not guarantee sound scholarship and reasoning. He pinned his colours to Newton and Locke having gained the Lucasian professorship in mathematics at Cambridge. However, he declared his allegiance to primitive Christianity and questioned the doctrine of the Trinity. This led to his being deprived of the post on the grounds of suspected Arianism (a heresy which denied the divinity of Christ) and afterwards he sought preferment in vain. Unintentionally, he entertained society with his publications and deductions. He gave a Newtonian account of Genesis in which he discovered that the deluge was the result of a collision by a comet. He informed Prince Eugène that the prince had fulfilled some of prophecies in Revelations. Eugène gave him 15 guineas, saying he had not been aware 'he had the honour of being known to St John'.

His scheme for finding the exact longitude he devised with Humphrey Ditton (1675–1715), mathematics master at Christ's Hospital. Their idea was to anchor boats over the oceans at fixed points 600 miles apart, erroneously believing the sea to be no deeper than 300 fathoms. From these, at stated times, shells would be fired, set to explode at 6440 feet. Mariners in the vicinity would be able to work out their distance from the boats using their knowledge of the speed of sound, as now computed by Newton, and timing the interval between flash and sound. The scheme was riddled with impractical-ities. It made false assumptions about the depth of the sea and there-fore failed to address how to secure the ships. It overlooked the problems of surviving violent weather without damage; of how to keep the ships supplied; of how to maintain a system of providing relief crews; and of how to protect each ship from piracy. Although his scheme was greeted with scepticism and eventually he was satir-ically portrayed in Hogarth's painting of a madhouse in *The Rake's Progress* (1753), Whiston nevertheless was able to figure in London society. His lectures in the coffee-house of Buttons were illustrated with experiments and encouraged by Addison and Steele. Steele advertised the longitude scheme on the 14 July 1713 in the *Guardian* and on 10 December 1713 in *The Englishman* .

Arbuthnot on reading the first advertisement wrote with testy amusement to Swift: 'Whetstone [i.e. Whiston] has at last publish'd his project of the longitude; the most ridiculous thing that was thought on, but a pox on him he has spoil'd one of my papers of Scriblerus', which was a proposal . . . [to] build two prodigious poles upon high mountains with a vast Light house to serve for a pole Star' (17 July 1714). Here was life outdoing the invention of the Scriblerians. But it would be wrong to construe their attack on mathematical method as wholesale and reactionary. Arbuthnot had, himself, been elected a fellow of the Royal Society on 30 November 1704. Using math-ematical reasoning, he had delivered a paper in 1710 on the average excess of male births to female births. He and his co-writers could discriminate between what they considered to be the use and abuse of mathematics. In the published *Memoirs . . . of Martinus Scriblerus*, Chapter xvii was probably written mainly by Arbuthnot, although he did not live to see it in print. Martin is identified by a number of so-called discoveries which show his false learning as a distortion of Newton's work. We are told 'he first discover'd the *Cause* of *Gravity* . . . To him we owe all the observations on the *Parallax* of the *Pole-Star*, and all the new *Theories* of the *Deluge* . . . His were the Projects of *Perpetuum Mobiles* . . . the Method of discovering the *Longitude* by *Bomb-Vessels*' and Martin advertises his intention to bore into the earth 'to refute Sir Isaac Newton's Theory of *Gravity*'. He is no follower of Newton not only for the obvious point of wishing to undermine (literally) the theory of universal gravitation but also for his concern with primary causes. Newton in his *General Scholium* explained his refusal to search for first causes, finding ample to do in his concern to define as accurately as possible what had been deter-mined by experiment. In part Martin sounds like Whiston with the bomb vessels and theory of deluge. But he also merges with another target of Arbuthnot's, a Dr Woodward who published another deluge theory in 1697.

Perhaps more surprising is the inclusion of observing the parallax as part of Martin's pseudo-learning, for this is a hit at John Flamsteed (1646–1719), the astronomer royal who produced highly accurate observations of the positions of stars. It referred to an attempt to discover the distance of the pole star from the earth by triangulation from two opposite points, either on the surface of the earth or at opposite positions in the earth's orbit. However, the change of the position of the observer introduced an apparent shift of the position ('parallax') of the pole star, much like the dance of trees and hills seen through the window of a moving railway carriage. Flamsteed's attempt to measure this as a constant was immediately contested and the matter was considered by so eminent an astronomer as Halley as incalculable. But it is not so much on the grounds of his false science[4] that he is included as for his arrogance. Flamsteed appears as part of this composite figure of Martin since it is an opportunity to score against a man whose jealousy and envy had made him a bitter opponent of Newton. Arbuthnot had a mediating role in settling for the Royal Society one of his quarrels over Newton's publication of his catalogue of stars. The Scriblerians were not writing as agents for Newton but their judgements on examples of human reasoning were moral, attacking the absurd and the self-boosting. A later time might prove the target's mathematics to be correct but, when the Scriblerians were writing, this was not obvious and usually they wrote from a good knowledge of the issues and an understanding of the Royal Society transactions. When we share this knowledge, we are better able to enjoy the joke and to appreciate the justice of the satire.

As we have seen, Swift knew almost all the members of the Dublin Philosophical Society in his school days and it is likely he was aware of their scientific pursuits. This may account for Gulliver's remark that 'I had my self been a sort of a Projector in my younger Days'. 'Projectors' unlike 'virtuosi' were, in broad terms, scientists rather than dabblers and Swift does not wholly distance himself from their activity. As in Arbuthnot's case, not all the science Swift brings into his satire is his target. The King of Brobdingnag's mathematics is 'wholly applied to what may be useful in Life, to the Improvement of Agriculture and all mechanical Arts'. The astronomers of Laputa sometimes work on sound principles:

They have likewise discovered two lesser Stars, or *Satellites*, which revolve about *Mars*, whereof the innermost is distant from the Center of the primary Planet exactly three of his Diameters, and the outermost five; the former revolves in the space of ten Hours, and the latter in twenty one and a half; so that the Squares of their Periodical Times are very near in the same Proportion with

153

the Cubes of their distance from the Center of *Mars*, which evidently shews them to be governed by the same Law of Gravitation, that influences the other Heavenly Bodies.

Although Swift does not tell us, this is based on Kepler's law which Newton had proved in his *Principia* to have mathematical accuracy. Swift's representation of it requires a little thinking about but the statement that the proportion is 'very near' is pleasingly accurate. If the diameter of Mars is x, then (working out the cubes of the distances and squares of the periodic times) $27x = 100$ and $125x = 462.25$. This give the proportion of distance^3 to time^2 as 3.704 in the first and 3.7 in the second.

Travelogues and 'my cousin Dampier'

Swift's pretence that Dampier was cousin to Gulliver again links him with the Royal Society. William Dampier (1652–1715), a reformed buccaneer, recounted his piratical adventures as though they were a voyage of exploration in a book, *A New Voyage Round the World* (1697), and dedicated it to the president of the Royal Society at that time, Charles Montagu, later Earl of Halifax. He also interested the Lord High Admiral, the Earl of Orford, by dedicating to him his *Voyages and Descriptions* (1699) with an account, highly practical to mariners, called a *Discourse of Trade Winds*. Montagu in return recommended him as suitable to lead a genuine voyage of exploration to Australia in 1699–1700, then known as New Holland, which Dampier published in two parts: *A Voyage to New Holland* (1702) and *A Continuation of a Voyage to New Holland* (1709).

Swift placed the locations of his fictitious voyages in regions which Dampier visited on the 1699 expedition or which were close enough. None can be exactly tied down specifically but Lilliput (Book I) is supposed to be between Van Diemen's Land (Tasmania) and the northern coasts of New Holland. The continent of Australia was only partially known so that this could be where we now know the outback to be. Similarly the land of the Houyhnhnms (Book IV) seems to be just south-west of Australia. Gulliver sails to Brobdingnag (Book II) from the Molucca isles (near New Guinea) and to Balnibarbi (Book III) from Tonkin. This places them in the Pacific, perhaps in the south and north respectively.

While it is easy to recognise the parody of the almost impossible technicality of mariner's language in the passage lifted from Sturmy (at the beginning of Book II) and to see in broad terms that the voyages of Gulliver mimic those of Dampier, the enjoyable cleverness of the parody becomes clearer when a closer comparison is made. In travelogues islands are represented in woodcuts as they would appear through a telescope. But having no sea represented and cut off at the base they appear as though flying through the air. An illustration of the Isle of St Jago in the Cape Verde Islands looks just like Laputa flying over Balnibarbi (see Plate 8). Dampier's tone is sometimes, like Gulliver's, Olympian in seeing better possibilities than the peoples he visited: 'if the Inhabitants [of Tenerife] were curious this way, they might have very pleasant Gardens'. He gives an extremely practical lesson to his sailors on how to make ropes from the fibre of Calabash and Maho. Gulliver also displays practicality, making boats for himself and an engine for reading. But his boast of 'Having a Head mechanically turned' has a sub-meaning of being mentally unbalanced by mechanics.

The range of Dampier's travelogue is shown by his plentiful descriptions of new things and novel customs in the new world (guinea fowl, salt pans, frape boats, clayed sugar, people resting in curtained hammocks suspended on something like musket rests); his sense of the political dimension such as commercial rivalry with the Dutch; his use of weapons to gain supremacy – he fired musket shots to terrorise natives and when on one occasion this failed to protect one of his sailors he became the first Englishman to shoot an aborigine. Constant danger and high adventure followed him. In the buccaneering account he marooned a sailor and was marooned himself. On the Royal Society exploration he was so fearful of his mutinous officers that he slept on deck with the weapons. He would not put himself to the danger of going ashore without a land fort to cover the boat with its guns. Counterparts of all these elements can be found in *Gulliver's Travels*. The Lilliputians 'bury their Dead with their Heads directly downwards'; the Dutch in two voyages threaten the safety of Gulliver; in Brobdingnag and Houyhnhnm land Gulliver urges the merits of gunpowder to subdue the natives; a treacherous mariner, James Welch, maroons him in Book IV.

Even the language of description is close to Swift's. Dampier praised the solidity of the town of Laguna. 'The Streets are not regular, yet they are mostly spacious and pretty handsome; and near the middle of the Town is a large Parade, which has good Buildings about it. There is a strong Prison on one side of it; near which is a large Conduit of good Water, that supplies all the Town.' This parallels the description of Mildendo where we imagine its grandeur until the delayed mention of the actual size threatens to undo our admiration. 'I thought that in all my Travels I had not seen a more populous place. The City is an exact Square, each side of the Wall being five hundred foot long. The two great Streets which run cross and divide it into four Quarters are five foot wide.'

Dampier describes an ingenious contraption, the crane at the Bay of all Saints. In order to overcome 'a Hill, too steep for drawing with Carts' he notes that 'the Merchants have also the Convenience of a great Crane that goes with Ropes or Pullies, one End of which goes up while the other goes down. The House in which this Crane is, stands on the Brow of the Hill towards the Sea, hanging over the Precipice; and there are Planks set shelving against the Bank from thence to the Bottom, against which the Goods lean or slide as they are hoisted up or let down.' In Lilliput Gulliver is hoisted on to a cart by means of an 'Eighty Poles', cords, hooks and pulleys. 'Nine hundred of the strongest Men were employed to draw up these Cords by many Pulleys fastned on the Poles, and thus in less than three Hours, I was raised and slung into the Engine, and there tyed fast.'

One of the animals Dampier encounters fills him with disgust. His description of it is meticulous, building up a picture which only gradually begins to make sense as a recognisable species:

> these had a larger and uglier Head, and had no Tail: And at the Rump, instead of the Tail there, they had a Stump of a Tail, which appear'd like another Head: but not really such, being without Mouth or Eyes: Yet this Creature seem'd by this Means to have a Head at each End; and . . . the Legs seem'd all 4 of them to be Fore-legs, being all alike in Shape and Length, and seeming by the Joints and Bending to be made as if they were to go indifferently either Head or Tail foremost. They were speckled black and yellow like Toads, and had Scales or Knobs on their Backs like those of Crocodiles, plated on to the Skin, or stuck into it, as part of the Skin. They are very slow in Motion; and when a Man comes nigh them they will stand and hiss, not endeavouring to get away. Their Livers are also spotted black and yellow: And the Body when opened hath a very unsavoury Smell. I did never see such ugly Creatures any where but here . . . the looks and smell of them being so offensive.

Just such a method Gulliver uses to describe his first sight of the offensive Yahoos who only towards the end of the description reveal themselves as bestial human beings. (Dampier's creatures are iguana. Mistakenly he calls them 'guanoes', associating them with the Spanish word for 'dung', and this parallels the sense of excretion which Swift associates with the Yahoos.)

Dampier also makes a connection for Swift with another potent symbol of the traveller's tale – the castaway, most notably celebrated in Defoe's *Robinson Crusoe*. On a privateering expedition (1703–07) for Queen Anne against the Spanish in the Pacific, Dampier rounded Cape Horn and soon after one of his officers, Alexander Selkirk, insisted on being marooned on Juan Fernandez Island as he believed the ship to be unsafe. Four years later in a second expedition (1708–11) serving as a pilot under Captain Woodes-Rogers, Dampier picked up Selkirk. Woodes Rogers published an account of this in *A Cruising*

Voyage Round the World, 1712, and if Swift did not read about it there he almost certainly did in Steele's *The Englishman*, no. 26, for 3 December 1713. Steele and Swift at that time were engaged in battle and the closing issue of *The Englishman*, 15 February 1714, was directly addressed to Swift as 'Mr. – at Windsor'. In Steele's account Selkirk 'grew reconciled to loneliness' and when brought back to civilisation 'The Man frequently bewailed his Return to the World, which could not, he said, with all its Enjoyments, restore him to the Tranquillity of Solitude.' Gulliver's distress in human society and wish to bed down in the stable near the horses parodies this.

Swift was well aware of a literature which presented the emotional impact of new nations and experiences as leading to reflection on the European condition, not always to European advantage. This was as fascinating as the new scientific discoveries and two instances involving Swift will illustrate how this entered into the popular consciousness as matter for everyday consideration. The European might sink to a degraded condition in the extremities of travel. In an amusing letter of July 1709, Anthony Henley advised Swift how extremity might teach him how to deal with his enemies. He had heard that Colonel Morrison's father in Virginia had been advised when starving 'Eat one another Pour passer le Tems'. Swift should resort to this, as the castaway's behaviour, showing 'the Use which may be made of modern Travels, and apply Mr Morrison's to your Condition'. He should imagine 'You are now Cast on an Inhospitable Island, noe Mathematical figures on the Sand, noe Vestigia hominum to be seen, perhaps at this very time reduc'd to one single Barrel of Damag'd Biscuit, and short allowance even of salt-water'. The solution to his sorry condition would be to 'gett an old piece of Iron and make a Harpoon' and eat his rivals. Gulliver very nearly does[5] this by covering his 'canoo' with the skins of Yahoos and using their tallow. The possibility that a savage might be noble, revealing by contrast the corruption of the 'civilised' voyager had already been examined in Aphra Behn's novel *Oroonoko* which subsequently was made into a play by Southerne and enjoyed a long run on the stage. In the *Journal to Stella* Swift wrote on 17 January 1711 about his personal contact with an actor in this play: 'for this very printer is my cousin, his name is Dryden Leach; did you never hear of Dryden Leach, he that prints the *Postman*? he acted Oronoko'. And in *Gulliver's Travels* he contrasts the superior form of government that the Houyhnhnms enjoy with that of the Europeans.

Locke: society and contract

Locke is once again a significant writer when it comes to discussing ideas of government. In 1690 he published *Two Treatises on Government* in which he argued for a social contract. He said that political power had one function which was that of 'regulating and preserving property' and that government had 'no other end but the preservation of property'. Productive labour on the land gives rights to its property because 'It is labour, then, which puts the greatest part of value upon land, without which it would scarcely be worth anything.' The form of government set up to protect this might be whatever the legislators 'thought fit' but once established the community was bound to surrender individual freedom to it until it ceased to fulfil its original function. Then it would be 'necessary to examine more carefully the original and rights of a government' and if there were a mismatch between the existing condition and the original to entertain the 'possibility of withdrawal'. The judges of this, when for instance a prince erred, would be the people 'for who so proper to judge as the body of the people (who at first lodged that trust in him) how far they meant it to extend?' 'Miscarriages of those in authority' entail forfeiture of their power 'and the people have a right to act as supreme, and continue the legislative in themselves or place it in a new form, or new hands, as they think fit.'

Swift had argued similarly in *A Discourse of the Contests and Dissensions . . . in Athens and Rome . . .* (1701) where the people 'whether by compact, or family government, as soon as they fall into any acts of civil society, do of themselves divide into three powers . . . The first is some one of eminent spirit . . . The second . . . is of such men who have acquired large possessions . . . The last division is of the mass or body of the people.' A variety of forms of government may follow and 'it is not necessary, that the power should be equally divided between these three; for the balance may be held by the weakest'. Danger to society occurs when 'the balance is broke' and in such cases 'in order to preserve the balance in a mixed state, the limits of power deposited with each party ought to be ascertained, and generally known'. As we saw in Chapter 2, Swift had argued against blind partisanship and how he believed there could be government by a non-partisan assembly 'proposing, debating, resolving, voting, according to the mere natural motions of their own little or much reason and understanding' where many 'pernicious and foolish overtures . . . would die and disappear. Because this must be said in behalf of human kind, that common sense and plain reason, while men are disengaged from acquired opinions, will ever have some general influence upon their minds.' In *Gulliver's Travels* this is close to the simple government of the king of Brobdingnag who 'confined the Knowledge of governing within very *narrow Bounds*; to common Sense and Reason, to Justice and Lenity, to the speedy Determination of civil and criminal Causes' and praised productive labour which 'could make two Ears of Corn, or two Blades of Grass to grow on a spot of Ground where only one grew before'. But soon after Gulliver dismissively comments 'The Learning of this People is very defective'. So, Swift in his later years consigns the optimism of Locke and his own *Discourse* to a fantasy world of benevolent giants, which the modern sees as ignorant, despite the fact that the ideas of government were ones that had currency and appeal for his contemporaries living under the revolution settlement which brought William and Mary to the throne.

In the matter of education Swift again echoes Locke, although he appears to emphasise more strongly than Locke the equality of females. Locke's *Some Thoughts Concerning Education* (1705) was written with the son of a gentleman in mind and so seems to concentrate on male gender. But early on, in paragraph 6, Locke wrote, 'I have said *He* here, because the principal Aim of my Discourse is, how a young Gentleman shall be brought up from his Infancy, which, in all things will not so perfectly suit the Education of *Daughters*; though where the Difference of Sex requires different Treatment, 'twill be no hard Matter to distinguish.' He describes an educational method that avoids as much as possible the extremes of cosseting and corporal punishment, for children 'distinguish early betwixt Passion and Reason'. Fantasies must be kept away. You must 'preserve his tender Mind from all Impressions and Notions of *Spirits* and *Goblings*, or any fearful Apprehensions especially in the dark. This he will be in danger of from the indiscretion of Servants, whose usual Method is to awe Children, and keep them in subjection, by telling them of *Raw-Head* and *Bloody Bones*, and such other Names ... Such *Bug-bear* Thoughts once got into the tender Minds of Children ... fasten themselves so as not easily, if ever, to be got out again.' Behind this is a humane concern for the vulnerability of the child and a belief in the attraction and clear appeal of truth, when it is not distorted by adults who abuse their position of power and superior understanding. Not that children are inevitably pure and require no guidance which may involve such power. 'The first time he is found in a *Lye*, it should rather be wondered at as a monstrous Thing in him, than reproved as an ordinary Fault.' If a sharp rebuke fails the next time and he persists 'you must come to blows'. Toys should not be bought for them 'whilst they lazily sit still, expecting to be furnish'd from other hands' unless they 'are above their Skill to make; as Tops, Gigs, Battledors, and the like which are to be used with labour' (i.e. require physical activity by the child). Their bodies should be hardened to cold by wearing less clothing and taking much exercise.

Swift does much the same with this 'ideal' education as he does with the simple government of 'Common Sense and Reason'. He does not take it over wholesale but critiques it by placing it in a context that contrasts with what we know. First, it is in an ideal past of a now corrupt Lilliput and, second, it is in the non-human society of the Houyhnhnms, ringed round by bestial Yahoos. In Lilliput the logical extension of the 'cool' parenting advocated by Locke is to put children in 'publick Nurseries' which separate male and female but, says Gulliver, 'neither did I perceive any Difference in their Education, made by their Difference of Sex, only that the Exercises of the Females were not altogether so robust, and that some Rules were given them relating to domestick Life, and a smaller Compass of Learning was enjoined them'. This pragmatically accepts that for females there were not equal opportunities for gaining the same jobs as males, therefore the same 'Compass of Learning' was not so necessary. Children in the nurseries were visited by parents no more than twice a year and they were allowed 'to kiss the Child at Meeting and Parting' but not 'to use any fondling Expressions, or bring any presents of Toys, Sweet-meats, and the like'. Self-reliance is emphasised and 'if it be found that these Nurses ever presume to entertain the Girls with frightful or foolish Stories . . . they are publickly whipped thrice about the City, imprisoned for a Year, and banished for Life to the most desolate Part of the Country'. At this point a contemporary reader would feel that the reasonable tone of Locke, already given a harder edge by institutionalising the parental relationship, has now an associated violence. This connects with the mordant tone describing the principle on which the nursery is established. We learn that a child is under no obligation to its parents for being born, 'which, considering the Miseries of human Life, was neither a Benefit in itself, or intended so by his Parents, whose Thoughts in their Love-Encounters were otherwise employ'd'.

A similar pattern of child-rearing among the Houyhnhnms develops Swift's criticism, raising questions of what is normative. Instead of the Houyhnhnms having an impersonal nursery, passion is expunged from the parents, permitting an education at home. 'They have no Fondness for their Colts or Foles, but the Care they take in educating them proceeds entirely from the Dictates of *Reason*.' Their regimen is also Spartan, running the young 'over hard stony Grounds', denying the desire for oats and milk and making do with plain grass. (Irresistibly one is reminded of Swift telling Stella in his *Journal* how 'I envy people maunching and maunching peaches' [1 September 1711] and 'my breakfast is milk porridge . . . faith I hate it' [15 May 1711].) Equality of the sexes in education is even more highly regarded:

And my Master thought it monstrous in us to give the Females a different kind of Education from the Males, except in some Articles of Domestick Management; whereby as he truly observed, one half of our Natives were good for nothing but bringing Children into the World: And to trust the Care of our Children to such useless Animals, he said was yet a greater Instance of Brutality.

Without the use of a developed reason the adult female is regarded as an animal, showing that brutality may be exercised in acts of omission as much as commission. This seems just, although force-fully expressed, and accords with Swift's concern that women should receive an education which values their minds as much as those of men. But it coexists with other instances of Houyhnhnm conduct and values. Gulliver notes that 'Friendship and Benevolence are the two principal Virtues' but when it comes to marriage 'Court-ship, Love, Presents, Joyntures, Settlements, have no place in their Thoughts . . . the married Pair pass their Lives with the same Friend-ship, and mutual Benevolence that they bear to all others of the same Species'. Although there is a shock in seeing 'Love' almost equated to the mercenary elements of 'Presents, Joyntures, Settle-ments' we can see that this relates to Swift's own preference for friendship over marriage and his self-characterisation that he was 'naturaly temperate'. But it leaves out another element which he said was strong in his own nature, the 'violence of friendship'. The Houyhnhnms have no sorrow.

Although Locke's ideas on education form the basis for the 'reason' of the institutions in Lilliput and the land of the Houyhnhnms, the various shocks we receive in relation to their transformations in these imagined worlds raise doubts about how desirable they may be in their entirety. Swift's known departures from some of the prescribed conduct have not been mentioned to show that these were his 'real' views. They are evidence of alternative ways of be-having that were certainly known to him when he wrote. We should take them into account when deciding what the significance of these episodes is in a work of art, where the language used and the march of events compose the meaning of the whole. At the end of this chapter we consider the overall shape of *Gulliver's Travels* in order to be in a position to give a better evaluation of such episodes.

Science and language

This last statement concerning the meaning of artistic expression would be contested if we were to adopt the views uttered by some members of the Royal Society. Thomas Sprat, the first official his-torian of the Royal Society, records that part of its agenda was to stabilise the fluidity of English and to use terms in a consistent manner in order to promote scientific understanding. Locke, also a fellow of the Society, had much of the same concern and again the model was that of mathematics. In both cases the creative function of language is either subordinated to or obliterated from the language of record. As Swift was most certainly a creative artist we would expect a clear divergence of opinion over the matter. However, the matter is more complex than simple opposition by statements of belief. In some respects Swift explicitly agreed to some of Locke's propositions and where he disagreed it was by implication through the function of language in his literary creations.

He voiced misgivings on contemporary English usage and spelling at first in the *Tatler* no. 230 and these he developed in *A Proposal for Correcting, Improving, and Ascertaining the English Tongue*, 22 February 1712. English seemed to him to be still developing so fast, like an unruly sapling, that some check or pruning of its growth would not harm it as it 'is not arrived to such a degree of perfection as to make us apprehend any thoughts of its decay'. This should be beneficial, for while the 'rude Latin of the monks is still very intelligible' vernacular English of the Middle Ages was not, having been 'so subject to continual succeeding changes'. That a process of obscuration might continue unchecked was a fear which not only the 'scientists' Sprat and Locke shared with Swift but others such as the poets Dryden and Waller, who wrote:

> Poets that lasting marble seek
> Must carve in Latin or in Greek.

Great social change was the cause of part of this flux. New words and expressions were coined 'from the mighty changes that have been made in law and religion, from the many terms of art required in trade and in war, from the new inventions that have happened in the world, from the vast spreading of navigation and commerce'. In addition popular usage changed meaning and confused the sense. Too many people 'spell as they speak' losing the etymological clues to the origin and meaning of the word. (Hence Swift's strictures on Stella's misspellings.) In everyday speech, users of the language invented slang words, truncated others and joined 'obdurate consonants' until the sense became obscured. Swift saw this as chaotic misuse rather than vernacular inventiveness. It appeared to have no rhyme or reason, as appeared from a limited experiment he seems to have conducted with mixed company to 'write down a number of letters' joined together. 'We found that which the men had wrote, by the frequent encountering of rough consonants, to sound like High Dutch; and the other, by the women, like Italian, abounding in vowels and liquids.' The exclusion of women from many arenas had impoverished the language and 'since they have been left out of all meetings, except parties at play or where worse designs are carried out, our conversation has very much degenerated'.

One of his concerns was to introduce 'into our style that simplicity which is the best and truest ornament of most things in life'. He justified this in the *Proposal* by remarking that 'the translators of the Bible were masters of an English style much fitter for that work than any we see in our present writings; which I take to be owing to the simplicity that runs through the whole'. The Bible's richness modifies his praise of 'simplicity'. As does one of the models he cited in the *Tatler* essay – the great Anglican theologian Richard Hooker (*c.* 1554–1600). So he did not equate simplicity with a lack of thought and vigour. In 1720 there is an amplification of this in *A Letter to a Young Clergyman* in which he advised the preacher to avoid 'hard words', the contemporary phrase for highly technical language, but not to descend into a 'flat kind of phraseology'. Meaning can be vigorously and clearly put over, he wrote. For example, without the knowledge of medical terms, a farmer is well able to inform you that his 'foot is out of joint'.

His solution, in the light of our present knowledge of the flow of language, seems authoritarian but it was a not unusual response for his time and reveals interesting aspects of his sense of the medium in which he excelled. He felt 'some method should be thought on for ascertaining and fixing our language for ever' although that was not to say it should 'never be enlarged'. He proposed that Oxford established an academy on the French model. While this was to be a Tory-inspired project and so gain party credit, its membership would not be as his critics suggested a means of rewarding camp followers. His plan for an academy had the ambitious role to bring together distinguished learned men from all parties, rather like the proposal for an ideal Parliament in *Dissensions*. Its attraction went beyond being the instrument to regulate language to providing a meeting of minds and cultural centrality for the group, unswayed by economic necessities. For, Swift noted with approval as a model that 'The French king bestows about half-a-dozen pensions to learned men in several parts of Europe, and perhaps a dozen in his own kingdom.'

Naturally Swift's own ambitions were tied up in this and his enthusiasm increased as church preferment eluded him. Oxford agreed to the scheme but procrastinated. Others encouraged him, such as Francis Atterbury and Archbishop King (no doubt hopeful of keeping this Irish priest on English soil). To him Swift wrote that Oxford 'and I have named above twenty Persons of both Parties to be Members' (29 March 1712). It went no further for the scheme was attacked in pamphlets by the Whigs, Mainwaring and Oldmixon. The latter argued that to fix the language was 'as visionary as the endeavours to discover the longitude, perpetual motion and the Grand Elixir'. Swift was accused of feathering a Tory nest and the subsequent death of the queen put paid to the matter. In Faulkner's collection of Swift's works (1735) an introductory note, perhaps by Swift, said 'It is well known, that if the Queen had lived a Year or two longer, the following Proposal would in all Probability have taken Effect.' This seems unlikely and if they are Swift's words they suggest bravado and a wish to turn back the clock.

Apart from the unreal expectation of rising above party dissension the academy would have somehow had to escape the direction of powerful patronage. Both the French Academy and the Royal Society began as free associations of intelligent and learned men but fell under the systematising hands of, respectively, Richelieu and Charles II. Just as Swift could no longer support the optimism of establishing the non-partisan Parliament proposed in *Dissensions* but instead located it in a land of benevolent but remote giants, so it is unlikely he could at heart believe in the continuing possibility of an English Academy. For his own part, the Scriblerus Club had fulfilled much of the projected academy's cultural function and in *Gulliver's Travels* a different voice is heard concerning the ease of regulating language. It gives some words he had spoken in self-deprecation in the *Proposal* a later ring of truth. In the *Proposal* he elegantly brought the work to a close lest he should 'find myself turning projector before I am aware'. In the guise of Gulliver about to visit the academy of Lagado, reflecting on his youthful proposals, he wrote 'I had my self been a sort of a Projector in my younger Days.' The implication is that he has outgrown this stage but is interested to know what others can do. Immediately he is shown crazy projects for shortening words by cutting all but the first syllable and a means of discoursing without words altogether.

The references to language in *Gulliver's Travels* collectively assume a larger importance, once we know of Swift's reasons for establishing an academy in his younger days. Gulliver's exceptional adeptness in learning and becoming fluent in foreign languages is a kind of bitter running joke for a man who feared that his own vernacular was subject to becoming intelligible. This fear was of key importance as another episode in the story shows. The immortal Struldbruggs were not able to understand each other, having been born in different ages and in the intervening years the flux of language had brought about so great a change that meanings had altered unrecognisably. When Gulliver imagined the felicity of being a Struldbrugg it was because he thought they were the repositories of wisdom and of the nation's history. Through them Swift expresses his concern for language as conveying the best that has been thought and said and a wish to prevent it silting over what was valuable in remote times so that it disappears from our collective use. This relates to his desire to be the queen's historiographer which was also part of the academy scheme. To achieve that position Swift, addressing Oxford with some flattery in the *Proposal*, wrote that it is 'your lordship's duty, as prime minister, to give order for inspecting our language, and rendering it fit to record the history of so great and good a princess'. The failure of communication between the Struldbruggs shows that behind the necessary public courtesies to Oxford and the queen was Swift's high concern for preserving the record of the nation and not simply a desire to take the post as a party reward and use it to perpetuate Tory propaganda.

Locke: empirical philosophy

In addition to raising the impracticality of regulating language that Locke hoped for, *Gulliver's Travels* challenges an aspect of Locke's view of language expressed in his philosophical writings. As his philosophical stance is also critiqued in *Gulliver's Travels* we need to turn aside to discuss Locke's *An Essay Concerning Human Understanding* (1690). This is Locke's most famous and longest work and took 19 years in the writing. It originated in the question whether one could apply the principle of mathematics to religious thought. Locke was concerned with the boundaries of knowledge. Early on in his *Essay* he likened the mind to a 'Darkened room dimly lit by windows'.

The style of his writing is modest, reasonable, unaffected, untechnical and enquiring. His language is simple in deference to the mathematical ideal he proposed. Each paragraph is set out with integer referencing, 'book, chapter, paragraph', for easy location and discussion. In broad terms the *Essay* attacks the idea of imagination as the key to knowledge in favour of recognising that the mind acquires knowledge through direct experience, that is to say, empirically.

The *Essay* has four books. The first disposes of the doctrine of innate ideas, that somehow we are born with prior knowledge and understanding, which had been part of the philosophy of Descartes. The second discusses the nature of simple and complex ideas, while the third discusses the nature of words. The fourth, and last, extends the survey into regions of morality and religion, touching on whether we have an immaterial soul. This movement through the books enacts the ideal enquiry, disposing of unproven hypotheses to find the most basic piece of evidence, how a simple idea is formed, and building on that to examine the wider systems of knowledge.

The argument in Book 2 is the core of his philosophy. Locke describes the mind at birth as a 'tabula rasa' – a wax tablet untouched by the marks that experience will write on it. Experience is something that the mind cannot refuse, rather as a mirror reflects an object that appears before it. It is a passive receptor of sensation which produces an idea in the understanding at the moment a sensum (the smallest part of sensation) is felt. The mind can and does exert

165

itself in several kinds of act, such as combining several sensa into a whole, relating one sensation to another, and abstracting a general idea derived from sensations. This is where there is a danger of introducing 'fantastical' ideas which are imaginary and not real. The test for their reality is to reduce complex ideas to the collection of simple ideas much as in the 'methods of algebra' and to 'search after moral as they do mathematical truth'. Always at the basic level will be the initial sensation in which the imprint has the relation of the die to the coin, or to use his technical terms, of 'archetype' to 'ectype'.

Locke knew that his appeal to reason to determine the truth of experience involved the thinker in no easy matter. He believed that there was a 'degree of madness in most men' which was often the effect of the power of the association of ideas. He described this in terms (which were to delight the author[6] of *Tristram Shandy*) of a badly worn grandfather clock whose internal system of chains and weights, the going and striking train, had become incapable of running true:

> there is a connexion of ideas wholly owing to chance or custom: ideas that in themselves are not at all of kin . . . the whole gang, always inseparable, show themselves together . . . all which seem to be but trains of motion in the animal spirits, which, once set a going, continue in the same steps they have been used to, which by often treading, are worn into a smooth path.

Locke provoked a debate about what is real. The materialism of objects external to the body seemed to be opposed to the sense of inner reality, of Descartes's famous 'cogito ergo sum' (I think therefore I am). Reason seemed to be elevated above spiritual revelation. Despite his orthodox Anglicanism, the methodology Locke had set free could easily be used to further the views of a deist (the 'Natural Religion' espoused by Bolingbroke), a free-thinker or an atheist. A worthy opponent of Locke was found in Bishop Berkeley. In his *Principles of Human Knowledge* (1710) he was concerned to defend the immateriality and actuality of the soul. He argued that one could not detach the object from the process of sensation. He did not question the existence of the object but its being perceived was inseparable from the mediation of the senses of the perceiver. Popularly this was crudified into a statement that if an object was not seen it did not exist and it was left to a later age for the subtleties of Immanuel Kant to pick up his true meaning in discussing the nature of the imagination. Berkeley's contribution to thinking about how the mind understands experience was therefore important. Nevertheless it was flawed. If the existence of 'thing' was inseparable from the perceiving how did one distinguish the imaginary from the real?

He proposed that the 'real' made a stronger and more durable impression but this does not rule out such things as hallucinations from shell shock. He also argued that the 'real' followed the laws of nature which were orderly and consistent but the laws of psychology produce a similar order and consistency.

Swift could have adopted (but did not) Berkeley's attack on materialism, for he knew his writings. As Berkeley was an inheritor of Vanessa's will and this has been seen as a snub to Swift (see Chapter 4) it is worth considering how Swift regarded him. He recommended him as chaplain to Lord Peterborough. He also promoted his interest with Lord Carteret, speaking of him with some fondness in a letter:

He was a fellow in the University here, and going young to England about 13 years ago, he there became the Founder of a Sect called the Immaterialists, by the force of a very curious Book which he had written upon that Subject . . . for three years past he has been struck with the Notion of founding an University at Bermudas . . . I do humbly entreat your Excellency either to use such Persuasions as will keep one of the first Men in this Kingdom for Virtue and Learning, quite at home, or assist him by Your Credit to compass his Romantick Design, which however is very noble and generous.

(4 September 1724)

Speaking of Berkeley's readiness to leave the well-paid Deanship of Derry, Swift told the 2nd Earl Oxford 'He is a true Philosopher and an excellent Scholar, but of very visionary Virtue and is endeavouring to quit a thousand Pounds a Year for a hundred at Bermudas.' No doubt the word 'visionary' made sly but sympathetic fun of his immaterial philosophy, for the Scriblerians had some difficulty taking in Berkeley's meaning. *Alciphron* 'is too Speculative for me' Swift wrote to Gay on 4 May 1732 and Gay agreed soon after, and so did Bolingbroke. Arbuthnot had some pleasure (again not malicious) in reporting Berkeley's medical condition on his return from Italy with Lord Peterborough in immaterialist terms: 'Poor philosopher Berkley has now the idea of health, which was very hard to produce in him, for he had an idea of fever upon him so strong' (to Swift, 19 October 1714). Pope numbered him with Swift among the Anglicans he hoped to meet again in heaven: 'yet am I of the Religion of Erasmus, a Catholick; so I live; so I shall die; and hope one day to meet you, Bishop Atterbury, the younger Craggs, Dr Garth, Dean Berkly, and Mr Hutchenson, in that place, To which God of his infinite mercy bring us, and every body!' (to Swift, 28 November 1729). But for all the friendly feeling, Swift's attack on Locke was not fuelled by Berkeley's vision but by his own sense of the writer's craft and by a seventeenth-century idea of reason.

Language in Gulliver's Travels

The passage in *Gulliver's Travels* which most directly refers to Locke's view of language occurs in the description of the academy of Lagado where Swift seems to show a bizarre version of the regulating academy he supported in his younger days as a projector. Two projects are closely related. One leaves out 'Verbs and Participles, because in reality all things imaginable are but Nouns'. The other is to do without words altogether 'since Words are only Names of *Things*, it would be more convenient for all Men to carry about them, such *Things* as were necessary to express the particular Business they are to discourse on'. The man who had more to say 'must be obliged in Proportion to carry a greater Bundle of *Things* upon his Back'. The first echoes the materialism of Locke's description of receiving sensa. In Locke's theory matter impinges on the body through the physics of contact. Even the sensation of seeing is the result of particles emanating from the object and being received by the eye. Swift deliberately uses the word 'imaginable' to raise the issue, as a subtext, of the process of the mind as an active rather than passive receptor, while ostensibly supporting the Lockean view. It links back to his earlier characterisation of the Lagadians: 'Imagination, Fancy, and Invention, they are wholly strangers to, nor have any Words in their Language by which those Ideas can be expressed; the whole compass of their Thoughts and Minds being shut up within the two forementioned Sciences' (Mathematics and Music). By excluding verbs and participles the Lagadians excise words of action, being and thinking and even their nouns are impoverished if they are to be confined to objects carried in a sack, leaving out the abstractions of joy, pleasure and sorrow. The imaginative loss is the result of minds that are indeed shut up by mathematics. And the second project parodies a passage in Book III of Locke's *Essay* where he argues that 'words enable us to discourse as it were in bundles' and goes on to the principle of reducing complex ideas to the collection of simple ideas derived from archetypes.

That language grows from a collection of nouns is deeply suspect. Chomsky has shown in *Cartesian Linguistics*[7] how in the seventeenth century at the Port Royal abbey in France a French grammar was constructed on the basis of phrases being the matrix from which a sentence emerges. Swift shows no knowledge of the Port Royal grammarians and his theory of language, judging from his earlier idea of an academy, is undeveloped. But it is as a practising writer that he opposes Locke's mechanisms. He wrote with a natural sense of metaphor which, for example, translated the remoteness felt by the Irish regarding communication with the Parliament in London into fluttering messages sent up a kite's string to the flying island;

which saw wisdom as 'a cheese, which by how much the richer, has the thicker, the homelier, and the coarser coat, and whereof to the judicious palate the maggots are the best'; and saw in the puritan's tatters and the high Roman Catholic's finery 'a kind of mock resemblance . . . there being a sort of fluttering appearance in both'.

In comparison with the conversation of objects drawn from a sack, there is nothing sedate about Swift's tumbling nouns that issue with the speed of wit from Gulliver in describing the consequences of British free trade:

> we sent away the greatest Part of our necessary Things to other Countries, from whence in return we brought the Materials of Diseases, Folly, and Vice, to spend among ourselves. Hence it follows of Necessity, that vast Numbers of our People are compelled to seek their Livelihood by Begging, Robbing, Stealing, Cheating, Pimping, Forswearing, Flattering, Suborning, Forging, Gaming, Lying, Fawning, Hectoring, Voting, Scribling, Stargazing, Poysoning, Whoring, Canting, Libelling, Free-thinking, and the like Occupations: Every one of which Terms, I was at much Pains to make him understand.

The argument appears to have sense in the general terms that the rich may have made many penniless through depriving them of necessities in order to purchase their luxuries. But as *we* are at pains to understand the terms Gulliver uses we find different reasons for the specific consequences being there. Some are to achieve money through crime or flattery. Others are the outcries of the oppressed. But 'voting? stargazing? canting?' – how did these come in? They can be harmonised after a fashion but the point of the medley is that each element has a different shade and some are more appropriate to Gulliver's tirade and others less. The case against free trade does sound powerful but we are constantly surprised by emotions of moral outrage, sympathy, incredulity, half-belief, amusement. Gulliver may be going mad but Swift ensures that we keep our minds alert and our footwork deft as a necessary consequence of engaging with his satirical vision. It is a use of language quite different from the 'methods of algebra'.

This links with Swift's constant play with language. From the ingenious games of the man of words – the prolific writer and indefatigable reader – to the creative play of wit in his satires is a continuous progression. There are various types of game. In the *Love Song of Dick Bettesworth* breaking words into other combinations makes them look like some cod Latin

> Mi de armis molli
> Ure mel an colli
> It is a folli;

> Fori alo ver,
> A ram lingat Do ver,
> Ure Dicke mecum o ver.

(My dear miss Molly, you're melancholy, It is a folly; For aye a lover, A-rambling at Dover, Your Dick may come over.)

Childish mispronunciation may produce a code. So in 'our richar gangridge' (our little language) r = l, ch = t(t), g = l, ri = ui (pronounced wi), idge = age (as in 'language, carriage'). And we have noticed in Chapter 4 that 'sollahs' means 'sirrahs' pronounced the Irish way 'sorrahs' with l = r. Sometimes a phonetic reading and recombining of misplaced words is necessary to get the sense. 'They have all got cold this Winter, big Owing tooth in lick lad ink old wet her, and dare ink you rabble.' (They have all got cold this Winter, by going too thinly clad in cold weather and are incurable.) Puns he adored, exchanging multitudes with Sheridan. In the *Journal to Stella* he says he must stop 'aboozing fine Radyes' (abusing fine ladies) and the pun hints at drinking toasts with them.

In *Gulliver's Travels* the games are thought-provokingly integrated with the satiric thrust. For example, by using a clever anagram (which is purposely strained) he holds up to scorn the impeachment and exile (1722) of his friend Francis Atterbury, Bishop of Rochester, for supposed involvement in a Jacobite plot on the basis of secret service decoding of intercepted messages. When the reader works out the detail (much as we are required to do with the list of the dire consequences of free trade) ramifications of the decoders' method cast doubt on the whole process.

> 'Our Brother Tom has just got the Piles'
> 'resist, – a PlOT js Brought home – the tour'

In Swift's first version the original message is homely and slightly indecorous, provoking some surprise at them poking their noses into a question of haemorrhoids. The letters of the original message do match those of the decoded sense, for the substitution of 'i' for 'j' is just about permissible although an archaic usage. But then other liberties have been taken. The decoded sentence has a wrenched syntax and unclear meaning which exposes the strenuously misguided effort of the 'translators' who are so intent on a conviction that they read what they expect into the most innocuous words. What they get is not even a coherent message but a collection of talismanic words representing vague dangers and this is sufficient proof of guilt to their prejudiced minds.

In a similar fashion, the decoding by substitution is undermined by the metaphoric life of the images. Again different shades of meaning operate. In the Atterbury plot 'a lame Dog' is supposed to signify an invader. This is a topical reference and absurd once we know that the bishop really had a dog which broke its leg on his return from France. The matching of these two things is straightforward but when we learn a 'Sieve [is] a Court Lady' there is a multiple appropriateness in the substitution. In the court world of backstairs intrigue and informers a court lady may be like a sieve, unable to hold a secret and, because of the sexual intrigue, may have had many penetrations. The indecency hovers over this as much as over the decoding of 'piles' to present the seaminess of the political manoeuvres. Swift's light touches often have the reader wondering whether indecency is in oneself or in the author. This one seems to be corroborated as Swift's since it is used once more, in a variant, in Book IV where Gulliver affirms that a chief minister in his own country 'is usually governed by a decayed Wench . . . the Tunnels through which all Graces are conveyed'. It again illustrates how the satire requires deft footwork and encourages the kind of scepticism which will resist the different and insidious sorts of corruption which are being exposed.

Other verbal games and codes have defeated systematic explanation. Some may have none, being Swift's joke at our expense and placing us alongside the Laputian decoders. Or they may relate to Swift's indulgence in private meanings to which we have already referred in discussing the role of the writer. If they belong to the latter, we may never have sufficient contextual reference to penetrate their puzzles. But attempts have often seemed to carry conviction, particularly in decoding the names of Gulliver's towns, countries and peoples. Two approaches have been used. One is to look for etymological roots, Latin, Greek, French and so on. The other is to apply the substitution rules as in 'ourichar gangridge' and the like. In both cases we come perilously close to the academicians of Lagado and that may be part of Swift's joke. However, the suggestion that 'Lindalino' is Dublin is immediately attractive, as it contains a double 'lin'. By the other method of etymology 'Munodi', the title of the lord disenchanted with his mad Lagadian world, may be a contraction of the Latin 'mundum odi' meaning 'I hate the world.'

Swift's technique could be a mixture of both approaches and some suggestions will illustrate methods of cracking the codes. Lilliput might mean 'little blockhead' – 'lil' being a contraction as in 'Lil' Abner' and 'put' meaning 'blockhead' as defined in the OED (substantive meaning 4) recording its use in 1720 and quoting from *The Tatler*, no. 230, and adding that it 'Arose in 17th c. slang; origin unascertained'. Maybe a closeness to the Latin 'caput' made it appeal to Swift. It reinforces the appeal of this interpretation to note symmetries between Lilliput having Little Endians and Blefuscu having Big Endians. Both nations are being considered as the places of heads and backsides. 'Blee + fuscu(s)' could then be 'swarthy faces' after 'blee' given by OED as 'colour of face' [substantive meaning 2] and cited in 1700, 'Ladies of so bright of blee'. 'Fuscous' from the Latin 'fuscus' means 'swarthy'. Naturally the Lilliputians would paint their enemies black.

Mildendo from the context is probably London so it could be formed from phonetics and contractions, such as Mi (= My) L(on)den -do.[8] If we admit an Irish dimension into the language game, 'Balnibarbi', the country oppressed by the remote flying island would appropriately be Ireland rendered partly in its own language. 'Bal' is 'Bally', Irish for 'settlement'; 'na' Irish for 'of'; 'barbi' the people who say 'bar'. The ancient 'barbarians' were so named because their alien language sounded to Greeks like 'bar bar'. So this means the settlement of the barbarians, meaning the Irish. The problem with all these suggestions is that so many liberties of method are allowed that there is no check to the reliability of the decoding apart from one's own tact. Often it is tempting, as in the following example, to believe that Swift is simply fooling. In Luggnag after licking the dusty floor (sometimes strewn with poison) the courtier has to address the king with the following formula: 'Ickpling Gloffthrobb Squutserumm blhiop Mlashnalt Zwin tnodbalkgufth Slhiophad Gurdulubh Asht.' Gulliver who had been forced to 'crawl on my Belly, and lick the Floor as I advanced' was pleased that the floor was 'swept so clean that the Dust was not offensive'. Nevertheless it was there and the clotted words mimic speaking with a mouthful of dust. Their sound is equivalent to, as near as can be made out, 'sicklied glottis-throb squitserum' ('sicklied', 'glottis', 'throb' and 'squitter' were current in Swift's day) followed by burps and gurgles and ending in 'ashes'.

Imagination in Gulliver's Travels

Much of what we have seen in relation to the language games is anti-system. It forces us into speculation which we hope to regulate by fitting it in to some wider vision and sense of purpose. As such it is a paradigm of Swift's sense of the relation of imagination to reason in his other great thrust against the materialism of Locke. There is a significant episode at Glubbdubdribb where Gulliver summons the shade of Aristotle, the Greek philosopher (384–322 BC) who in many ways was a systematiser of ethical and political practice, derived from the collected observations of his own academy. In the Middle Ages Aristotle was regarded as the highest authority in scholastic teaching. In the Renaissance, when the study of his original Greek texts superseded the Latin derivatives, his inconsistencies (which may have been because the texts were unedited lecture notes) were noticed and his position was modified from being the supreme philosopher to that of a highly significant contributor to philosophy, especially the study of logic. Swift turns his imperfections into a merit: 'This great Philosopher freely acknowledged his own Mistakes in Natural Philosophy, because he proceeded in many things upon Conjecture, as all Men must do; and he found, that . . . the *Vortices* of *Descartes* were . . . exploded. He predicted the same Fate to *Attraction*.' The great philosopher, according to Swift, can proceed in many things only upon conjecture. In the examples of mistaken philosophy which Aristotle cites the contemporary reader would have known that Newton exploded Descartes's theory of the vortices but that Newton himself was responsible for the theory of attraction, the theory of gravity. According to Aristotle even Newtonian mathematics was provisional and might pass away. But Locke, despite the humility of seeing the mind as a darkened room, considered that mathematics ensured certainty.

Behind Swift's endorsement of 'conjecture' is his view of the relation of imagination to reason. Reason, according to Luther, was the handmaid of God when it was subordinate to demonstrating the truths of divine revelation. In his terms it was 'regenerate reason'. But when it set itself up as the measure of all men then it was arrogant reason and the devil's whore. Something like this is behind Swift's view which, like his sense of the corruption of the human body, is closer to seventeenth-century thought than that of the eighteenth. In *A Letter to a Young Clergyman* (1720) he warns against 'attempting to explain the mysteries of the Christian religion. And indeed, since Providence intended there should be mysteries, I do not see how it can be agreeable to piety, orthodoxy, or good sense to go about such a work.' Both seventeenth-century representations of the body and of reason seem to be behind his savage attack at the end of *Gulliver's Travels* on man as a 'lump of Deformity and Disease smitten with Pride'. Man's pride impels him to think that he can explain all things. In *The Battle of the Books* the spider represents the modern as a mathematical technician spinning his web from his entrails, confident of himself as the origin and measure of all things. Similarly, in *A Tale of a Tub* reason has the Procrustean reductiveness of wishing to 'reduce notions to the same length, breadth and height'.

The place of imagination in relation to reason as the handmaid of God is shown in a celebrated passage of *A Tale of a Tub* where both are counterpoised in an image of imperfect and self-contradictory mankind. In a digression concerned with madness, the narrator presents imagination like some jockey on the horse of reason or bullying landlord kicking out common sense, the legitimate tenant of the house of the body. 'But when a man's fancy gets *astride* on his reason, when imagination is at cuffs with the senses, and common understanding as well as common sense, is kicked out of doors; the first proselyte he makes is himself.' This has the ring of Locke's approval of the supremacy of reason and his belief that there is something mad in most men which produces delusion within – 'the first proselyte (convert) he makes is himself'. However, later in the passage it is reason's turn to come under attack. It parodies Locke's discussion of simple ideas where he argued that there are four irreducible 'primary qualities' which a body has when it impinges on the senses. Locke says that no matter how you dissect an object these qualities remain unimpaired:

> take a grain of wheat, divide it into two parts, each part has still solidity, extension, figure, and mobility; divide it again, and it retains still the same qualities: and so divide it on till the parts become insensible, they must retain still each of them all those qualities. For, division (which is all that a mill or pestle or any other body does upon another, in reducing it to insensible parts) can never take away either solidity, extension, figure, or mobility from any body, but only makes two or more distinct masses of matter of that which was one before.

To explain the four qualities through illustration, imagine squeezing the grain and you feel resistance (solidity); it occupies a certain space (extension); it has a certain shape (figure); it is either at rest or moving (mobility). Swift parodies the philosophical language of primary qualities and endows the image of division with the blood-curdling nature of a busybody inept surgeon:

> The two senses to which all objects first address themselves are the sight and the touch. These never examine further than the colour, shape, the size, and whatever other qualities dwell, or are drawn by art, upon the outward of bodies; and then comes reason officiously, with tools for cutting, and opening, and mangling, and piercing, offering to demonstrate that they are not of the same consistence quite through.

Reason, the dissector, kills while it analyses, leaving mangled and therefore indeterminate remains, insisting ('officiously') on a superior understanding that it does not deserve. The result is lack of imagination in foreseeing consequences which the 'reasonable' narrator, who seems to exemplify the madness he discusses, shows with his unimaginative and unfeeling comment, 'Last week I saw a woman flayed; and you will hardly believe how much it altered her person for the worse.'

Neither reason nor imagination hold the sole key to understanding in a world where all men must proceed by conjecture. The

Laputians lacked imagination in their mathematical reasoning and the Houyhnhnms have no imagination in their passionless social reason. They 'laugh at valuing other people's conjectures'. Also they have no books and so are denied imaginative art in which, as we have discussed, it can be said that the 'truest poetry is the most feigning'. Literature has been described as a noble lie and the Houyhnhnms have no concept of a lie. So it could be argued that they have no concept of truth, since in normal discourse hypothesis is tested by counter instance. We are told that '*Doubting* or *not believing* are so little known in this Country, that the Inhabitants cannot tell how to behave under such Circumstances.' So that when there is an opposing view (say, false or lying) the person has '*said the Thing which was not*' and this was seen to defeat the end of conversation 'to receive Information of Facts' and 'these were all the Notions he had concerning that Faculty of *Lying*'. However a contrary instance might not be a lie or false statement but could be an exception to a general truth. Not to admit it suggests an intellectual fascism and a frozen imagination, unable to accept the proposition that 'on at least one occasion x occurred'. In fact there is demonstration of this in Swift's text. Gulliver attempts to point out an island that is indisputably there since he sails to it and lands on it. But the sorrel nag has no conception of it and can only see a blue haze. In direct contrast to Aristotle, the Houyhnhnm master of Gulliver had extreme difficulty in understanding the 'meaning of the Word *Opinion*, or how a Point could be disputable' and when Gulliver 'used to explain our several Systems of *Natural Philosophy*, he would laugh that a Creature pretending to *Reason*, should value itself upon the Knowledge of other People's Conjectures'.

The society of the Houyhnhnms seems moderate but it is not 'wise as the serpent' since it believes reason will in time always prevail against brute strength. In political Britain Swift had ample evidence of corruption and lying to see that this is normal in human affairs and inability to recognise it is a vulnerable condition. And the horses actually exhibit unreasonable behaviour in expelling Gulliver merely because in their senate 'the Representatives had taken Offence at his keeping a *Yahoo* (meaning myself)'. No evidence is offered of any danger from Gulliver but only the possibility of it. While the decree of the general assembly is called an exhortation it works as a decree since 'no Person can disobey Reason, without giving up his Claim to be a Rational Creature'. What has been said, being the voice of reason, admits no counter instance. And implicitly threatened is Gulliver's master since his opposition would class him with the Yahoo-like, subject to the pains and penalties that now threaten Gulliver. (This sheds doubt on the statement that they had no conception of 'Power, Government, War, Law, Punishment'.)

Although the superiority of the Houyhnhnms as an ideal for humanity has its adherents among critics there are good grounds for not accepting this valuation. Gulliver at the end of the book has become unhinged, so that his testimony is dangerous. The philosophical ends served by the Houyhnhnms run counter to much of the anti-Lockean outcomes of *Gulliver's Travels*. It is part of Swift's art to produce willing suspension of disbelief when faced by the incredible. We swallow the fantasy for the pleasure it gives but our monitoring self appreciates the absurdities that undermine the belief. For example, Lilliput's Mildendo is a credible great 'populous' city but also in danger of much damage from Gulliver's waistcoat. Gulliver sees a horse 'put his Fore-hoof to his Mouth, at which I was much surprized' and in our everyday minds we recognise the comedy if we try to imagine how the leg joints would permit this. Similarly anyone who has sat on the box of a carriage, daily viewing the obvious rear quarters of a horse, which in a day are computed to produce 48 lbs of droppings, may have difficulty in ascribing superior cleanliness to the beasts. (There is a nice irony in knowing that hard by Swift's lodgings in Suffolk Street was a stable known as the Dunghill Mews.) When Gulliver on his return trots like a horse, can we repress the smile we would give to a favourite relative doing this as an imitation of a horse in charade? Don't we feel the limitations of Houyhnhnm society's ability to build a house since it has no 'Use of Iron', when we see that they are dependent on a miraculous tree which grows 'very strait' so that it needs no shaping and 'at Forty Years old . . . falls with the first Storm' so that it needs no felling? Significantly Swift gives a pointer on how to see the Houyhnhnms in a flourish that Gulliver makes as an elegant author, quoting some improving lines from Virgil:

> I imposed upon myself as a Maxim, never to be swerved from, that I would *strictly adhere to Truth;* neither indeed can I be ever under the least Temptation to vary from it, while I retain in my Mind the Lectures and Example of my Noble Master, and other Illustrious *Houyhnhnms*, of whom I has so long the Honour to be an humble Hearer.
>
> *– Nec si miserum Fortuna Sinonem*
> *Finxit, vanum etiam, mendacemque improba finget.*

He links his truth-telling to the model of the Houyhnhnms which we have already seen as flawed, since they cannot detect the difference between a lie, a figment of the imagination and an exception to a rule. The Latin quotation is spoken by a Greek who warred with the Trojans and helped to sack their great city of Troy. The Latin translates as 'Although Fortune has moulded Sinon to misery, she shall not through malice make him a cheat and a liar.' Like so many of Swift's satiric touches it has undercurrents that alert the reader. While Sinon asserts his purity, in actual history he was a great liar who managed to bring about the sacking of Troy by a lying deception. He made the Trojans believe that a giant effigy inside which were concealed some of the best Greek soldiers was an object of veneration and that their capture and installation of it inside the city would bring them good fortune. At midnight the hidden soldiers stole out, opened the city gates and with their fellows sacked, pillaged and burned the buildings, and raped and slew the inhabitants. The effigy was of a wooden horse reminiscent, for readers of *Gulliver's Travels*, of the inflexible or wooden intelligences of the Houyhnhnms. Swift/Gulliver is behaving like Sinon in introducing a 'Trojan horse' or rather a society of Trojan horses in the invention of the Houyhnhnms. Their 'reason' threatens to make the breach which wipes out mankind as effectively as the Trojan horse which enabled the sacking of Troy.

There is a specific political reference too which warns against Gulliver's identification with the horses. In a sub-meaning of the book Swift draws an implicit parallel between the Irish and the Yahoos and the colonising English and the Trojan horse of reason. This develops from an anti-Irish tradition, endorsed by the outrageous history of the Welsh historian, Giraldus Cambrensis, which William Temple's father drew on in his book *The Irish Rebellion* (1646) which it is likely that Swift knew, possessing a copy in his library. According to this viewpoint the Irish were savage, primitive, naked, warlike, dirty, dishonest and lazy. In the fourth of *The Drapier's Letters* Swift remarks of the English that 'They look upon Us as a sort of *Savage Irish*, whom our Ancestors conquered several hundred Years ago . . . hearing only *one Side of the Cause* . . . they *believe a Lye* merely for their Ease, and conclude, because Mr. *Wood* pretends to have *Power*, he hath also *Reason* on his Side.'

The progress of the fable

The examination of Swift's fiction engaging with contemporary ideas is incomplete if it remains only with the exegesis of particular passages. In the preceding discussion threads of engagement with discovery, invention, mathematics, government and philosophy, invoking the names of Newton and Locke, emerge. This suggests an overall strategy to the four books and the way they interact is part of the meaning of the whole. In the eighteenth century Dr Johnson prized this quality in no less than Shakespeare's plays as 'the progress of the fable'.

In the original sequence of *Gulliver's Travels* (which reversed the order of Books III and IV) there is a clear progression. In a manner reminiscent of the Elizabethan travellers' tales the wonders increase: Gulliver meets little men, then giants, followed by talking horses and a galaxy of magicians/philosophers, immortals and spirits. The *Voyage to Laputa* completes a cycle. Lilliput represented British politics mainly under Queen Anne. Laputa (etymologically similar) returns to Britain after two fantasy worlds to show its culture. Its approach seems determined by the attitude to the moderns which Swift expressed in *The Battle of the Books*. Here he finally comes to dwell on contemporary society which seems fragmented, an archipelago of islands divided by war and self-interest where the practical agriculture of Lord Munodi has no hope against the crazy decoctions and machines of Lagado. As a termination of the series of tales it is fitting it should dwell on an historical perspective and then on the 'last things' of life. In Glubbdubdribb Gulliver calls up Homer, Aristotle and Agrippa. Unlike *The Battle of the Books* the history is not wholly advantageous to the past, for Swift has matured into the would–be historiographer for Queen Anne. After this, in Luggnagg the peevish, diseased, deformed and witless Struldbruggs reveal the body as a living mortification of the spirit, reconciling Gulliver to the necessity of death. As a conclusion to the tales, the book has a reflective function which begins by reviewing modern science, broadens into an historical retrospect and concludes naturally with a meditation on the process of ageing and death. (If Gulliver's return through Japan belongs with this tale in the earlier structure, his refusal to debase the crucifix by trampling on it shows an appropriate sensitivity to Christian salvation, brought about by his concern with 'last things'.)

We do not know what alterations Swift made when rearranging the last two books, but assuming that the broad pattern remained the same within each book, the original sequence presents a psychological progression in Gulliver's behaviour. The first three books represent Gulliver as a weapon of war: capturing the Blefuscudian fleet, unsuccessfully promoting the killing and maiming power of cannonades in Lorbrulgrud, and loftily instructing his Houyhnhnm master in the arts of battle. This is absent from *A Voyage to Laputa . . .* where Gulliver acts mainly as a sane observer, approving Lord Munodi and chastened by the sight of the Struldbruggs.

By putting the land of horses last, Swift revives the idea that Gulliver's enthusiasm for and knowledge of the grisly detail of war represent a real threat to humankind and in his maddened state unlikely to show mercy to what he can only perceive as Yahoos. But neither are the Houyhnhnms, masters of reason, much more well-disposed to humanity. There seems no escape. However, Swift lifts the veil by his parallel between Gulliver and Sinon, another successful weapon of war. In recommending the reasonable but deadly horses, Swift has altered the focus of his criticism from the evidently mad chaos of Laputa (prefigured by the *Battle of Books*) to the almost invulnerable science and logic of a more polished age. This looks ahead to the unmoved scientific 'philanthropist' of *A Modest Proposal* who coolly recommends spit-roasting the babies of the poor to solve in one the overpopulation and food shortage in Ireland.

Within this broad movement to a darker conclusion the role of Gulliver is constantly shifting. For example, he is humane towards the Blefuscudians whom he refuses to annihilate and callous towards the death of friends which would be no more than the 'annual succession of pinks and tulips'. He is a blind patriot praising the valour of England in plundering, stripping, ravishing, burning and destroying. He is half-right (properly sceptical but unidealistic) when exclaiming against a political system that would 'reward merit and promote great abilities'. He is completely right when approving the neatly built farmhouses of Lord Munodi. In relating to Gulliver the reader cannot take him at a constant face value but has to show intellectual suppleness and the responsible moral judgement of a concerned but detached observer.

Notes

1 Joseph McMinn, *Jonathan's Travels*, 17.
2 He was knighted in Cambridge on 15 April 1715. He had been made a fellow of the Royal Society on 11 January 1672.
3 See further, Oldmixon's attack on Swift.
4 In fact it led to a better understanding of the problem, although contempory scientists were not to know this. Re-examination of the findings of Flamsteed and others led to Bradley's discovery (1728) that another factor of distortion had occurred to interfere with the calculation – the aberration of light.
5 Maybe this contributed to the idea in *A Modest Proposal* of eating baby Irish Yahoos.
6 Laurence Sterne who made it the basis of this inventive and chaotic fiction, published 1759–67.
7 Noam Chomsky, *Cartesian Linguistics: A Chapter in the History of Rationalist Thought*, Harper & Row, 1966.
8 There was a project to sweeten the roughness of plain English by making it sound more Italian by tacking the suffix '-o' on to as many words as would take it.

Part Two
Critical Survey

Critical survey of selected passages

The passages chosen for comment in this section indicate something of Swift's range in poetry and prose. They are supplementary to other passages already considered in the discussion of topics earlier in the book and, where appropriate, reference is made to them. Collectively they show how Swift both engages attention and demands a very high level of reading skills. He prefers a simple and clear expression, which does not rely on the rhetorical tricks of patterned words and phrases but nevertheless has many resources. The virtue of simplicity is readability, immediacy and vigour, coming from a conversational ease which can turn to colloquial energy, such as 'Bless me! what a devil has raked this rabble together! Z – ds, what squeezing is this! Honest friend, remove your elbow.' Swift's turns of phrase often, as we have seen, depend on a lively appreciation of metaphor, often developed to surprising and appealing applications – wisdom is 'a nut, which unless you choose with judgment may cost you a tooth, and pay you with nothing but a worm'. Such a style coupled with his ability to create convincing imagined worlds seduces the attention of a reader.

However, the satiric resources of the text discompose a comfortable engagement with the narrative, since they are likely to turn round and bite the reader. Caustic invective excoriates its targets and, while we may feel that we stand beside the speaker attacking a 'royal prude' or lawyers (see the following passages), at some point we find ourselves in danger of being included in 'the most pernicious Race of odious vermin that Nature ever suffered to crawl upon the Surface of the Earth'. One of Swift's devices is to pile up an accumulation of details which bear down on the folly and wickedness of mankind and, as we saw in Chapter 5, varying responses are called out by the inclusion of dissimilar but linked features, which require a constant vigilance and receptiveness in reading and marking every item of moral censure. At other times, Swift works through allegory (such as the three brothers in *A Tale of a Tub* and the flying island in *Gulliver's Travels*) where we follow and judge its appropriateness by substituting elements of a known actuality. An offshoot of this technique is his parody, such as mimicking textual scholars' wrenching the meaning of the Bible: ' "Tis true," said he, "the word Calendæ hath in Q.V.C. [some ancient manuscripts] been sometimes writ with a *K*, but erroneously, for in the best copies, it is ever spelt with a *C*." '

These qualities require energetic attention enough from the reader but reach a point of athleticism when it comes to Swift's irony. A sense of irony is bound up with a sensitivity to style – an ability to catch underlying nuances in the particular phrases – and staying-power to see the dramatic irony of structural features, such as the progression of the books of *Gulliver's Travels* or the outcome of events, like Gulliver behaving like a horse.

Swift's use of a narrator assists the reader to stand apart from the text in judging his ironic manner. But it also introduces further complication. *A Tale of a Tub* forces the reader to listen to different voices, which distance the views it puts forward. There is a babble from the bookseller, the fawning dedicator and the supposedly real author who mentions names of actual people in his defence of the fiction. This is enough to put us in a discriminating mode, ready for the two most important voices: the narrator of the digressions and the story-teller.

The digressor is a vehicle for contextualising the satire when he expresses the threat to true religion of 'new levies of wits, all appointed (as there is reason to fear) with pen, ink, and paper, which may at an hour's warning be drawn out into pamphlets' but rapidly he is exposed as one of the pamphleteers himself. He professes 'to be a most devoted servant of all *modern* forms' and irrepressibly disregards sensible objections, being 'resolved to establish whatever argument it might cost me' his own point of view and leaving gaps in the manuscript when the fancy takes him that he no longer cares or is able to argue. His statements are increasingly mad: 'Last week I saw a woman *flayed*, and you will hardly believe how much it altered her person for the worse.' So he becomes an object lesson for the reader.

The story and digressions progress by turns. And while the narrator is also the story-teller, Swift makes use of literary conventions which give the story an independent life, without its allegory being subverted by having come from the mouth of a man in important respects mad. The tale begins with the conventional formula which announces a story of never-never land: 'Once upon a time, there was a man who had three sons by one wife, and all at a birth.' The reader accepts the bargain offered: suspend your disbelief for the gain of entering a fantasy world. The narrator intervenes with 'Here the story says this good father died' and later 'I shall not trouble you farther with recounting.' Interruption by the narrator is one of the arts of story-telling – of withholding as well as supplying – in order to create suspense or advance the plot. Inartistically done, it will focus too much on the inventor making it up but the story has sufficient momentum to allow the game of willing suspension of disbelief to continue. The function of the narrator here is that of a story-teller, to draw attention to the allegory being a sport, a literary device to 'fling out an empty *tub* by way of amusement, to divert [a whale, i.e. enemies] from laying violent hands upon the ship [i.e. the church]'.

In *Gulliver's Travels* the narrator no longer stands aloof from the story but is also a participant, who becomes unbalanced by the experiences he recounts. His reliability is therefore variable and interpretation of his view and of the drift of the events is thrown on the reader, who is by turns sympathetic, hostile and half-approving. In *A Modest Proposal* the narrator sustains a wholly unacceptable view, presented in reasonable and humane language which is attributed as belonging to our own value system. While the narrator is an object lesson for moral censure in his view of mankind, Swift's presentation of his arguments implies that we are collaborators.

Poetry

Extract from *Baucis and Philemon*, 1709

This poem belongs to the period of urban pastorals that Swift wrote for the *Tatler* (see Chapter 3). Swift made many revisions under the guidance of Addison but unlike the polite verse of *A Description of the Morning* it describes a more rural way of life with charm, invention and humour. Nevertheless, it seems intended to capture admiration from the same audience that appreciated the urban pastorals. The care that he took, consulting Addison whose taste counted in the fashionable world, and the poem's allusions to its literary antecedents both suggest that the author wished to appear as a man of polished refinement. Swift's older cousin, the established poet John Dryden, had written on the same subject and might be expected to be in the reader's mind when appreciating Swift's turns of phrase. Swift sets out, from this point of view, to outdo the performance of Dryden who is supposed to have said to him that he 'would never be a poet'. Both Dryden and Swift derive their poems from the same celebrated source which would be known and appeal to the classically educated. They translate and adapt from the Roman poet Ovid an incident in his *Metamorphosis*. This described how Jupiter and Hermes travelled among ordinary people, meeting rebuffs until they were welcomed into the humble dwelling of Baucis and Philemon. Swift transformed the Roman gods into saints and gave the whole a more domestic touch which is conveyed with light cheerfulness by the verse, Swift's favourite tetrameter with a regular stress pattern and neat couplet rhymes.

> Our wandering saints in woeful state,
> Treated at this ungodly rate,
> Having through all the village passed,
> To a small cottage came at last;

Where dwelt a good old honest yeoman,
Called in the neighbourhood, Philemon
Who kindly did the saints invite
In his poor hut to pass the night;
And then the hospitable sire
Bid Goody Baucis mend the fire;
While he from out the chimney took
A flitch of bacon off the hook;
And freely from the fattest side,
Cut out large slices to be fried:
Then stepped aside to fetch 'em drink,
Filled a large jug up to the brink;
And saw it fairly twice go round;
Yet (what was wonderful) they found
'Twas replenished to the top,
As if they ne'er had touched a drop.
The good old couple was amazed,
And often on each other gazed:
For both were frighted to the heart,
And just began to cry, 'What art!'
Then softly turned aside to view
Whether the lights were burning blue.
The gentle pilgrims soon aware on't,
Told them their calling, and their errand:
'Good folks, you need not be afraid,
We are but saints,' the hermits said;
'No hurt shall come to you, or yours;
But, for that pack of churlish boors,
Not fit to live on Christian ground,
They and their houses shall be drowned:
Whilst you shall see your cottage rise,
And grow a church before your eyes.'

They scarce had spoke; when fair and soft
The roof began to mount aloft;
Aloft rose every beam and rafter;
The heavy wall climbed slowly after.

The chimney widened, and grew higher,
Became a steeple with a spire.

The kettle to the top was hoist,
And there stood fastened to a joist:
But with the upside down, to show
Its inclination for below;
In vain; for some superior force

Applied at bottom, stops its course,
Doomed ever in suspense to dwell,
'Tis now no kettle, but a bell.

A wooden jack, which had almost
Lost, by disuse, the art to roast,
A sudden alteration feels,
Increased by new intestine wheels:
And what exalts the wonder more,
The number made the motion slower,
The flier, which though't had leaden feet,
Turned round so quick you scarce could see't;
Now slackened by some secret power,
Can hardly move an inch an hour.
The jack and chimney, near allied,
Had never left each other's side;
The chimney to a steeple grown,
The jack would not be left alone;
But up against the steeple reared,
Became a clock, and still adhered:
And still its love to household cares
By a shrill voice at noon declares,
Warning the cook-maid not to burn
That roast meat which it cannot turn.

The groaning chair was seen to crawl,
Like an huge snail half up the wall;
There stuck aloft, in public view;
And with small change, a pulpit grew.

One of the pleasures of this poem is the sense of assured control
with which the story is told – what a contemporary would have
called 'easy and familiar'. The expectations set up by the easy jog
trot of the four stresses to a line and the inevitability of the rhymed
couplets encounter pleasant surprises. 'Feminine' rhymes, where the
end of line acquires an extra lightly stressed syllable, interrupt the
flow at points of dramatic significance: where we meet the 'yeoman
. . . Philemon', where the 'rafter' is followed by the wall 'after', and
the chimney grows 'higher' to become a 'spire'. This comes over as
playfulness in which an Irish half-rhyme brings together 'aware on't'
and 'their errand'. For much of the time, the sense unit coincides
with the end of the couplet, so that the verse paragraph running
over six lines pronouncing the curse on the rest of the village takes
on a greater emphasis.

Swift represents his Baucis and Philemon in comfortable domest-
icity that would not be out of place in Ireland with the flitch of bacon

to be fried and the jug of drink passing round freely. Instead of focusing on some high morality the narrator shares the couple's interest in the 'drop' of drink which ever renews itself, expressing his own sense of the matter in a conversational aside '(but what was wonderful)'. The folk wisdom that spirits might turn the lights blue even the saints understand and it may be no surprise that in Ireland the saints were 'lusty drinkers' and yet were the most ordinary things – 'we are but saints' – in that land of saints and miracles.

The transformation of the humble cottage to a church shows great imagination and ingenuity. Objects acquire a life of their own in the witty double meanings of the words that describe them. The 'heavy' wall both solid and reluctant climbs slowly after the roof; the kettle turns upside down to become a bell and express its 'inclination for below; In vain'; and the wooden jack which becomes the works of the clock will not leave its ally the chimney now become a steeple. The jack's feeling a 'sudden alteration' is a nice touch, reminding us that it was unused to rotate as the old couple were too poor to have a roast. Sympathy informs Swift's presentation and this is continued in a gentle satire on churchgoing in lines not quoted where the ballads pasted on the wall of the cottage to commemorate folk heroes become the heraldry of monuments and a bedstead becomes a pew still 'lodging folk disposed to sleep'.

A comparison of the poem with that of Dryden shows a considerable change in interest. Dryden gave 77 lines to the hospitality given by the couple. The details suggest a more idyllic rural plenty than the fatty bacon offers:

> A Garden-Sallad was the third Supply,
> Of Endive, Radishes, and Succory:
> Then Curds and Cream, the Flow'r of Country-Fare,
> And new-laid Eggs, which Baucis busie Care
> Turn'd by a gentle Fire, and roasted rear.

Dryden draws upon the appeal of the country life to the man-about-town for which eighteenth-century classicising poets had a special affinity. They looked to ancient Rome and found it in Virgil's *Georgics*, celebrating peasant life and bee-keeping, and Martial's pleasure in the 'rus in urbe' (the country in the town) afforded by the enclosure of a fine garden by the Roman town villa. Dryden's adaptation of Ovid to produce a version which sounds this note requires the reader to be ready to catch allusions which are implicit in the text. When Swift produced his version, adapting gods to saints and shifting the focus of the poem to the transformation of the cottage, Dryden is added to the list of poets the reader is expected to remember. This trait in contemporary literary taste has been called the 'poetry of allusion'.

Swift's more elaborate description of the church growing before our eyes also gives an image that is more humble than Dryden's short account:

> A stately Temple shoots within the Skies:
> The Crotches of their Cot in Columns rise:
> The Pavement polish'd Marble they behold,
> The Gates with Sculpture grac'd, the Spires and Tiles of Gold.

Dryden is closer to the original here but neither poet is relying simply on accurate translation to recommend his performance. Both are variations on a theme. Dryden chooses the stately at this juncture but had been quite at ease with the humorous, describing an amusing episode where the peasants discover the godhead of their visitors when a 'sagacious goose' outruns their butchering pursuit and lays its head as a suppliant between the feet of Jove. If Dryden's uplift is that of the civilised gentleman, Swift's celebration is of the clergyman in touch with the common people and the glebe of Laracor where he once visualised 'the willows begin to peep, and the quicks to bud'.

Extract from *The Author Upon Himself*, 1714

Swift probably wrote this poem just before the despondent *In Sickness* (see Chapter 3) contemplating the recent death of Queen Anne and the sense of exile in Ireland:

> By an old red-pate, murdering hag pursued,
> A crazy prelate, and a royal prude.
> By dull divines, who look with envious eyes,
> On every genius that attempts to rise;
> And pausing o'er a pipe, with doubtful nod,
> Give hints, that poets ne'er believe in God.
> So, clowns on scholars as on wizards look,
> And take a folio for a conjuring book.
>   Swift had the sin of wit, no venial crime;
> Nay, 'twas affirmed, he sometimes dealt in rhyme:
> Humour, and mirth, had place in all he writ:
> He reconciled divinity and wit.
> He moved, and bowed, and talked with too much grace;
> Nor showed the parson in his gait or face;
> Despised luxurious wines, and costly meat;
> Yet, still was at the tables of the great.
> Frequented lords; saw those that saw the Queen;
> At Child's or Truby's never once had been;
> Where town and country vicars flock in tribes,
> Secured by numbers from the laymen's gibes;

And deal in vices of the graver sort,
Tobacco, censure, coffee, pride, and port.
  But, after sage monitions from his friends,
His talents to employ for nobler ends;
To better judgements willing to submit,
He turns to politics his dangerous wit.
  And now, the public interest to support,
By Harley Swift invited comes to court.
In favour grows with ministers of state;
Admitted private, when superiors wait:
And, Harley, not ashamed his choice to own,
Takes him to Windsor in his coach, alone.
At Windsor Swift no sooner can appear,
But, St John comes and whispers in his ear;
The waiters stand in ranks; the yeomen cry,
'Make room', as if a duke were passing by.

This poem is remarkable for its openness, unreserve and self-revelation. It was not published until 1735 in Faulkner's collection of Swift's works when the embers of the quarrels it describes had almost ceased to glow. Like the *Windsor Prophecy* (see Chapter 2) it makes a direct attack on the Duchess of Somerset but widens the scope of its targets. It begins vigorously with the author seen as the victim of lesser beings but well able to defend himself with his invective, powerfully hitting out in each descriptive epithet of the opening couplets. The Duchess is seen as triply disqualified from reasonable judgement by her age, hot blood (suggested by 'red-pate') and the reputation of having been an accomplice in the murder of her second husband by her lover, Count von Köningsmark. The Archbishop of York, John Sharp, was the 'crazy prelate' who opposed Swift's preferment after the offence given by *A Tale of a Tub* and is said to have tried and failed to achieve a reconciliation with Swift later. As the poem progresses other divines are included who are probably men like the Bishop of Kildare, who tried to wrest the credit of the First Fruits from him, and the Archbishop of Dublin, William King, who failed to promote Swift's interests. (Both are discussed in Chapter 1.) More surprising, given Harley's loyalty to the queen, is Swift's bitter attack on her as a 'royal prude'. She never gave him an audience and probably did resist his advancement, shocked by the improprieties that Sharp was zealous to show.

  The lines of Swift's self-defence against these enemies give a lively picture of eighteenth-century politics, a reasonably accurate autobiography and sometimes implicate himself in the reader's critical judgement. He was indignant at accusations of infidelity ('poets ne'er believe') and would not, he said, stoop to defend himself. So in this poem he deals in personalities rather than theological debate, taking the high ground of a man of learning, ranking himself with 'scholars' and most divines as 'clowns'. Shrewdly he recognises that his raillery was a major offence against the stuffiness of the clergy, conspiring and gossiping ('twas affirmed, he sometimes dealt in rhyme'), who see his wit as sin (rather than merely a crime) and his graceful circulation among the great as insufficiently parsonical. Swift displays his humour in the specific details of his characterisation of them 'pausing o'er a pipe, with doubtful nod' and giving 'hints' while too craven to come out in the open. But the underlying energy shows that he was touched to the quick and the strategy of self-justification is an uneasy one. We know he was abstemious in his drinking and eating but there is some unintended pathos in the accuracy of his account which forces him to show he didn't meet the queen but only 'saw those that saw the Queen' and that he prides himself on having been 'at the tables of the great'.

He turns his intimate knowledge of the town to advantage when imagining the lesser clergy flocking to Child's coffee-house and Truby's tavern in St Paul's churchyard. The siting of these establishments close to the city's principal place of worship enabled an easy and almost imperceptible diversion for the procession of these men. Here the divines who do not practise his stricter regimen are able to hide in numbers secure from reports to their parishes of being seen there. The tumble of their animated conversation coloured by the moral censure, which is the trademark of the godly, is enacted in a compressed couplet, stringing greater with lesser vices:

> And deal in vices of the graver sort,
> Tobacco, censure, coffee, pride, and port.

The reader forced to discriminate between the grave and less grave (remembering Swift's memorable attack on humanity 'puffed up with Pride') goes another step to examine the nature of the 'dealing'. While the clerics deal, in the sense of swapping, examples of how corrupt the world has become, are they not themselves drinking coffee and port, smoking tobacco, indulging in censure and puffed with pride of religious certainty? Perhaps they are as tainted as the objects of their condemnation. A dull divine might not be certain that was the meaning, however. Swift's suavity makes him a difficult target for the affronted clergyman which therefore irritates all the more.

In pursuing his own self-promotion Swift is less in control. He stacks the argument about his political involvement telling us that his turning that way was the result of 'sage' advice, a 'nobler' task and in the 'public interest'. But we may feel that he has the thrill of power in speaking of his 'dangerous wit'. In justice to this master of ambiguity we may also admit that his wit was dangerous to his own prospects too and that meaning may also be contained in the description. Some smug self-satisfaction lurks in his boast of being seen 'while superiors wait' but this is astonishingly open about his feelings, and does not have the protective layer of the satirist in *Gulliver's Travels*. While we may feel that he reduces his consequence when hitching his wagon to Harley's star we may remember that he had an unaffected admiration for his friend and a wish to honour him.

The poem (in lines not quoted) progresses through the events of Harley's ministry and the rupture between him and St John. So the truth of his being flattered by Harley's attentions gains a dramatic significance in his account of a failure to bring them together which resolves the poem:

> By faction tired, with grief he waits a while,
> His great contending friends to reconcile.
> Performs what friendship, justice, truth require:
> What could he more, but decently retire?

The authenticity of the history (admittedly seen through Swift's eyes) validates the virtues of friendship, justice and truth against the madness, prudery and envy represented in the opening lines. Swift did indeed, at the fall of Harley, retire to be with his friend the Reverend John Geree, rector of Letcombe Bassett in Berkshire, near Wantage. But for his restless spirit this was only a temporary stasis.

Extract from *On Poetry: A Rhapsody*, 1733

This poem is roughly contemporaneous with the scatological poems discussed in Chapter 4. Unlike them it has a more public role and range since it surveys the role of poetry in the contemporary social scene. It is in the form of a monologue spoken by an experienced and successful poet. Beginning with his amazement at the rage to have a reputation as a poet he advises the would-be poet on his conduct in society, the subjects he may hope to profit by and the persons he must flatter, almost incidentally revealing the necessity of compromise of moral position at every turn. The intense competition for literary fame in Grub Street is expressed in the famous lines:

> So, naturalists observe, a flea
> Hath smaller fleas that on him prey,
> And these a smaller yet to bite 'em,
> And so proceed ad infinitum:

The passage chosen here follows an apparent shift of the narrator's position in exempting the British monarch, George II, and his prime minister Robert Walpole from the charge of corruption. It also seems to be a demonstration to the tyro how to praise in verse:

Now sing the minister of state,
Who shines alone, without a mate.
Observe with what majestic port
This Atlas stands to prop the court:
Intent the public debts to pay,
Like prudent Fabius by delay.
Thou great viceregent of the King,
Thy praises every muse shall sing:
In all affairs thou sole director,
Of wit and learning chief protector;
Though small the time thou hast to spare,
The church is thy peculiar care.
Of pious prelates what a stock
You choose to rule the sable flock.
You raise the honour of the peerage,
Proud to attend you at the steerage.
You dignify the noble race,
Content yourself with humbler place,
Now learning, valour, virtue, sense,
To titles give the sole pretence.
St George beheld thee with delight,
Vouchsafe to be an azure knight,
When on thy breast and sides Herculean,
He fixed the star and string cerulean.

Say, poet, in what other nation,
Shone ever such a constellation.
Attend ye Popes, and Youngs, and Gays,
And tune your harps, and strow your bays.
Your panegyrics here provide,
You cannot err on flattery's side.
Above the stars exalt your style,
You still are low ten thousand mile.
On Lewis all his bards bestowed,
Of incense many a thousand load;
But Europe mortified his pride,
And swore the fawning rascals lied:
Yet what the world refused to Lewis,
Applied to George exactly true is:
Exactly true! Invidious poet!
'Tis fifty thousand times below it.

Translate me now some lines, if you can,
From Virgil, Martial, Ovid, Lucan;
They could all power in heaven divide,
And do no wrong to either side:

They teach you how to split a hair,
Give George and Jove an equal share.
Yet, why should we be laced so straight;
I'll give my monarch butter-weight.
And reason good; for many a year
Jove never intermeddled here:
Nor, though his priests be duly paid,
Did we ever desire his aid:
We now can better do without him,
Since Woolston gave us arms to rout him.

The stealth, grace and silkiness of Swift's approach here belies his deadly power and shows him at his most feline. (It contrasts greatly with the direct attack on the court in his *Author upon Himself*.) Queen Caroline, the consort of George, was fooled into thinking that the poem was indeed complimentary about her as an arbiter of taste in the immediately preceding section which has the tone experienced here. (In fact Walpole and the monarchy are to be seen as birds of the same feather since he is called 'great viceregent to the King'.) So many of the words praising Walpole are barbed with a submerged meaning that to the alert reader it becomes apparent that far from being the secondary sense the compliments exist to cast an ironic light on Walpole's pretension and to reveal the disreputable side of him. Walpole 'shines alone' because his wife was unfaithful to him and he earned the nickname Atlas because he was stout. The Roman hero Fabius (Quintus Fabius Maximus) was celebrated for delaying engagement in battle with Rome's enemies in order to wear them down. Walpole wears the public down in not paying them what he owes. 'In all affairs . . . sole director' he may seem to be the unique leader, but as directorship had a bad name from association with ruin of many speculators in the government South Sea company it is not the compliment that would please Walpole. This is particularly the case since he had been out of power during the financial crash and had owed his return for the reputation of being clean in this respect. Swift's appellation suggests that this Whig grandee is no different from the one that went before.

The entourage of Walpole are also suspect. Remembering the 'dull divines' in the previous extract, we realise that a shift of tone is all that is necessary to express distaste rather than admiration for Walpole's 'peculiar care' ('peculiar' meaning either 'special' or 'abnormal') and in the exclamation 'what a stock'. Naturally one would think of churchmen as a flock following the Good Shepherd and because of their clerical cassocks they would be sable in colour, but a 'sable flock' is a synonym for black sheep. The peers who are proud to attend Walpole in the 'steerage' may feel they have their hands on the helm of state but the steerage was also the cabin aft of the main cabin and was allocated to the inferior officers and the crew. The gentry wait on the monied interest and feel 'proud' to do so. Natural dignity has been lost. What dignities there are seem to be a substitute for the civic virtues in an ambiguous couplet:

> Now learning, valour, virtue, sense,
> To titles give the sole pretence.

Either this means that these four qualities are to be found only in conferred titles or that titled aristocrats (a metonymy, where the attribute stands for the whole, as the crown stands for the monarch) are the only ones who may lay claim to them. Neither is satisfactory, morally speaking, and the succeeding mention of Walpole's being invested with the blue ribbon and silver star of the Order of the Garter confirms it. The ribbon is merely 'string' and the grand adjective 'cerulean' is undermined by the triple rhyme and jangling difference of stressed emphasis of 'Herculean' (which continues the sense of obesity raised by the comparison with Atlas).

The next verse paragraph returns to the royal family in the context of this entourage and to the instruction to the would-be poet. Pope, Young and Gay who are asked to celebrate the monarch in different ways represent the infelicity of such a request. Pope would have no dealings with the court. Gay (and the Duchess of Queensberry) were turned out of court on a trumped charge of sedition in his ballad opera *Polly*. Young was a poet respected by Pope but had been forced in his poem *The Universal Passion* to face both ways by criticising the vices of society and praising its leaders. *A Rhapsody* is partly a riposte to Young's poem and at this juncture has said enough concerning the responsibility of leaders for the society they encouraged to make Young pause before renewing his praise. So 'you cannot err on flattery's side' which initially is taken to mean 'no flattery can be too much for him' (his worth is so great or his appetite is inexhaustible) becomes 'you cannot make the mistake of joining in the flattery'. After this sobering actuality the extravagance of the instructing poet is felt to be marked, especially as one point of reference is to Louis XIV, the sun king felt to be the enemy of Protestant Britain and a type of overblown majesty.

After the conversational ease and sense of interchange of the paragraph of soaring praise the next section begins haltingly. Again there is a couplet which runs slightly counter to the regular pattern. It has a double rhyme with an extra syllable and the stress falls on the last one of the first line and the penultimate of the second: 'if you can . . . Ovid, Lucan'. There is something negligent about the scansion which is also there in the Roman authors chosen to adorn the praise. The effect of the stumble is to make us consider the choice of words.

In *Baucis and Philemon* we have seen how Virgil, Martial and Ovid might represent an ideal countryside for the eighteenth-century city-dweller. They could even be trotted out here as the usual decoration somewhat half-thought, not requiring anything specifically apt but, as the narrator says, just 'some lines'. But then there is Lucan. Rather like Gulliver's attempt to embellish his prose with an allusion to Sinon, the poet's inclusion of Lucan introduces a sinister note. For he was the poet best known for his *Pharsalia*, a description of the ruin of the Roman nation under the ravages of war. Marvell had used him to warn of the perils of civil war during the time of Cromwell. Swift adduces him to suggest the disintegration of contemporary Britain which is exemplified in the next lines. The extravagance of praise given to George is the sign of a godless country. The king is offered butter-weight which gave an extra two ounces to the pound while Jove gets the standard measure since he is not to be 'buttered up'. In fact he has not had dealings 'here' 'for many a year' so that any intervention now would be seen as 'intermeddling' – interfering with matters outside his sphere. Society is better off since it knows how to overcome the divinity with the help of Thomas Woolston, the free-thinker. He has shown us that miracles do not happen and that divine intervention, therefore, is not a possibility.

Prose

A Tale of a Tub, 1704

In Chapter 1 we examined two extracts from *A Tale of a Tub*, one of which came from the allegorical story of Peter, Martin and Jack, who represent different churches, and another which came from a passage justifying the use of clothing as a metaphor for religious belief. In the following extract the irrepressible narrator, a type of the Grub Street paper-mongering hack, makes his farewell to the gentle reader:

> *Going on too long* is a cause of abortion as effectual, though not so frequent, as *going too short*; and holds true especially in the *labours* of the brain. Well fare the heart of that noble Jesuit[+] who first adventured to confess in print that books must be suited to their several seasons, like dress, and diet, and diversions. And better fare our noble nation for refining upon this among other French modes. I am living fast to see the time when a *book* that misses its tide shall be neglected as the *moon* by day, or like *mackerel* a week after the season. No man hath more nicely observed our climate than the bookseller who bought the copy of this work. He knows to a tittle what subjects will best go off in a *dry year*, and which it is proper to

expose foremost when the weather-glass is fallen to *much rain*. When he had seen this treatise and consulted his *almanac* upon it, he gave me to understand that he had maturely considered the two principal things which were the *bulk* and the *subject*, and found it would never *take* but after a long vacation, and then only in case it should happen to be a hard year for turnips. Upon which I desired to know, *considering my urgent necessities*, what he thought might be acceptable this month. He looked westward and said, 'I doubt we shall have a fit of bad weather. However, if you could prepare some pretty little *banter (but not in verse)* or a small treatise upon the –, it would run like wildfire. But *if it hold up*, I have already hired an author to write something against Dr. B[en]tl[e]y, which I am sure will turn to account.'

At length we agreed upon this expedient; that when a customer comes for one of these and desires in confidence to know the author, he will tell him very privately as a friend, naming whichever of the wits shall happen to be that week in vogue; and if Durfey's last play should be in course, I would as lieve he may be the person as Congreve. This I mention, because I am wonderfully well acquainted with the present relish of courteous readers, and have often observed with singular pleasure, that a *fly* driven from a *honey-pot* will immediately, with very good appetite, alight and finish his meal on an *excrement*.

I have one word to say upon the subject of *profound writers*, who are grown very numerous of late and I know very well the judicious world is resolved to list me in that number. I conceive therefore, as to the business of being *profound*, that it is with *writers* as with *wells* – a person with good eyes may see to the bottom of the deepest provided any *water* be there, and that often when there is nothing in the world at the bottom besides *dryness* and *dirt*, though it be but a yard and half underground it shall pass, however, for wondrous *deep*, upon no wiser a reason than because it is wondrous *dark*.

I am now trying an experiment very frequent among modern authors, which is *to write upon nothing*; when the subject is utterly exhausted, to let the pen still move on; by some called the ghost of wit, delighting to walk after the death of its body. And to say the truth, there seems to be no part of knowledge in fewer hands than that of discerning *when to have done*. By the time that an author hath writ out a book, he and his readers are become old acquaintance and grow very loth to part; so that I have sometimes known it to be in writing as in visiting, where the ceremony of taking leave has employed more time than the whole conversation before.

[⁺ footnote in the original: Père d'Orléans]

In this engaging farewell there is no sense of conclusion since the author never seems to run out of steam and is as happy to ridicule his reader as any of his multifarious targets. Fascinated interest in what he will do next and rapid decoding of barbed meanings hold our attention. While there is not the considered effect of sustained ironic presentation as in *Gulliver's Travels*, there is a vivacity in the brilliance of performance. The narrator's witty parallel, between the creative act of writing and that of bearing a child, becomes inelegant as the word 'abortion' takes on the meaning of 'misshapen' and the sense of premature or overdue birth becomes actual. In the next breath he assumes the role of a person of wide learning who refers to 'that noble Jesuit' expecting us not to need the support of a footnote but nonetheless supplying it. The honour of the French he subverts with the word 'modes', suggesting 'modishness' and his praise of the English contained in 'noble nation'. But what makes the English noble? A science of publishing which operates in an almost Laputian fashion. Initially this science conjures up an attractive image of the moon naturally coexisting with the tides (whose ebb and flow it controls) and with shoals of mackerel (which teem with the tides). But behind this is the eighteenth-century sense of the printing press producing an information explosion in the overproduction of books of pamphlets. (Samuel Johnson, using a similar 'birthing' metaphor in 1778, spoke of the 'superfoetation' of the press.) Swift draws on the discredited quackery of the almanac-mongers to advance a mock argument about the propitious time for publishing a book based on its 'bulk' and 'subject'. The readership this suggests is one that is more interested in the fashionable topic and the weight of the reading rather than its rational argument or emotional appeal. So cloddish an interest brings us to the rural context of agriculture and turnips, with the opposition of country lore to city smartness. This is opportunistic, since the rural commended itself elsewhere and in Swift's day the rhythm of the seasons affected the city to the extent that the Law Courts had a long summer vacation in order to let the gentlemen see to the harvest of their estates. But the language of the bookseller has all the hallmarks of country colloquial: what will 'go off in a dry year' ('explode' like gunpowder, metaphorically speaking), using 'I doubt' to mean 'I expect', and saying 'if it hold up' to mean if it is held back. This contrasts nicely with the circumlocution of the needy Grub Street writer whose 'urgent necessities' may suggest his being 'caught short'. (Swift's interest in the use of colloquial phrases in common speech is shown at length in his three dialogues composed entirely of such forms, known by its short title of the *Polite Conversation*. In the introduction to this he writes 'I always kept a large Table-Book [i.e. a memorandum book] in my Pocket; and as soon as I left the

Company, I immediately entred the choicest Expressions that passed during the Visit.')

One interest of this imagined trade talk is the closeness it shows of writer to bookseller and to customer. The system of publishing is still on the old-fashioned scale, despite the increase in production. It is a close community. All are assumed to know the 'notoriety' and therefore the commercial value of Dr Bentley (the object of the satire of *The Battle of the Books* discussed in Chapter 2) as a name that sells a pamphlet. The writer disarms the reader with his exposé of the tricks of the trade, just as Thomas Nashe did, a century before, in his popular pamphlets (see p. 224. In assigning any author to the text so long as it sells, the bookseller and hack are happy to practise their roguery unblinkingly on the public. Swift drives the point home by likening Congreve (a personal and honoured friend) to a honey pot and the then-fashionable Durfey to excrement, while the singularly pleased and relishing fly corresponds to the reader. This is the after-reading effect of a sentence that separates the 'courteous reader' from the seemingly innocent image of the fly and the postponed word at the end of the paragraph of 'excrement'. (The notion of writing as excrement reacts with the idea of it as birth. In *Gulliver's Travels* the Yahoos who excrete on Gulliver may be seen as producing the filth of the gutter press.)

Fertile as ever, the narrator skips from this inelegance to a boast of the 'judicious world' seeing him as a profound writer. Given the airy knowingness of the whole we probably read this 'world' as the social set he happens to frequent in London. But the metaphor that follows in its developed detail really does claim some merit in its clever appropriateness. It is often the case that Swift's language has this poetic resource. His equation of the profound with the deep, based on a pun being taken literally, is a joke that continued to attract his contemporaries, particularly Pope in his later mock treatise on the profound or the bathetic (*Peri Bathous, or the Art of Sinking*). What gives this originality here is seeing the true and false profundities as wells, one with water and one without. Water deep down is refreshing, has clarity and reflects light. The dry bottom has no freshness, associates with filth through its 'dirt', and gives a false sense of being far down. Connecting the two is the idea that darkness of soul often masquerades as wisdom. It takes an eighteenth-century view of the need for clear statement and for opposition to obscure seventeenth-century metaphysics.

In the next paragraph, Swift hits at the modern writer who writes nullities in an automatic fashion, glancing also at such *tours de force* as Rochester's Restoration poem written on the topic of 'Nothing'. His confidential tone makes the reader an associate in the experiment, reinforcing a sense that has prevailed throughout the work with its easy flow, multiple digressions and loss of formal shape. (In this literary device *A Tale of a Tub* prefigures *Tristram Shandy* and is unlike *Gulliver's Travels*.) Once again the intimate tone of the close community surfaces, when the reader is the anxious host trying to shut the door on his buttonholing guest. But only half-wishing to rid himself since there is a truth in the idea that some books enchant so much that we would wish them longer.

Gulliver's Travels 1726
Book I extract

The Reader may remember, that when I signed those Articles upon which I recovered my Liberty, there were some which I disliked upon account of their being too servile, neither could any thing but extreme Necessity have forced me to submit. But being now a *Nardac*, of the highest Rank in that Empire, such Offices were looked upon as below my Dignity, and the Emperor (to do him Justice) never once mentioned them to me. However, it was not long before I had an Opportunity of doing his Majesty, at least, as I then thought, a most signal Service. I was alarmed at Midnight with the Cries of many hundred People at my Door; by which being suddenly awaked, I was in some kind of Terror. I heard the word *Burglum* repeated incessantly: several of the Emperor's Court making their Way through the Croud, intreated me to come immediately to the Palace, where her Imperial Majesty's Apartment was on fire, by the carelessness of a Maid of Honour, who fell asleep while she was reading a Romance. I got up in an instant; and Orders being given to clear the way before me, and it likewise being a Moonshine Night, I made shift to get to the Palace without trampling on any of the People. I found they had already applied Ladders to the Walls of the Apartment, and were well provided with Buckets, but the Water was at some distance. These Buckets were about the size of a large Thimble, and the poor People supplied me with them as fast they could; but the Flame was so violent, that they did little good. I might easily have stifled it with my Coat, which I unfortunately left behind me for haste, and came away only in my Leathern Jerkin. The Case seemed wholly desperate and deplorable, and this magnificent Palace would have infallibly been burnt down to the ground, if, by a Presence of Mind, unusual to me, I had not suddenly thought of an Expedient. I had the Evening before drank plentifully of a most delicious wine, called *Glimigrim*, (the *Blefuscudians* call it *Flunec*, but ours is esteemed the better sort) which is very Diuretick. By the luckiest Chance in the World, I had not discharged myself from any part of it. The Heat I had contracted by coming very near the Flames, and by my labouring to quench them, made the Wine begin to operate by Urine; which I voided in such a Quantity, and applied so well to the proper Places, that in three minutes the Fire was wholly extinguished, and the rest of that noble Pile, which had cost so many Ages in erecting, preserved from destruction.

It was now Day-light, and I returned to my House, without waiting to congratulate with the Emperor; because, although I had done a very eminent piece of Service, yet I could not tell how his Majesty might resent the manner by which I had performed it; For, by the fundamental Laws of the Realm, it is Capital in any Person, of what Quality soever, to make water within the Precincts of the Palace. But I was a little comforted by a Message from his Majesty, that he would give Orders to the Grand Justiciary for passing my Pardon in form; which, however I could not obtain. And I was privately assured, the Empress, conceiving the greatest Abhorrence of what I had done, removed to the distant side of the Court, firmly resolved that those Buildings should never be repaired for her Use; and, in the presence of her chief Confidents, could not forbear vowing Revenge.

The comedy of this incident rests upon Gulliver's preening himself on the dignity of being a Nardac and therefore exempted from 'servile offices' describing his urinating as a 'signal Service'. This is undignified in normal circumstances and when 'voided in such Quantity' by a giant is particularly unpleasant. The joke could easily have come from Rabelais's tales of Gargantua and Pantagruel which Swift admired (see Chapter 2). But the manner of telling the tale introduces a great deal more subtlety. Within this framework, Swift hits a number of targets and at the same time tells a story with convincing detail. In true travelogue style the narrator preens himself on his foreign title where the reader, reflecting on the triviality, cruelty and power-seeking qualities of the Lilliputians, questions the worth of royal honours. The reader adopts an attitude in tune with Locke's *Two Treatises of Government* which was discussed in relation to the passages in *Gulliver's Travels* about education and society (Chapter 5). Locke contrasted the condition of kings in America with the condition of the labourer in England: 'a king of a large and fruitful territory there feeds, lodges, and is clad worse than a day labourer in England'. Locke's and Swift's participation in the post-revolution sentiment which disestablished the Stuart monarchy produced a lack of reverence for kings and an enquiry into the quality of the life of men, whether king or subject. The emperor of Lilliput has an impressive looking urban-centred civilisation but the pursuits are as trivial as dancing over ropes and slicing the tops of eggs.

As a piece of story-telling, the incident has much attraction. Scraps of the language of the country establish the foreignness and also have a strange resonance within our own, just as French words are allied to English but have another meaning (the 'faux amis', such as the word 'populace'). 'Burglum' sounds like 'burglar' and 'flunec' is reminiscent of flowing nectar. There is an observed journalistic quality in the descriptions of ladders, buckets and the people supplying the willing giant as fast as they can. His regret for not wearing his coat sounds like a man thinking to some purpose in the imagined event and his haste which made him not put it on adds to the urgency of concern for the 'magnificent palace . . . that noble Pile, which cost so many Ages in erecting'. The action of heat and the diuretic qualities of the wine account partly for the lack of inhibition in Gulliver (although one does not expect consistency in the character who modestly relieves himself – when the 'offence' is scarcely visible – using a sorrel leaf in Book II) and the rest is accounted for in his unthinking wish to please, a lack of thought which has been already demonstrated in his pride in being a Nardac. The quality of this writing is to encourage belief in the authenticity of the event, a technique in which Swift is adept throughout the work, often producing descriptions of considerable charm, such as when Gulliver sees a crowd of ladies below him seeming 'to resemble a Petticoat spread on the Ground, embroidered with Figures of Gold and Silver'.

The incident is also a representation of Swift's own experience at the reception of *A Tale of a Tub*. The palace is being consumed by fires which have been the result of the carelessness of a Maid of Honour reading herself to sleep with a romance. *A Tale of a Tub* was intended to dampen the fires of religious controversy, an action which Queen Anne as the head of the church he expected to approve under the moderating Revolution Settlement. As we know she did not appreciate this form of defence and in the poem the *Author upon Himself* Swift sees this as the effect of her prudery and of the Archbishop of York's destruction of his good character. However, the poem begins with an attack on the Duchess of Somerset who was a Maid of Honour and she has some claim to be the maid of honour represented here. For in 1709 the Duchess wrote to her aunt, the widow of Sir William Temple, that Swift was 'a man of no principle either of honour or religion'. The immediate cause of this remark was their annoyance at Swift's publication of the third part of Temple's *Memoirs*, although this had been his responsibility as secretary to the great man. The other cause was the distaste she had for *A Tale of a Tub* published in 1704. Later, with her husband, she worked on behalf of the Whig Junto against the Tory negotiations for peace in 1712 to end the war of the Spanish Succession (which had put Catholic against Protestant). And she actively discredited Swift with the queen. The effectiveness of her advice to the queen is glanced at in the words 'the Empress, conceiving the greatest

Abhorrence'. In addition the Duchess's connection with 'reading a Romance' may be seen in her having two husbands and a lover who killed her second husband.

There is yet another layer of meaning. It is a story of a 'moonshine night' when tom-fooling is in order. The ineffective ladders and thimbleful buckets of water may refer to the Test Acts which allowed a non-Anglican to hold on to the 'ladder' of preferment. In essence, this was by observing some of the practices of the Church of England – nominally baptised by a sprinkling of its 'holy' water. But this is insufficient to put out the fires of religious controversy. So, to the rescue comes the fluent art of the young Swift. 'By the luckiest Chance in the World' Gulliver's urine flowed so plentifully and was 'applied so well'. This also recalls the link between excretion and writing (referred to in the previous criticism of the passage from *A Tale of a Tub*). Gulliver is sent up for boasting of his efficacy much as Pope satirised the pissing contest between Curl and another bookseller in *The Dunciad*. (Although this was not published until 1728, it is still relevant to *Gulliver's Travels* for Swift had some part in the early draft of it, possibly nine years in the making.) In so far as Gulliver is Swift there is some self-satire at the propensity of his writing to 'indecent' scatology. But there is much more criticism of the prudery of a court whose protocol made it impossible to answer a call of nature. Crossed legs must have been frequently the order of the day during a lengthy audience 'For, by the fundamental [a probable pun here!] laws of the realm, it is Capital in any Person, of what quality soever, to make water within the Precincts of the Palace'. The three concentric courtyards of the palace when scaled to human measure cover 21 400 square metres, with no loo.

Book II extract

Their Stile is clear, masculine, and smooth, but not florid, for they avoid nothing more than multiplying unnecessary Words, or using various Expressions. I have perused many of their Books, especially those in History and Morality. Among the rest I was much diverted with a little old Treatise, which always lay in *Glumdalclitch's* Bed-chamber, and belonged to her Governess, a grave elderly Gentlewoman, who dealt in Writings of Morality and Devotion. The Book treats of the Weakness of Human kind, and is in little Esteem except among the Women and the Vulgar. However, I was curious to see what an Author of that Country could say upon such a Subject. This Writer went through all the usual Topicks of *European* Moralists, shewing how diminutive, contemptible, and helpless an Animal was man in his own nature; how unable to defend himself from the Inclemencies of the Air or the Fury of wild Beasts. How much he was excelled by one Creature in Strength, by another in Speed, by a third in Foresight, by a fourth in Industry. He added that Nature was degenerated in these latter declining Ages of the World, and could produce only small abortive Births in comparison of those in ancient Times. He said it was very reasonable to think, not only that the Species of Men were originally much larger, but also there must have been Giants in former Ages, which, as it is asserted by History and Tradition, so it hath been confirmed by huge Bones and Sculls casually dug up in several Parts of the Kingdom, far exceeding the common dwindled Race of Man in our Days. He argued that the very Laws of Nature absolutely required we should have been made in the beginning, of a size more large and robust, not so liable to Destruction from every little Accident of a Tile falling from an House, or a Stone cast from the Hand of a Boy, or of being drowned in a little Brook. From this way of Reasoning the Author drew several moral Applications useful in the Conduct of Life, but needless here to repeat. For my own part, I could not avoid reflecting how universally this Talent was spread of drawing Lectures in Morality, or indeed rather matter of Discontent and repining from the Quarrels we raise with Nature. And, I believe upon a strict Enquiry, those Quarrels might be shewn as ill-grounded among us, as they are among that People.

Overall the second book of *Gulliver's Travels* is more discursive and morally reflective than the first. The value for Swift of a clear style (already discussed in Chapter 5) leads the reader to expect well of the books which the Brobdingnagians value sufficiently to keep in their small libraries. Perhaps Swift forgot in Gulliver's claiming to 'peruse many of their Books' that it was difficult for his size and that he had described before a 'wooden machine' which cumbersomely helped his difficulty. More likely it is a form of boasting in the style of the comments where in a matter of weeks he is master of the language of the country. The book he chooses to describe shows a serpentine meaning underneath. As the treatise is esteemed only by 'the Women and the Vulgar' we may wish to endorse Gulliver's rejection of it as 'ill-grounded'. It has some of the amateur archaeo-logical approach of virtuosi inspecting 'huge Bones and Sculls casu-ally dug up'. But it also has striking similarities with *Gulliver's Travels*. They are to be found in the comparison of man's physical and mental qualities with those of animals which Gulliver dismisses as 'all the usual Topicks'. But Gulliver is happy with such analogies elsewhere. Gulliver had already argued with the king of Brobdingnag that his smallness did not disqualify him from being paid attention for 'among other Animals, Bees and Ants had the Reputation of more Industry, Art, and sagacity than many of the larger kinds'.

This requires crediting the bees and ants with these qualities if Gulliver is also to be heard. There is a danger in adducing the wrong qualities, for an academician at Lagado later justifies building a house from the roof downwards 'by the like Practice of those two prudent Insects the Bee and the Spider'. In addition, the last book of these travels presents a beast fable in which the virtues of horses are equivocally recommended above those of humans. So it would seem that whether the writer of the treatise is to be listened to depends on the persuasiveness of his comparisons rather than questioning the method. Such a critique as that of the 'little old Treatise' had been made by the French philosopher, Montaigne, in his *Essays* (translated into English in 1603 and again in 1685) whose concern was to abase human pride – a concern shared by Swift. What brings it even nearer to Swift is that *Gulliver's Travels* echoes the sense of degeneration. In Glubbdubdrib Gulliver experiences 'melancholy Reflections to observe how much the Race of human kind was degenerate among us' reducing the size of their bodies. And, the giants of Brobdingnag do represent a more ideal agricultural society close to that adumbrated in *Contests and Dissensions* (see Chapter 5) as do the 'Giants of former Ages' mentioned here.

This line of argument encourages us to question the direction that seemed to be offered by the 'little old Treatise' not being esteemed 'except among the Women and the Vulgar'. Perhaps the young giantess Glumdalclitch who carries Gulliver like a doll or pet stands in some way for Stella who is represented as his governess in the *Journal to Stella* and who is imagined in the intimacy of a 'Bed-chamber' (see Chapter 4). A counterpart for her companion, Mrs Dingley, may then be found in 'the grave elderly Gentlewoman', which has the humorous exaggeration which Swift enjoyed. And the 'Vulgar' would be just the people who praised and supported the Dean as the Drapier. Swift's wit now seems like Shakespeare's 'chervil glove' that looks right whether it is turned inside out or not.

Perhaps neither approach is wholly true or false. There is after all a lack of logic in the idea of a more robust existence in the days of the giant forbears. Why should a giant more robustly stand the dangers referred to? Tiles, stones and boys would all be larger, representing as much danger in either scale of dimensions. As so often, we have to pick our way through the moral points, evaluating and discriminating. In the process we consider the overall effect of the book, its relation to Swift's published writings such as *Contests and Dissensions* (also *A Proposal to Correct the English Tongue*), and its relation to semi-private meanings for intimate friends. These considerations subvert relying on discovering in *Gulliver's Travels* a normative character or voice to act as a continuing reference point for sanity. They warn us against siding, for example, with either Yahoo or

Houyhnhnm. The introduction of the 'little old Treatise' is Swift's helpful pointer on how to read his satire. If it is taken simply as picturesque meditation we will believe, as the Countess of Berkeley did, when Swift read her his parody of a sermon that a broomstick may teach us much about life.

Book III extract

The flying island of Laputa has the ability to land on a rebellious city, crushing the life out of its inhabitants. But, Gulliver tells us, this sanction is not favoured:

> But there is still indeed a more weighty Reason, why the Kings of this Country have been always averse from executing so terrible an Action, unless upon the utmost necessity. For if the Town intended to be destroyed should have in it any tall Rocks, as it generally falls out in the larger Cities, a Scituation probably chosen at first with a View to prevent such a Catastrophe; or if it abound in high Spires or Pillars of Stone, a sudden Fall might endanger the Bottom or under Surface of the Island, which although it consist as I have said of one entire Adamant two hundred Yards thick, might happen to crack by too great a Choque, or burst by approaching too near the Fires from the Houses below, as the Backs both of Iron and Stone will often do in our Chimneys. Of all this the People are well apprized, and understand how far to carry their Obstinacy, where their Liberty or Property is concerned. And the King, when he is highest provoked, and most determined to press a City to Rubbish, orders the Island to descend with great gentleness, out of a Pretence of Tenderness to his People, but indeed for fear of breaking the Adamantine Bottom; in which Case it is the Opinion of all their Philosophers, that the Load-stone could no longer hold it up, and the whole Mass would fall to the Ground.
>
> About three Years before my Arrival among them, while the King was in his Progress over his Dominions there happened an extraordinary Accident which had like to have put a Period to the Fate of that Monarchy, at least as it is now instituted. Lindalino the second City in that Kingdom was the first his Majesty visited in his Progress. Three Days after his Departure, the Inhabitants who had often complained of great Oppressions, shut the Town Gates, seized on the Governor, and with incredible Speed and Labour erected four large Towers, one at every Corner of the City. Upon the Top of each Tower, as well as upon the Rock, they fixed a great Loadstone, and in case their Design should fail they had provided a vast Quantity of the most combustible Fewel,

hoping to burst therewith the adamantine Bottom of the Island, if the Loadstone Project should miscarry.

It was eight Months before the King had perfect Notice that the Lindalinians were in Rebellion. He then commanded that the Island should be wafted over the City. The People were unanimous, and had lain in Store of Provisions, and a great River runs through the middle of the Town. The King hovered over them several Days to deprive them of the Sun and Rain. He ordered many Packthreads to be let down, yet not a Person offered to send up a Petition, but instead thereof, very bold Demands, the Redress of all their Grievances, great Immunitys, the Choice of their own Governor, and other like Exorbitances. Upon which his Majesty commanded all the Inhabitants of the Island to cast great Stones from the lower gallery into the Town; but the Citizens had provided against this Mischief by conveying their Persons and Effects into the four Towers, and other strong Buildings, and Vaults under Ground.

The description of an abortive attempt by the flying island to put down a rebellion in Lindalino is a sustained allegory of the relation between London and Dublin, probably centring on the outcry about the Annesley case and the resistance to the introduction of Wood's halfpence (see Chapter 3). Swift's own feelings are directly involved in the matter when Gulliver describes his first impression of the island as 'the most delicious Spot of Ground in the World'. But while London held the attraction of being the centre of politics and providing the stimulation of the Scriblerians, like Laputa its treatment of Ireland (Balnibarbi) was that of a conqueror. It had already used trade sanctions to advantage its own commerce and, to Swift's eyes, impoverish the Irish. The success of London literally overshadows Dublin as the island hovers depriving them 'of the Sun and Rain' which are essential for good agriculture and healthy living (elsewhere, Swift says such deprivation produces 'dearth and disease'). When this fails, the stones cast down are the policing actions of informers and the intimidations of guardians of the law, such as the Lord Chief Justice Whitshed. But for the island to 'drop directly on their heads' would require a full-scale invasion and occupation of the city which had been attempted in the time of Cromwell but no longer made political sense. Absentee landlords had property in Ireland as the grandees of Laputa had in Balnibarbi, an example of the interdependence of court and country. England required the economy of Ireland for its own needs and although it could perhaps destroy the trade structure, the revolution of 1688 was close enough in memory to imagine what resistance it might provoke: to 'kill the King and all his Servants, and entirely change the Government'.

There are also satisfyingly appropriate parallels in the fantasy of Laputa and the actuality of Ireland. Verisimilitude in the pseudo-science of why the island does not flatten the city is gained by the domestic image of the fireback whose iron casing expands to burst the stone it contains. This shows the dependence of London on Dublin and the false 'Tenderness to his People' of the king. Extrapolated it shows that the fires of religion were what he has most to fear in an alliance between churches, civic authorities and native ruggedness (spires, towers and rocks). In this rebellion the 'People were unanimous, and had lain in Store of Provisions' which recalls the immunity their support gave the Drapier and the juries which refused to be swayed. In the allegory, the Lindalinians derive further support as 'a great River runs through the middle of the Town'. This affords the inhabitants life-giving water when the island deprived them of rain. The actual river in Dublin is the Liffey which James Joyce used later as a punning reference to life itself. It is tempting to think that such a pun was in Swift's mind too, referring to the native vigour of the Dubliner. The 'Exorbitances' of the Lindalinians were demands as reasonable as those of the Dubliners: for 'the Redress of all their Grievances' (such as the imposition of the halfpence) and 'the Choice of their own Governor' (the replacement of the antipathetic Charles Fitzroy, 2nd Duke of Grafton, with Lord Carteret). In the later part of the allegory (not quoted) the king is 'forced to give the Town their own Conditions'. Here there is some licence in the parallel, for while Wood's halfpence were withdrawn, the appointment of Carteret was a piece of luck, resulting from Walpole's wishing to saddle this rival with what seemed an impossible task. And the subservience of the Irish Parliament and other grievances remained.

Although the fiction of a successful Lindalinian rebellion seems a little optimistic when applied to Ireland, it interestingly reflects the closeness of the events to the writing about them and indicates something of Swift's shaping process. He was writing this part of the book on 19 January 1724, when he wrote that he was in the flying island, and it was not until 31 August 1725 that he was convinced that the Drapier had won. This was the last book to be written but was revised to stand as the third (see Chapter 5). Some of the expression here seems to echo language used in the Irish Parliament on 21 September 1725. The king of Laputa professes tenderness and exercises great gentleness. The Irish Parliament was invited to approve King George's 'most mild and gracious government' which after debate they did, also inserting with sly insinuation their approval of his 'great Wisdom'. This victory was a high point which events afterwards showed to be only of a battle and not a campaign. But had this recollection of recent triumph been in the concluding section of

Gulliver's Travels the work would have been a history beginning with Oxford's ministry and the succession of Walpole in the first book, brought up to date in the last with the condition of Ireland after Wood's halfpence and all placed in the greater retrospect afforded by summoning up the ghosts of Agrippa and Aristotle. We do not know what revisions were made in the restructuring but the distaste for the monarch in England takes a sharper edge and insolent meaning at the end of this episode when we are told that the king was forbidden by law 'to leave the island'. This is a reference to a clause in the Act of Settlement of 1701, which George I had repealed in 1715, in order to visit Hanover which he preferred. Swift gives it a sting in saying that the law also included the queen 'till she is past Child-bearing', suggesting doubts of her marital fidelity.

Book IV extract

It is a Maxim among these Lawyers, that whatever hath been done before, may legally be done again: And therefore they take special Care to record all the Decisions formerly made against common Justice, and the general Reason of Mankind. These, under the Name of Precedents they produce as Authoritys to justify the most iniquitous Opinions; and the Judges never fail of decreeing accordingly.

In pleading, they studiously avoid entring into the *Merits* of the Cause; but are loud, violent and tedious in dwelling upon all *Circumstances* which are not to the Purpose. For Instance, in the Case already mentioned; They never desire to know what the Claim or Title my Adversary hath to my *Cow*, but whether the said *Cow* were Red or Black, her Horns long or short; whether the Field I graze her in be round or square, whether she was milked at home or abroad, what Diseases she is subject to, and the like; after which they consult *Precedents*, adjourn the Cause from Time to Time, and in Ten, Twenty, or Thirty Years come to an Issue.

It is likewise to be observed that this Society hath a peculiar Cant and Jargon of their own, that no other Mortal can understand, and wherein all their Laws are written, which they take special Care to multiply; whereby they have wholly confounded the very Essence of Truth and Falsehood, of Right and Wrong; so that it will take Thirty Years to decide whether the Field left me by my Ancestors for six Generations, belongs to me or to a Stranger three hundred Miles off.

In the Tryal of Persons accused for Crimes against the State the Method is much more short and commendable: The Judge first sends to sound the Disposition of those in Power, after which he can easily hang or save the Criminal, strictly preserving all due Forms of Law.

> Here my Master interposing, said it was a Pity, that Creatures endowed with such prodigious Abilities of Mind as these Lawyers by the Description I gave of them must certainly be, were not encouraged to be Instructors of others in Wisdom and Knowledge. In answer to which I assured his Honour, that in all Points out of their own Trade they were the most ignorant and stupid Generation among us, the most despicable in common Conversation, avowed Enemys to all Knowledge and Learning, and equally disposed to pervert the general Reason of Mankind in every other Subject of Discourse, as in that of their Profession.

Swift's attack on lawyers is undisguised. There have been occasions in previous books where indignation against abuses surfaces in unmistakeable criticism. The king of Brobdingnag concludes that Gulliver has been praising 'pernicious little vermin' and in Laputa rewarding wisdom, capacity and virtue or setting a tax on the chastity of women is represented as patently absurd in the corrupt world we live in. In the fourth book this note is more sustained and the satire is often diatribe. Gulliver later tells the reader that after the rational analysis of his country with his Master he considered the 'Honour of my own Kind not worth managing'. As he becomes more anxious to identify with the horses, using the skins of Yahoos, hating the smell of his wife and stabling in the hay, he loses credibility and value as a critic. But this passage is before such excess has mounted up and although there is a heightened and simplified account of the law the argument hits home as a piece of good propaganda.

The account of obfuscation through circumstantial argument is necessarily simplified to something that can be understood by the layman – quibbling about the horns of a cow and the shape of its field. The reader, amused by the *reductio ad absurdum*, can recognise that this has its unfairness but that it is compensated by the truth of cases where complainants had been ruined at law and lawyers had prospered. Dickens was to make the same charge as a leading theme in his novel, *Bleak House*. Gulliver felt he could expertly advise the king of Brobdingnag on the law, having been himself almost ruined in a 'suit in chancery'. Behind the criticism is discontent with the adversarial nature of the legal system. The king of Brobdingnag asked pointedly whether lawyers 'pleaded for and against the same Cause'. In this passage the fact that they do lends credence to the sense of their being unprincipled in determining what is 'legal' in opposition to 'common Justice'.

Their 'peculiar Cant and Jargon' in Swift's day was more than the necessary technicalities of a particular branch of learning. The highly formal language did oppress and confuse the non-specialist and the judicial system was intimidating. It wasn't until much later –

1873 – that the Judicature Act reformed the Court of Chancery to bring it within the Supreme Court of Judicature. This was the beginning of the process which consolidated separate courts each with its own peculiar machinery, to harmonise and simplify systems of pleading and put them all under the same rule of law. In Ireland such complication had the additional disadvantage of the final appeal being situated in England. Later Swift was to write in *A Short View of Ireland* (1728) that Ireland failed the test of 'being Governed only by Laws made with their own Consent, for otherwise they are not a free People. And therefore all Appeals for Justice, or Applications for Favour or Preferment to another Country, are so many grievous Impoverishments.'

If the system was defective, corrupt men made it worse. Lawyers are dismissed here as 'the most ignorant and stupid generation among us, the most despicable in common Conversation, avowed Enemys to all Knowledge and Learning'. The judges who rise from these ranks are implicated as being the worst. The political trial was much in Swift's mind, noting the 'judge first sends to sound the Disposition of those in Power' and remembering, no doubt, his enemy in the Drapier trial, Lord Chief Justice Whitshed, whose coach bore the hypocritical Latin motto: *Libertas et natale solum* ('liberty and my country first').

A Modest Proposal, 1729

The dense working and controlled modulation of the tone of *A Modest Proposal* is best seen in a number of short excerpts taken at some distance from each other. In some isolation from the development of the argument they show the variety of its satiric method. Part of Swift's concern is to establish information about the condition of Ireland. He does this through the mouth of a heartless 'projector' who begins with a statement of facts:

> The number of souls in this kingdom being usually reckoned one million and a half, of these I calculate there may be about two hundred thousand couple whose wives are breeders, from which number I subtract thirty thousand couples who are able to maintain their own children, although I apprehend there cannot be so many under *the present distresses of the kingdom,* but this being granted, there will remain an hundred and seventy thousand breeders. I again subtract fifty thousand for those who miscarry, or whose children die by accident, or disease within a year.

The statistical account gives the scale of the issue and confronts the sceptical and over-comfortable English traveller with a substratum of solid fact, endorsing that years of famine entail years of living at subsistence level in between. English pamphlets had asserted the contrary, referring to 'the Quays almost cover'd w[i]th Hogsheads of Wine' and the 'fertil Arable Fields, with Flocks of Cattle'. The 'present distresses' of Ireland are implied in the collection of data by the unimpassioned observer: the reduction in numbers from the effects of miscarriage, accidents and disease. From these we can infer that Ireland suffers from wringing poverty, producing malnutrition, and from the listlessness of living without hope. Swift follows this up with a mention of possible remedies, most of which he had recommended without success, such as the *Proposal for the Universal Use of Irish Manufacture*. The failure of these to be adopted gives force to the savage plan to cannibalise as the only option left. In preparation for this transition, the Irish poor are first referred to as 'souls', often used as a variation for 'individuals'. But it also reminds us of their religious worth and this meaning is sharpened when they come to be discussed in terms of livestock as 'breeders'.

In the moderate tones of the proposer a savage process is recommended. Such words as 'flay' and 'carcass', applied to the idea of flaying a human being, become more repellent when the speaker is unconscious of their enormity. And his unconcern suggests that his English readers will be similarly minded in accepting his 'reasonable' proposal.

> Those who are more thrifty (*as I must confess the times require*) may flay the carcass; the skin of which artificially dressed, will make admirable *gloves for ladies*, and *summer boots for fine gentlemen*.

The common excuse for not giving charitable donations that times are difficult the proposer accepts without demur ('as I confess the times require') leaving the reader to contrast those wealthy enough to be ladies and gentlemen, wearing fine gloves and summer boots, with the miserable and hungry poor of Ireland. Forcing us to consider the suppleness of the child's skin, suitable enough for glove leather, Swift shows us their tender vulnerability.

In the midst of such horrific details the narrator blithely indulges in speculation, designed to show he is a loyal Protestant.

> Infants' flesh will be in season throughout the year, but more plentiful in *March*, and a little before and after, for we are told by a grave author, and eminent French physician, that *fish being a prolific diet*, there are more children born in *Roman Catholic countries* about nine months after *Lent*, than at any other season; therefore reckoning a year after *Lent*, the markets will be more glutted than usual, because the number of *Popish infants* is at least three to one in this kingdom, and therefore it will have one other collateral advantage by lessening the number of *Papists* among us.

The pseudo-science that eating fish encourages sexual activity and therefore a higher birth-rate is grist to his mill, as he will snatch opportunistically at any reasoning to advance his proposal. It was a folk-belief in Shakspeare's day that fish-eating encouraged lechery and in the eighteenth-century slaves were not permitted to marry in the belief that promiscuity would increase the population of slaves. So the idea did not seem so unlikely. But the application of it to 'lessening the number of *Papists*' betrays a concern for trying out the proposal beyond remedying the current distresses. Roman Catholicism was not one of the distresses the philanthropist needed to relieve but a bigoted Englishman, looking to self-interest, would enjoy the idea of reducing their number, in addition to the usual methods of conversion or emigration. Swift himself considered the dissenters as a greater threat to the Anglican church than Roman Catholics (see Chapter 1). There is probably a play on the meaning of the 'grave author' as one who is a serious writer and one who opens up the way to the grave.

Not all Swift's criticism is directed at the English. The Irish who are imagined to accept the proposal bear some blame:

> *Sixthly*, this would be a great inducement to marriage, which all wise nations have encouraged either by rewards, or enforced by laws and penalties. It would increase the care and tenderness of mothers toward their children, when they were sure of a settlement for life to the poor babes, provided in some sort by the public to their annual profit instead of expense. We should see an honest emulation among the married women, *which of them could bring the fattest child to the market.* Men would become as *fond* of their wives, during the time of their pregnancy, as they are now of their *mares* in foal, their *cows* in calf, or *sows* when they are ready to farrow; nor offer to beat or kick them (as is too *frequent* a practice) for fear of a miscarriage.

Swift did not romanticise the condition of the poor, noting that there were thieves under the age of six in Cavan. But the lack of family commitment (offering 'to beat or kick them as is too *frequent* a practice') leading to what he later calls 'animosities and factions' and lack of patriotism, wherein the Irish 'differ even from LAPLANDERS and the inhabitants of TOPINAMBOO', is suggested to be the result of tough circumstances and probably contributing to their subjection to the English.

The tone of reason in this passage is marked by the numbering of points ('Sixthly') and the enlightened survey of different cultures ('all wise nations'). The language of humaneness: 'marriage, wise, tenderness, honest' collides with the brutish 'in foal, in calf, farrow, beat, kick'. Civilisation should raise humans from animal necessity

213

to social kindness. But given the purpose of butchering and eating the children such civilisation as is presented here is decidedly illusory. The reassuring words tremble over an unacceptable horror so that 'a settlement for life' which is offered as 'a prudent provision' colours into 'a bargain in which life is forfeit' and the 'poor' children are seen as not only 'impecunious' but in a 'sorry state' which is heart-breaking.

Part Three

Reference Section

Biographical list

These biographical notes give further information about individuals mentioned in this book. They supplement the histories which have been related in discussing aspects of Swift and in order to assist the reader to combine the two the index has been arranged to recapitulate the previous detail in summary. Two classes of individual are noted here. Contemporaries are included who played a significant part in Swift's life (as described here) and whose own histories have a richness which indicates the interest of other aspects of the period. Some non-contemporary writers whom Swift read are also described in order to give a ready reference to his literary context. Where notes interlock and another entry should also be seen, there is the mark '(q.v.)'.

JOSEPH ADDISON, 1672–1719. Essayist, poet, politician. Educated at the Charterhouse where, 1686, he made the friendship of Steele (q.v.), and at Oxford University where he became fellow of Magdalen College, 1698–1711. A fluent classicist he wrote a number of Latin poems designed to show his allegiance to William III and one, on the peace of Ryswick, dedicated to Charles Montague, later the Earl of Halifax, secured a pension of £300 per annum for him (1698). However, he enjoyed this for only a year since William died in 1701. In 1699 he spent a year in France learning the language and meeting the philosopher, Malebranche, and the critic and poet, Boileau, following this with a tour of Italy (1700–01) which gave rise to his poem, *A Letter from Italy*, which was acclaimed. In London he became a member of the Whig Kitcat Club and in 1704 wrote the *Campaign* celebrating Marlborough's victory at Blenheim. Godolphin made him under-secretary for state and he was appointed commissioner of appeals, 1704–08. In 1709 he was secretary to Wharton, lord-lieutenant of Ireland. At the coffee-house, Buttons, he presided over a company which included Swift, Steele, Pope (q.v.), Tickell, Davenant and Ambrose Philips. He was a Member of Parliament 1708–19. He assisted Steele in the later numbers of *The Tatler* and wrote 274 numbers of their joint periodical, *The Spectator*. He was largely responsible for the development of the character of Sir Roger de Coverley in its pages and wrote papers on 'The Pleasures of the Imagination' which are interesting to students of the aesthetics of the time. In 1713 he finished his play, *Cato*, which probably had been inspired in Venice at the turn of the century. His espousal of

Tickell's translation of Homer and of Philips' pastoral verse, both in opposition to Pope's rising star, incurred Pope's displeasure and satiric attention. With the return of the Whigs he became under-secretary to Sunderland (1714) and fellow secretary of state (1717). He retired in 1718 and, after a growing disaffection with Steele over his failure to repay loans, fell out with him concerning his attack on Sunderland's bill to limit the peerage.

QUEEN ANNE, 1665–1714. Queen of Great Britain and Ireland 1702–14, younger daughter of James II by his first wife and last of the Stuarts, under whose reign the party system of Whig and Tory evolved, through political managers, and the power of the crown was reduced. Born with a sickly constitution and suffering various maladies through her life, including the small-pox, she adopted a strict orthodox Anglicanism and proved obstinate and dull in her judgements. She married (1683) Prince George of Denmark (died 1708), soldier son of Frederick III of Denmark. By him she had 18 pregnancies; none of her children survived into adulthood.

DR JOHN ARBUTHNOT, 1667–1735. Physician in ordinary to Queen Anne, fellow of the Royal Society (1704), wit and writer. Key member of the Scriblerus group, epitomising constancy in friendship, humour and compassion. Befriended Swift 1710. Invented the character of John Bull in a Tory satire promoting peace and gave a major impetus to the *Memoirs of Martinus Scriblerus*.

FRANCIS ATTERBURY, 1662–1732. A staunch Tory, friend to Swift and defender of Sacheverell (see Chapter 2). When he was Bishop of Rochester and Dean of Westminster, he was accused of complicity in a Jacobite plot, 1722, and exiled the following year when he joined the Pretender. Swift satirised in Book III of *Gulliver's Travels* the proceedings taken by Walpole (q.v.) to implicate the bishop as an example of the authoritarian single party rule which had earlier impeached Oxford and Bolingbroke (1715) and at every opportunity had stigmatised the opposition as Jacobite. The details of the case against Atterbury lent themselves to ridicule, since much was made of a lame spaniel named Harlequin sent him by the Pretender and of some letters hidden in the bishop's privy. No evidence was brought forward at the time to directly prove Atterbury's involvement, although later historians have now done so.

RICHARD BENTLEY, 1662–1742. Classical scholar and critic. A man of considerable learning whose combative and derisive manner earned him many enemies. From 1683–9 he was tutor to the son of Dr Stillingfleet, dean of St Paul's, and protector of Anglicanism in the

Restoration. In 1691 he established his reputation with annotations to the *Chronicles of Malelas* which mapped out a wide range of classical references and literary examples which helped to establish a chronology of ancient times. The following year he gave eight lectures in a series instituted by Robert Boyle to prove 'christian religion against notorious infidels' which were remarkable for drawing on the ideas of Newton with whom he corresponded. He made improvements to the organisation of the Cambridge University Press and was appointed, 1694, keeper of the royal libraries and fellow of the Royal Society. The following year he became chaplain in ordinary to the king. He was drawn into the controversy regarding the Ancients and Moderns (see the episode of *The Battle of the Books* in Chapter 1) by slighting remarks of Charles Boyle in his edition of *The Letters of Phalaris*, which implied (unjustifiably) that he had withdrawn permission for his collator to examine the original. In 1700 he was appointed Master of Trinity College, Cambridge, and vice-chancellor of the university. The rest of his life at Trinity was marked by dissension with the fellows for having infringed the statutes and for his arrogant and absolutist manner. Twice he was put on trial before the college visitor (the office of the Bishop of Ely). In 1714 an adverse verdict was interrupted by the death of the visitor and also of Queen Anne. In 1734 he was sentenced to be deprived of the mastership but successive vice-masters refused to carry out the punishment. During his time at Trinity Bentley did much to improve the academic standing of the college. His edition of Milton's *Paradise Lost* was based on the idea that the amanuensis of the blind poet introduced mistakes and interpolated bad verses.

GEORGE BERKELEY, BISHOP OF CLOYNE, 1685–1753. Philosopher and cleric. Educated at Kilkenny College and Trinity College, Dublin, but met Swift in London in 1713 and others of his circle. 1728 unsuccessfully tried to set up a missionary college in Bermuda. Wrote his *Treatise* in 1710 (revised 1734) and a number of other philosophical works. Took issue with Newton's calculus, then called 'fluxions', in *The Analyst* (1734).

BOLINGBROKE: see HENRY ST JOHN.

CHARLES II, 1630–1685. King of Great Britain and Ireland. Elder son of Charles I. In 1660 he was restored to the throne after a short interregnum following the death of Cromwell in 1658. Extravagant and licentious he set the tone of a libertine court but he was also initially skilful in managing his own pro-French and pro-Roman Catholic policies. However, public feeling was whipped into anti-Catholic fear. The Great Fire of London, 1666, was rumoured to have been started by Catholics and in 1678 there was uncovered a supposed Popish Plot to kill the king and substitute his Catholic brother, James (q.v.). On the false information of Titus Oates, 35 Catholics were executed. Legislation was passed to exclude Catholics from Parliament and measures were discussed to exclude any Catholic from succession to the throne. With financial support from Louis XIV, Charles was able to prorogue at will the Parliament which he would otherwise have needed to vote him money. But after three dissolutions he was forced to rule without Parliament from 1681–85 to avoid its further determined confrontation.

JOHN CHURCHILL, DUKE OF MARLBOROUGH, 1650–1722. Commander of British forces. In 1672 he served under the Duke of Monmouth, illegitimate son of Charles II, who became the Protestant candidate of some Whigs to exclude the Catholic Duke of York (James II) from succession to the throne. Followed him into exile and in his illegal return to Scotland, 1679. He married the vigorous and dominating Lady-in-Waiting to Princess Anne, Sarah Jennings, 1678, and from then they contrived together their mutually successful future careers. He switched sides to accept a colonelcy under Charles II and became Baron Churchill and major-general under James II, defeating Monmouth's rebellion at Sedgemoor (1685). In 1688 as lieutenant-general he assured both James II and William of Orange of his loyalty, defecting to William's side at Axminster and progressing to Earl of Marlborough in 1689. He continued to play both sides: leading an expedition against James in Ireland (1690), obtaining a pardon from James the following year and betraying to him in 1694 the British expedition against the French in Brest. In 1692 he was dismissed and his wife and Princess Anne fled Queen Mary's displeasure. Mary died in 1694 and a gradual reconciliation with William permitted Marlborough to resume all his titles in 1698. Marriages of two of his daughters, respectively to Godolphin (1698) and the son of Lord Sunderland (1701), strengthened his political position. The accession of Anne in 1702 brought him the dukedom of Marlborough and the post of captain-general of the forces fighting against the French. It also brought further honours for his wife. He successfully urged that England should play a principal and not auxiliary role in the war. He conducted a series of brilliant campaigns, co-ordinating a disparate set of allies. He captured Bonn (1703), and won victories in Bavaria: Blenheim (1704), and in The Netherlands: Ramillies, (1706), Oudenarde (1708), and Malplaquet (1709). He was rewarded for the success at Blenheim by the queen with the lands of Woodstock and the construction of a palace and by the Emperor Leopold with the princedom of Mindelheim. However, at Malplaquet the allies suffered greater losses than the French forces and Abigail Hill (later

Mrs Masham) was supplanting the Duchess of Marlborough in the queen's confidence. In 1710 Harley's ministry began and the Duchess overplayed her hand by hectoring the queen too many times. She and then her husband were dismissed in 1711, leaving England in 1712 to settle eventually in Frankfurt. When George I became king, 1714, Marlborough was restored to his former posts but took a less active role after suffering two paralytic strokes in 1716. Leslie Stephen wrote of him as 'supreme as a man of business, he allowed no scruples to interfere with the main chance'. His frequent changes of allegiance may also be seen to reflect the volatility of the politics of his time.

WILLIAM CONGREVE, 1670–1729. Playwright. Fellow student with Swift at Kilkenny school and Trinity College, Dublin. Initially studied for law but turned to drama and achieved fame with *The Old Bachelor* (1693) a social comedy which Steele noticed in the same issue of *The Tatler* in which he introduced Swift's *A Description of Morning*, with words which characterise the social comedy for which Congreve became famed: 'The Part of *Fondlewife* is a lively Image of the unseasonable Fondness of Age.' Several successful comedies followed, reflecting wittily, often with bawdy exchanges, on sexual intrigue and marriage in the fashionable world.

ABRAHAM COWLEY, 1618–67. Poet. Wrote an epic on the Biblical King David, the *Davideis* (1656), but especially known in the eighteenth century for his love poems and odes which introduced a fashion for irregular metrication as the sign of passion or conviction. The knotty, conversational and elaborated conceits of poems, such as *To the Royal Society*, appealed as models to Swift in his early public verse. Cowley embraced the advancement of contemporary science and praised the Royal Society's historian Thomas Sprat, who later wrote a complimentary life of him prefixed to his works.

DANIEL DEFOE, 1660/1–1731. Prolific writer, who excelled in the detailed realism of his accounts of contemporary society in fictions such as *Robinson Crusoe* (1719), *Moll Flanders* and *A Journal of the Plague Year* (1722). Although he fought with Monmouth he joined William III and satirised British insularity in *A True-Born Englishman* (1701) and also Tory intolerance with an ironical pamphlet to stamp out Non-conformity called *The Shortest Way with Dissenters* (1702). For this he was pilloried and imprisoned. From 1703 to 1714 Harley employed him to discover public opinion and to assist, probably without Swift's knowledge, the Tory propaganda machine with his pamphlets. His last works drew on his extensive knowledge from his travels of the state of Great Britain and of the commercial world.

JOHN DONNE, 1573–1631. Poet and divine. Studied law and entered the service of Essex and Raleigh. 1601 married secretly, Ann More, a niece by marriage of his employer, Sir Thomas Egerton, Lord Keeper of the Great Seal. Disgraced and possibly debarred from office by suspicion of Catholic tendencies, he entered the Anglican church in 1615, becoming Dean of St Paul's in 1621. Celebrated for his passionate and metaphysical love and religious poetry, he was also a powerful preacher.

JOHN DRYDEN, 1631–1700. Poet, dramatist and critic. Prolific writer, excelling in tragi-comedy. Some of his plays were adaptations of Shakespeare. His satirical poetry reflected on the politics of the period and his religious poems went to the heart of the Anglican/Catholic schism, defending first one side and then the other in separate poems before and after his conversion to Rome. His critical essays often arose as defensive prefaces to his works. He was made Poet Laureate, 1688, and Historiographer Royal, 1670. Alexander Pope (q.v.) acknowledged him as a major influence on his own writing and Swift seems to have vied to rival him, as his distant cousin.

JOHN GAY, 1685–1732. Poet and dramatist. His poetry is gently mocking, following in the paths of Pope and Swift in their urban/urbane guise. His ballad opera, *The Beggars' Opera*, 1728, which mocked fashionable society with a mirror of itself among the rogues, had an additional common touch in being set to the music of popular songs. He also wrote the libretto for Handel's touching and graceful *Acis and Galatea*, 1718.

GEORGE I, 1660–1727. George Lewis, king of Great Britain and Ireland (1714–27). The son of the granddaughter of James I, Sophia, he married his cousin, Sophia Dorothea of Celle in 1682. By her he had a son, George Augustus, the future George II (q.v.) in 1683. Alleging her infidelity in 1696, he divorced her and had her confined in a castle at Ahlden until her death, in 1726. He fought under Leopold I at the siege of Vienna, 1683, (see Chapter 2) and gained the reputation of a leader with considerable military knowledge and personal courage. Marlborough (q.v.) as captain-general of the forces fighting Louis XIV visited him in 1704 and 1705, winning his confidence and crucially his support for the Whigs' war policy and his later dependence on them. (George had no English so they conversed in Latin.) After George was made Elector of Hanover in 1708, Marlborough kept in touch and turned him against Tory overtures, such as their offer of giving him command of the forces of the Low Countries. When Queen Anne (q.v.) expressed displeasure (1714) at his requirement that his son, George Augustus, should sit in the House of Lords by virtue of his title of Duke of Cambridge, he saw in this the hand of Bolingbroke and it completed his alienation from the Tories. He was an unpopular king and preferred his links with Hanover. This led to his total reliance on Walpole (q.v.) in 1721 to persuade Parliament to rescind the clause of the Act of Settlement which prohibited his visits there. In addition he appeared awkward, selfish, over-privileged and infatuated. He heaped honours on his two German mistresses who became respectively the Duchess of Kendal, 1719, and the Countess Darlington, 1721.

GEORGE II, 1683–1760. George Augustus, king of Great Britain and Ireland (1727–60). By contrast with his father, he could speak in French and English, as well as Latin. He was also soldierly, fighting at the battle of Oudenarde (1708) and being the last British king to command in battle – at Dettingen (1743). In 1705 he married Wilhelmina Charlotte Caroline of Brandenburg-Anspach (1683–1737), usually known as Caroline of Anspach or, after 1726, Queen Caroline. An ambitious and intelligent woman, she proved to be a major influence on his reign, particularly when acting as regent during his absences in Hanover and in her tolerance and manipulation of his succession of mistresses. These included (from 1716 to 1734) Henrietta Howard, Countess of Suffolk (see Chapter 4), who was installed at court after his accession. His father's dislike he returned, probably disaffected by his father's treatment of his mother. As a result of one of their quarrels in 1717 he was banished from the court of St James and set up in 1718 with Caroline an alternative and brilliant court in Leicester House, Leicester Fields. This enabled Walpole (q.v.) to exert leverage when out of office and to gain the lifelong support of Caroline. (Walpole supported George Augustus's opposition to Sunderland's Bill to limit the peerage in 1719 which would have restricted the future king's room for conferring privileges and as the price of steering George Lewis's amendment to the Act of Settlement – see entry for George I – he imposed a cold reconciliation between the two.) On his accession George II identified Walpole as one of his father's ministers and tried to do without him but within 24 hours reinstated him as the result of the persuasion of Caroline and in recognition of Walpole's ability to lead Parliament to increase the moneys paid from the civil list to the king and queen.

ROBERT HARLEY, FIRST EARL OF OXFORD, 1661–1724. Swift literature calls him either 'Harley' or 'Oxford'. He entered Parliament in 1689 and from 1690–1711 he represented New Radnor in Herefordshire. He was made Speaker of the Commons in 1701 in recognition of his formidable Parliamentary knowledge and acted as a moderate, combining Whig and Tory elements. His belief in Parliamentary process was early attested by his successful introduction of a Bill to force elections every three years (Triennial Act, 1695) and his reduction of the size of the army in 1698. His most powerful period in government began with his appointment as secretary of state (North) which led to the Tory Junto (see Chapter 2) to engineer his resignation in 1708. In 1711 he returned as the chief minister and formed an administration with Henry St John (q.v.). He was created First Earl of Oxford on 23 May 1711. His masterly handling of political propaganda, involving Swift and Defoe, is discussed in Chapter 2. Dismissed in 1714, he courageously refused to flee and was imprisoned in the Tower (1715) for two years and was then released when the attempted impeachment collapsed. King George I's animosity to him excepted him from the Act of Grace, denying him access to court politics. For a further two years he debated in the House of Lords, before ceasing to participate in Parliamentary activity.

JAMES II, 1633–1701. King of Great Britain and Ireland, 1685–88. Younger son of Charles I. Schemed to establish an absolute monarchy and Roman Catholicism as the state religion. Installed Catholics as army officers and as replacement fellows at Magdalen College, Oxford, and tried several measures to repeal the Test Acts which barred non-Anglicans from public office, ostensibly as his attempt to introduce toleration for both dissenters and Catholics. In December 1688, following the invasion of William of Orange (q.v.) he fled to France from where he invaded Ireland with French troops in 1690. His defeat by William in the Battle of the Boyne, 11 July 1690, led to his permanent exile back in France.

BEN JONSON, 1572/3–1637. Poet and playwright. Formidably learned, Jonson was nevertheless accomplished in his handling of dramatic suspense and in the fertility of his linguistic invention, ranging from racy colloquialism to the imaginatively powerful, especially in *Volpone* (1605) and *The Alchemist* (1610). He also wrote masques which exhibit grace, elegance and tenderness. All these qualities may be found in his poems, some of which celebrate the virtues of hospitality, friendship and social stability. In his enjoyment of his works, Swift may well have identified with the variety of tone which Jonson had at his command: subtle, moral, witty and sometimes crude.

THOMAS NASHE, 1567–1601. Popular writer and pamphleteer. A lively Grub Street writer who adopted many styles and entertained with his iconoclastic attacks on stuffy academicism. In his pamphlet war with the Cambridge scholar, Gabriel Harvey, which had to be stopped by authorities, he mixed conversational rudery with learned embellishment, delighting in the medium of the print, wittily exposing the methods of the hack writer.

OXFORD: see ROBERT HARLEY

ALEXANDER POPE, 1688–1744. The major poet in England of the first half of the eighteenth century. Pope wrote with extraordinary facility, developing the range of the heroic couplet. This form had lines of ten syllables with five stresses in the regular pattern of 'unstressed/ stressed' and the lines rhymed in pairs. Pope used it to encompass the epigram and verse paragraphs of imaginative power, wit, great beauty, conversational ease or withering invective. He wrote pastorals; translated Homer into verse; composed morally instructive poems; and created satires in the manner of Dryden (q.v.) or of the classical writer Horace in such a way as to produce an original work, whose exhilaration partly depends on understanding the allusions to its literary tradition.

SIR RICHARD STEELE, 1672–1729. Writer, playwright, politician. Born in Dublin and educated at the Charterhouse where he and Addison (q.v.) became friends, he studied at Merton College, Oxford, which he left, 1694, without taking a degree. He became a gentleman-volunteer in the life-guards under the second Duke of Ormonde and rose to the rank of captain. In 1700 he seriously wounded Captain Kelley in a duel and he became disaffected with the military way of life. He wrote four unsuccessful plays between 1701 and 1705, two of which were based on French models: *The Lying Lover* (Corneille) and *The Tender Husband* (Molière). In 1705 he married Margaret Stretch, an heiress to land in Barbados, who died in 1706. In 1707 he married Mary Scurlock whom he called his 'Ruler' and 'Absolute Governess'. Often in debt he secured a number of posts: gentleman waiter to George, Prince of Denmark (1706), gazetteer (1707), commissioner of stamps (1710). In 1709 he began the periodical *The Tatler* which came out three times a week, writing 188 of its 271 numbers, and was aided by Addison. This ceased in 1711, probably to placate Harley (q.v.) who had deprived him of the post of gazetteer for his anti-government writings. With Addison he brought out *The Spectator* from 1711 to 1712, writing 236 of its numbers. He attacked the Tories in *The Englishman's Thanks to the Duke of Marlborough*, August 1713, and was elected MP for Stockbridge the following March. Charged with seditious libel he was expelled from the House of Commons 16 days later. A string of short-lived periodicals were begun and abandoned by him: *The Guardian* (1713), *The Lover* and *The Reader* (April-May, 1713), *The Englishman* (1714), *Town Talk*, *The Tea Table*, *Chit-Chat* (March 1718). His attack on the peerage bill in his periodical *The Plebian* (1719) was answered by Addison in *The Old Whig* and the two became estranged. The accession of George I (q.v.) brought him rewards: the offices of Justice of the Peace, deputy lieutenant for the county of Middlesex, surveyor to the royal stables at Hampton Court, supervisor to the Theatre Royal at Drury Lane. In 1715 he became MP for Boroughbridge, Yorkshire, and in 1722 MP for Wendover, Buckinghamshire. His last play, *The Conscious Lovers*, had some success but he fell more into debt and retired to Wales.

HENRY ST JOHN, FIRST VISCOUNT BOLINGBROKE, 1678–1751. Known in Swift literature as either 'St John' or 'Bolingbroke'. He served in Parliament, 1701–1708 as MP for Wootton Bassett in Wiltshire. For two years he retired from politics and then joined Harley (q.v.) to become secretary of state (North) in 1710. Created First Viscount Bolingbroke in June 1712, he was a 'root and branch' Tory, meaning that he sought to exclude all Whigs from office. This and his own personal ambition led to his attempts to dislodge Harley. He too was dismissed (1715) and joined in France the Old Pretender, James Edward, son of James II (q.v.) in the hope of stirring rebellion against the House of Hanover in favour of the Stuart line of royal descent. In 1723 he bought his pardon and returned to England and purchased the restoration of his titles in 1725. He wrote on philosophy and a theory of government (derived from Harley). His discussions with Alexander Pope (q.v.) and Swift are reflected in their writings.

EDMUND WALLER, 1606–87. Poet. Wrote in the cavalier cause and was celebrated in the eighteenth century for his graceful and complimentary strain of love poetry. His smooth simplicity accords with part of Swift's concern to purify the English language and his exaltation of his mistress provides a foil for Swift's poems to Vanessa and Stella.

ROBERT WALPOLE, 1676–1745. Politician, usually seen as the first prime minister of Great Britain. Twenty stone MP for King's Lynn, Norfolk, he ensured the Whig majority by branding the Tories Jacobites, helped by the unsuccessful rebellion of 1715, and by passing the Septennial Act (1716), which allowed Parliaments to run for seven years before a general election. He controlled his party position by reducing the circle of powerful ministers to an intimate cabinet of five or six, by his ascendancy over successive kings (George I and George II q.v.) which enabled him to dispense patronage effectively, and by his common touch and effective oratory. He found means of sidelining able and independent-minded rivals within the Whig ranks: denying office to Pulteney, sending Carteret to Ireland and blocking the foreign policies of Townshend.

WILLIAM III, PRINCE OF ORANGE, 1650–1702. Defended the United Provinces, which included Holland, against the expansion of Louis XIV, 1672–88. In 1688, intended to invade Britain which was increasingly supporting the French when he was invited by influential Whigs to curb the excesses of James II (q.v.) who eventually was deemed to have 'abdicated'. William was related to the Stuart dynasty through his mother, the elder daughter of Charles I, and by his marriage (1677) to Mary the elder daughter of James II by his first wife. When the throne was offered to them both he insisted on ruling with equal status as king and not as consort. Successfully removed the threat of James II's return and through mixed ministries at first and then with the Whig war party prosecuted the campaign against France. His wife, Queen Mary II, died in 1694.

Gazetteer

Ireland

Kilkenny

Kilkenny Castle and its grounds are open to visitors. Within are portraits of the Butler family dating back to the fourteenth century.

St Canice's Cathedral an Anglicisation of the Irish 'Cainneach' (pronounced 'Kenny') still has the ancient Round Tower (31 metres) standing by.

Kilkenny College in Lower St John Street is a later building (1780) than the school Swift attended.

Dublin

7 Hoey's Court where Swift was born was on the corner of Werburgh Street and Ship Street. A plaque by the castle gate marks the spot.

St Patrick's Cathedral. In Swift's time the cathedral had no steeple and has been much restored since. The west end of the nave has Swift's bust and the epitaph he composed with the famous phrase of his 'saeva indignatio' ('fierce indignation'), a memorial to Stella and the graves of Swift (marked by a simple lozenge-shaped brass plate) and of Stella. The north transept has Swift's corner containing items associated with him. There is a movable wooden pulpit from which he preached, reminiscent of his description of a tub; his altar table from Laracor; and a case with some of his publications and his death mask. (The north transept in Swift's day was separate and used as the church of St Nicholas Without. He unsuccessfully tried to have his fellow Scriblerian, Thomas Parnell, installed as its priest.) In the north choir aisle there is a black marble monument to the Duke of Schomberg which Swift and his chapter had erected, with a Latin inscription attacking the duke's relations for leaving it to strangers to honour the hero of the Battle of the Boyne. In the south transept there is Swift's grateful and affectionate memorial to his servant, Alexander McGee ('in memory of his discretion, fidelity and diligence').

Marsh's Library was designed by Sir William Robinson and founded in 1702. It stands near to the deanery (rebuilt after Swift's day). Although Swift felt Archbishop Narcissus Marsh had obstructed his career, he refused an opportunistic attempt by some of the clergy to torpedo the foundation. Characteristically he stood aloof from both sides, agreeing that there was a danger that the funding of the first Librarian verged on simony but refusing to oppose its being built on a dubious procedural technicality. It contains Swift's own copy of Clarendon's *History of the Great Rebellion* with his pencilled notes, some of which attack the Scots.

St Stephen's Green, which Swift, inviting Stella to live in Dublin, recommended to her as having the 'finest walking gravel in Europe', was improved by Ormonde to the current shape but the Georgian buildings date from a time later than Swift and it has undergone considerable alteration in layout.

Trinity College in Swift's day comprised a quadrangle (1593) and Marsh's chapel and hall. The oldest building which survives now is the Old Library, built between 1712 and 1732 to the design of Thomas Burgh.

Parliament House, now the Bank of Ireland, built in 1729 is opposite Trinity College and is mentioned in Swift's attack on Irish parliamentarians in *A Character, Panegyric and Description of the Legion Club*:

> As I stroll the city, oft I
> Spy a building large and lofty,
> Not a bow-shot from the College,
> Half a globe from sense and knowledge.

Steevens Hospital, founded by the will of Dr Richard Steevens, a Dublin physician, in 1721, opened in 1733. Stella's will funded the chaplain for this hospital which was already being constructed at her death and for which Swift acted as trustee and then governor. It is near the corner of Steeven's Lane and St John's Road West.

St Patrick's Hospital, Steeven's Lane, designed by George Semple, opened in 1757. Swift endowed its foundation in his will. *Verses on the Death of Dr Swift* refer to his bequest for it thus:

> He gave the little wealth he had,
> To build a house for fools and mad:
> And showed by one satiric touch,
> No nation wanted it so much

Meath

Laracor near Trim still has Swift's little church but it has been converted into a private dwelling and is not open to the public.

Cavan

Quilca (Quilcagh) the home of Dr Thomas Sheridan has been mainly rebuilt and is not open to the public.

Kildare

Celbridge, is a village 13 miles west of Dublin where Vanessa made her home in Celbridge Abbey, now owned by a religious order (viewing by permission). It was remodelled in the late eighteenth century.

England

London

A plaque on the corner of Fountain Court and the Strand marks the Fountain Tavern which Swift visited. Although the streets in which Swift lived remain, little of the early eighteenth-century housing remains after Regency (Regent Street) and Victorian improvements. Some idea of the domestic architecture may be had by looking at an almost perfect range of contemporary houses (*c.* 1704) at Queen Anne's Gate on the south side of St James's Park. By walking from Leicester Square (formerly 'Fields') to Suffolk Street (just off Trafalgar Square) and then to St James Street it is still possible to get a sense of the proximity to St James and to imagine the closeness of his London. (Similarly it is still possible to travel along much of the old Watling Street and the coach road to Chester, using the A5–A51–A534–A51.)

Cheshire

Chester. The Yacht Inn on the corner of Nicholas Street was Swift's lodging when embarking for Ireland.

Surrey

Moor Park, near Farnham, Surrey, England. Originally Compton Hall and renamed by Sir William Temple after a mansion in Hertfordshire of the same name belonging to the family of his wife. The seventeenth-century house, where Swift was Temple's secretary and Stella's tutor, has been much altered and became an educational centre.

Illustrations

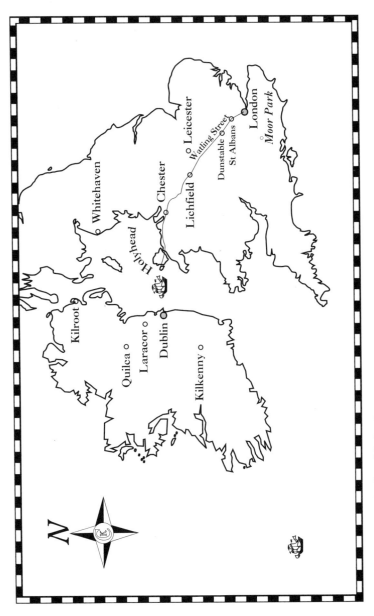

Fig. 1: *Swift's England and Ireland*

The illustrations have been chosen as another source of evidence to understand Swift's context and the captions here are intended to encourage a closer look than a passing glance.

Fig. 1: *Swift's England and Ireland*

Marked on this map are places where Swift lived: Dublin (where he was born, educated as an undergraduate and to which he returned in later life), Whitehaven (where his nurse took him for 'almost three years'), Kilkenny (where he was schooled), Moor Park (Sir William Temple's estate near Farnham in Surrey), London, Kilroot, Laracor. Quilca was where his friend Thomas Sheridan resided. On his journeys between the two countries he crossed the Irish Sea between Holyhead (or Chester) and Dublin. From London he went by the old Roman Road of Watling Street through St Albans and Dunstable as far as Lichfield. The coach road then wound its way to Chester before striking west to Holyhead. Swift rode on horseback, sometimes visiting friends. The fastest time he took from London to Holyhead was nine days, excluding a two-night stay to recover at Dunstable. Leicester is where his mother spent her last years.

Plate 1: *A Panorama of Kilkenny*, Irish School, 1760/1800

To the left of the River Nore is Ormonde's Kilkenny Castle and his mills by the river. A symbol of Anglo–Norman strength and the independence of the city (with the marks of Cromwell's cannon shot on its walls) it is balanced by imposing buildings (some in decay) witnessing the presence of Anglican and Roman Catholic Christianity. The city is to the right with the small tower of its town hall just beside that of St Mary's church seen through the centre group of trees. On the far right is the Anglican St Canice's cathedral with an ancient round tower in front of it. To its right are the ruins of the abbey of St Francis belonging to the Greyfriars. At the centre behind the group of people is one of the city gates, the Maudlin Gate which heads Maudlin Street leading past Swift's school situated in the large wooded park in front of St Mary's and the town hall. In the distance behind Maudlin Gate are the ruins of the priory of St John the Evangelist built for the Austin canons and also the Black Abbey, rebuilt by Dominican friars after the dissolution of the monasteries, but abandoned by the time of Swift. Although this painting postdates Swift's life, the city is little different from a careful topographical drawing by Francis Place taken from the same vantage point in 1699. The town hall here is a later one, built in 1760, and the unknown artist has given more of the atmosphere of Kilkenny than Francis Place did.

Plate 1: *A Panorama of Kilkenny*
Courtesy of the National Gallery of Ireland

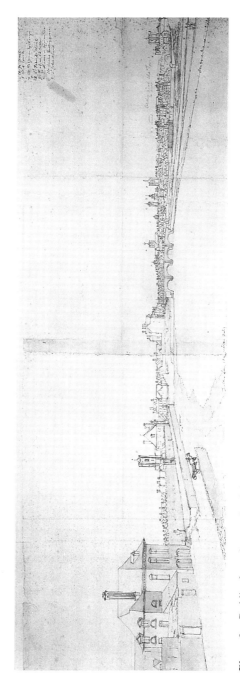

Plate 2: *Dublin from the wooden bridge*
Courtesy of the National Gallery of Ireland

Plate 2: *Dublin from the wooden bridge*, Francis Place, 1698

Francis Place drew this view in 1698 from the western edge of Dublin standing on a wooden bridge which was later washed away. The nineteenth-century O'More bridge stands there now. The arched bridge in front was known as Arran bridge, connecting Arran Quay with Ussher's Quay (on the right), but it too has been replaced, by Liam Mellows bridge. The towers and steeples of churches on the right bank are all close to St Patrick's cathedral on the extreme right, and show St Audeon's, Christchurch, St James, St Werburgh's and the town hall. This is the fearsome skyline that threatened to pierce the underside of the flying island of Laputa. The broad river, Liffey, supplies water when the island prevents rain from falling on the city – less grand than London (see plate 5).

Plate 3: *St James's Palace and environs*, John Rocque's map of London, 1746

The Palace of St James is in the angle where Green Park meets St James's Park. Buckingham House, not yet a palace, is just off the lower left hand (west) corner at the head of a number of tree-lined avenues and the 'Canal' which today is a lake. Modern Piccadilly Circus is where the Hay Market meets Piccadilly and Coventry Street. With these as reference points it should be simple to pick out areas which figure in Swift's life. To the east of the Hay Market is Leicester Fields where Swift first stayed with Sir Andrew Fountaine and where the son of George I, after a quarrel with his father, set up an alternative court in waiting. Swift lived in a number of lodgings between Leicester Fields and St James's palace: at Berry Street (a misspelling of 'Bury Street') just off St James's Street, near to the palace and also to the Vanhomrighs who lived in the same street. When they moved, he followed to nearby Great Suffolk Street to the east of the Hay Market. Then he went to St Martin's Street, leading south from Leicester Fields; to Little Panton Street, just west of the Hay Market; and finally to Little Rider Street, crossing Berry Street. The whole area had much to do with horses. Suffolk Street was built at the end of the seventeenth century over the Earl of Suffolk's stables. Nearby, several times a week, a major sale of hay and straw was conducted in the Hay Market, bringing in many carts to clog the streets. In this vicinity there were a number of stables (called 'mews' since they were originally places for keeping hawks). The Royal, by the palace, the Dunghill, by Great Suffolk Street, and the Greene Mews, by Leicester Fields (just going off the page). The name of the Dunghill Mews suggests that the horse manure was inescapably present and that Swift's Houyhnhnms were a considerably sanitised version of the reality he experienced. The stench of the gutter (called the 'sink') in the road outside his lodgings was enough to provoke him to remark in his *Journal*: 'I am almost st – k out of this with the sink, and it helps me to verses in my [poem, *A Description of a*] *Shower*.' Wren had supported plans for Little Panton Street as a route to avoid the congestion and smell which he called 'noysomness'.

Plate 3: *St James's Palace and environs*
Courtesy of the Museum of London

Plate 4: *The Old Stocks Market*
© The Governor and the Company of the Bank of England

Plate 4: *The Old Stocks Market*, Josef van Aken, *c.* 1730

The Old Stocks Market between the Royal Exchange and Gresham
College. This was in London's commercial centre dominated by the
Grocers' Company who patronised the new domed church of St
Stephen's Walbrook shown overlooking the stalls. It was built by
Wren (from 1672–1687) and they presented him with 'twenty guineas
in a silk purse.' Swift, seeing the sights in 1710, dined at a chop house
nearby and visited Gresham, in such a hackney coach as shown here.
He located Gulliver in Old Jewry a step away, so that he would
have been able to buy the drugs and oriental spices used in medicine
from the market here. Gulliver's settling here also underlines the
commercialism of his travels. The equestrian statue is of Charles II
trampling upon Oliver Cromwell. Marking the rapid changes to
political sentiment, it had been remodelled in a Tory spirit from an
original statue of John Sobieski trampling upon the Turk. In a further political twist, a spirit of Whig free trade now (1730) makes a
Turk part of this cosmopolitan scene and orderliness and prosperity
prevail. In 1738 it all disappeared to become the site for the residence of the Lord Mayor – the Mansion House.

Plate 5: *The View from One-Tree Hill in Greenwich Park*
© The Governor and the Company of the Bank of England

Plate 5: *The View from One-Tree Hill in Greenwich Park,* an etching from an original picture by Peter Tillemans, *c.* 1718

On a sight-seeing trip in 1707 with Stella and her dog, Pug, which chased deer in this park, Swift came to see Wren's unfinished Naval Hospital (centre), an enormous building when it was finished. This building evidences the importance of the Navy to the British economy for it was able to give the best medical treatment to large numbers of sailors. Nearby, the Royal Observatory helped to establish the navigational superiority of the fleet (see Chapter 5) and to the right is a ship in full sail from Gulliver's Wapping or from Deptford (which is near his Redriff) putting out to the North Sea, the gateway to many expeditionary voyages. To the left, London stretches out along the Thames with St Paul's rising in the distance above many other spires, which were also the work of Wren.

Plate 6: *A Description of a City Shower*
Courtesy of the Museum of London

Plate 6: *A Description of a City Shower*, Edward Penny, 1761

This represents an actual incident in Swift's poem where the 'first drizling shower' is likened to the 'sprinkling which some careless quean/Flirts on you from her mop'. Although rather stagey in the prim heels-together attitude of the servant and the aghast warding-off of the man of fashion, the picture catches the poem's sense of observed urban detail in costume, buildings and street furniture. On a closer look the stageyness is part of a pictorial counterpart to the urbane manner of Swift's poem with its underlying mockery of social decorum. The painter reveals the meaning below the surface of the apparently careless behaviour. The mop is rolled elegantly between the fetching bare arms of the pretty woman who looks away, apparently unaware that she is attracting attention. But a 'quean' is both a 'hussy' and a 'harlot' and the flirting of the mop has a sexual undertone, suggested here by the position and appearance of the mop end.

Plate 7: *The Humble Representation made to the King's Majesty*, by the Lords Spiritual and Temporal in Parliament Assembled; And by them Ordered to be Printed and Published, Samuel FAIR-BROTHER, Dublin, 1719

This document contained the argument of the Irish Lords about their constitutional role, sparked off by the appeal of Maurice Annesley over their heads to the English Parliament. These are the first two pages which go straight to the heart of the matter of the separate nature of Ireland as a 'Kingdom *being of it self a Distinct Dominion, and no Part of the Kingdom of* England, none can Determine concerning the Affairs thereof, unless Authorized' by the king himself. It appeals not to natural justice but to a legal obligation, impressively buttressed by quotation, going back to the reign of Elizabeth I. It has a distinctly Anglo–Irish flavour, noting 'a great Encouragement to many of the *English* to come over and Settle' and emphasising that by the independent constitution 'the *English* Subjects of this Kingdom have been Enabled faithfully to Discharge their Duty to the Crown of *England*'. This pamphlet was also sold in London in 1720 with the detailed report of their dealing with the Annesley case. The anger aroused by the English assertion of supremacy in the Declaratory Act of 1720, fuelled the resistance to Wood's halfpence.

(5)

TO THE

KING's

Most Excellent Majesty,

THE HUMBLE

REPRESENTATION

OF THE

LORDS *Spiritual* and *Temporal*, in Parliament Affembled.

Moſt Gracious Sovereign,

IT is with the greateſt concern, That We, Your Majeſty's moſt Dutiful and Loyal Subjects, the Lords *Spiritual* and *Temporal* in Parliament aſſembled, do find our ſelves under a neceſſity of making this our Humble Repreſentation to Your Majeſty.

It

(6)

It evidently appears by many Ancient Records and ſundry Acts of Parliament paſſed in this Kingdom, and particularly by one in the Eleventh of Queen *Elizabeth*, Entitled, *An Act for Attainder of Shane O Neil, &c.* That the King, with all the Princes and Men of Value of the Land, did, of their own good Will, and without any War or Chivalry, ſubmit themſelves to Your Majeſty's Royal Anceſtor King Henry the Second, took Oaths of Fidelity to him, and became His Liege Subjects, Who (as it is aſſerted by the Lord Chief Juſtice * *Coke*, and others) did Ordain and Command, at the † Inſtance of the *Iriſh*, *That ſuch Laws as be Bad in England, ſhould be of Force and obſerved in Ireland*. By this Agreement the People of *Ireland* obtained the ‡ Benefit of the *Engliſh* Laws, and many Privileges, particularly that of having a diſtinct Parliament here as in *England*, and of having ‖ *weighty and momentous matters relating to this Kingdom Treated of, Diſcuſſed and Determined in the ſaid PARLIAMENT.*

* *Coke* 4*th* Inſt. *pag.* 349.
‡ *Matth. Paris Ann.* 1172. *pag.* 105.
‡ *Coke* 4*th* Inſt. *p.* 350.
‖ *Prys* on 4*th* Inſt. *Pag.* 287. *Autem* 31. *Ed.* 3. Rex Juſtic. & Cancellar. ſuis *Hibern.* ſalutem, *&c.* Item voluimus & præcipimus quod noſtra & ipſius Terræ negotia, præſertim Majora & Ardua in Conciliis, per petitos Conſiliarios noſtros ac Prælatos & Magnates, & quoſdam de diſcretioribus & probioribus Hominibus de partibus vicinis, ubi ipſa Concilia teneri contigerit propter hoc evocandos: In PARLIAMENTIS vero, per ipſos Conſiliarios noſtros, ac Prælatos & Proceres, alioſque de Terrâ prædictâ, prout mos exigit, ſecundum Juſtitiam. Legem, Conſuetudinem & Rationem tractentur, deniantur, & fideliter timore, favore, odio aut pretio poſtpoſitis, dicuntantur & etiam Terminentur.

This

(7)

This Conceſſion and Compact thus made, and afterwards by ſucceeding Kings Confirmed to the People of this Land, in Proceſs of Time. proved a great Encouragement to many of the *Engliſh* to come over and Settle themſelves in *Ireland*, where they were to enjoy the ſame Laws and Liberties, and live under the like Conſtitution as they had formerly done in the Kingdom of *England*, which thro' God's good Providence has proved a Means of Securing this Kingdom to the Crown of *England*, and we truſt will do to all Futurity. By this happy Conſtitution, and theſe Privileges by us for ſo many Years enjoyed, the *Engliſh* Subjects of this Kingdom have been Enabled faithfully to Diſcharge their Duty to the Crown of *England*; and vigorouſly ſet themſelves upon all Occaſions, to aſſert the Rights thereof againſt all the Rebellions which have been Raiſed by the *Iriſh* Enemies: And therefore We Your Majeſty's Loyal Subjects do, with all Submiſſion to Your Majeſty, inſiſt upon them, and hope through Your Majeſty's Goodneſs, to have them Preſerved inviolable.

And We beg leave to Repreſent to Your Majeſty, That though the * *Imperial Crown* of this Realm was formerly inſeparably Annexed to that of *Great-Britain*; yet this Kingdom † *being of it ſelf a Diſtinct Dominion, and no Part of the Kingdom of England*, none can Determine concerning the Affairs thereof, unleſs

* *Anne* 2 *Eliz. p.* 214. *C.* 5. *c.* 7. *pag.* 218.
† *Coke* 4*th* Inſt. *pag.* 349.

Authorized

Plate 7: *A Humble Representation made to the King's Majesty*

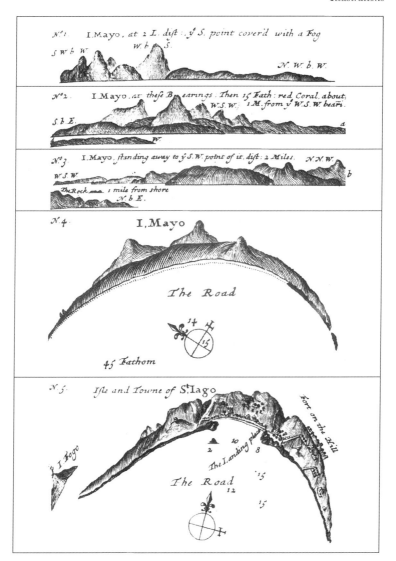

Plate 8: *Cape Verd Islands*
By Permission of the British Library (shelfmark 1045f3)

Plate 8: *Cape Verd Islands*, cut from William Dampier's *Voyage to New Holland*, 1703

The use of wood engravings (cuts) in travelogues to show the outline of islands as they might appear through the telescope heightened the immediacy of the account of the voyage. From afar, distinctive group-ings of mountains enabled identification of the landfall. With bear-ings and soundings and line-of-sight landmarks, the readers could imagine feeling their way in past rocks and shoals to 'The Landing Place'. It is tempting to see in the cut of St Iago, through the trick of perspective, the Island of Togo as flying through the air like Laputa.

Plate 9: *Wild horses in a Wood*, Hans Baldung Grien, 1534

This illustrates the tradition which associates horses with unrestrained animality discussed in Chapter 3. It can be traced back to Plato's *Phaedrus*, written in the fourth century BC. Swift would have known this source as he had two editions of Plato's works in his library, prizing his three volume Estienne edition of 1578, and used Plato to bolster his arguments with Bolingbroke. Hans Baldung Grien's engraving is the second in a series of three representations of horses. The first shows a violent mêlée of horses, biting and kicking each other in battle. Here they are clearly sexually roused, manes and tails flying, teeth bared and wild eyed. The stallion in the foreground is excited by the mare to the right and in the third picture of the sequence, she kicks him and he ejaculates on the ground. The mon-key, a symbol of lust, looks relatively demure, while an elk, interpreted as a symbol of melancholy, stalks away from the scene. A prudent man in civilised bonnet and robe – dress which is contemporary to Baldung – takes cover behind a tree. The value of this engraving is to sharpen the reader's awareness of an alternative to the idealised literary presentation of noble steeds, particularly when now the experience of the physical actuality of a horse is less common than in Swift's day. The satire of the Houyhnhnms works partly through the surprise of inverting preconceptions of the animal nature of horses (not simply their being non-rational), leading variously to humour, burlesque or the shock of disgust.

Plate 9: *Wild Horses in a Wood*
The Metropolitan Museum of Art, Rogers Fund, 1922 (22.67.58).

Plate 10: *Death and a Woman (Hans Baldung Grien)*
Öffentliche Kunstsammlung Basel, Kunstmuseum
Photo: Öffentliche Kunstsammlung Basel, Martin Bühler

Plate 10: *Death and a Woman*, Hans Baldung Grien, *c.* 1519

Feeling an embrace from behind, the woman has turned in expectation of the lover's kiss, only to react with horror at a love bite from a being whose nose and lips have rotted away. She is enclosed in the arch of his legs and we notice that his left foot has fallen off. Death represents the decay to which her body will come (see the discussion of *A Beautiful Nymph Going to Bed* in Chapter 4). Like the Struldbrugg, death can never die but does show all the marks of mortality. Baldung Grien frequently painted or engraved variations of this subject, including macabre details of peeling flesh, crooked spines, gangrenous wounds, hanging entrails. These motifs were repeated in popular woodcuts, tomb effigies and church wall paintings. Apart from these enduring reminders of an old tradition, there were literary descendants in Swift's day. Ehrenpreis notices a prose translation of Quevedo's *Visions*, detailing a woman's raddled body under her artificial trappings, and this went through 11 editions between 1667 and 1715. Swift's own poems of decay and corruption became part of such popular reading. In *Death and Daphne* Swift grotesquely parodies the image of death as lover and the energy of the imagined situation reveals an underlying unease.

Bibliography

Works

The Drapier's Letters to the People of Ireland . . . , (ed.) Herbert Davis, Clarendon Press, Oxford, 1935.

The Prose Works of Jonathan Swift, (ed.) Herbert Davis *et al.*, 14 vols, Clarendon Press, Oxford, 1939–68. This is the standard edition but it is out of print.

Jonathan Swift: Journal to Stella, (ed.) Harold Williams, 2 vols, Clarendon Press, Oxford, 1948, repr. 1975.

The Correspondence of Jonathan Swift, (ed.) Harold Williams, 5 vols, Clarendon Press, Oxford, 1963–65.

Gulliver's Travels by Jonathan Swift, (ed.) Angus Ross, Longman, London, 1972. Although out of print, this is worth tracking down for its helpful annotations and short essays on topics relevant to the text.

Jonathan Swift: The Complete Poems, (ed.) Pat Rogers, Penguin Books, Harmondsworth, 1983. Thoroughly edited and approachable edition with many helpful notes.

Jonathan Swift, The Oxford Authors series, (ed.) Angus Ross and David Woolley, Oxford University Press, Oxford, 1984, corr. 1989. This is an anthology with scholarly and informative introductions and notes. As a source of primary texts it contains most of the writings of Swift discussed in *A Preface to Swift*, except for *Gulliver's Travels* which, as the editors say, is readily available in a number of cheap editions.

Jonathan Swift/A Tale of a Tub and Other Works, (ed.) Angus Ross and David Woolley, World's Classics, Oxford University Press, Oxford, 1986.

The Memoirs of the Extraordinary Life, Works, and Discoveries of Martinus Scriblerus, (ed.) Charles Kerby-Miller, Oxford University Press, Oxford, 1988.

Criticism

Biographical

Swift, Leslie Stephen, English Men of Letters Series, Macmillan, London, 1899.

Swift, The Man, his Works, and the Age, Irvin Ehrenpreis, 3 vols, Methuen 1962–1983. This is the standard life of Swift. Unfortunately the first two volumes are out of print.

Jonathan Swift, A Hypocrite Reversed: A Critical Biography, David Nokes, Oxford University Press, Oxford, 1985. This is an entertaining, well-researched one-volume biography.

Critical studies

Dean Swift's Library, (ed.) Harold Williams, Cambridge University Press, Cambridge, 1932.

Jonathan Swift: a list of critical studies, compiled James J. Stahis, Vanderbilt University Press, Nashville, 1967.

Jonathan Swift, the critical heritage, (ed.) Kathleen Williams, Routledge & Kegan Paul, London, 1970, repr. 1995.

Focus: Swift, (ed.) C.J. Rawson, Sphere Books, London, 1971.

The Irish Perspective of Jonathan Swift, Andrew Carpenter, P. Hammer, Wuppertal, 1978.

The Art of Jonathan Swift, (ed.) Clive T. Probyn, Vision Press, London, 1978.

Hacks and Dunces: Pope, Swift and Grub Street, Pat Rogers, Methuen, London, 1980.

Swift Studies 1965–1980, an Annotated Bibliography, Bernard Tucker, Gill and Macmillan, London, 1983.

Order from Confusion Sprung: Studies in Eighteenth Century Literature from Swift to Cowper, Claude Rawson, Allen & Unwin, London, 1985.

The Body in Swift and Defoe, Carol Houlihan Flynn, Cambridge University Press, Cambridge, 1990.

Critical Approaches to Teaching Swift, (ed.) Peter J. Schakel, AMS Press, New York, 1992.

Critical Essays on Jonathan Swift, (ed.) Frank Palmer, Macmillan, London, 1993.

Jonathan Swift: Gulliver's Travels, Howard Erskine-Hill, Cambridge University Press, Cambridge (Landmarks of world literature), 1993.

Jonathan Swift and the Burden of the Future, Alan D. Chalmers, University of Delaware Press, Newark, 1995.

Jonathan Swift: The Irish Identity, Robert Mahoney, Yale University Press, New Haven, 1995.

Historical context

Specifically on Swift

Swift and the Church of Ireland, Louis Landa, Clarendon Press, Oxford, 1954.

Jonathan Swift: Political Writer, J.A. Downie, Routledge & Kegan Paul, London, 1984.

Jonathan's Travels/Swift and Ireland, Joseph McMinn, Appletree Press, Belfast, 1994.

On the Irish context

The Irish Comic Tradition, Vivian Mercier, Clarendon Press, Oxford, 1962, repr. Souvenir Press, London, 1991.
Modern Ireland 1600–1972, R.F. Foster, Penguin Books, Harmondsworth, 1989.
The Oxford Illustrated History of Ireland, (ed.) R.F. Foster, Oxford University Press, Oxford, 1989.
Irish Literature: A Social History, Norman Vance, Blackwell, Oxford, 1990.

On British politics

Britain after the Glorious Revolution 1689–1714, (ed.) G. Holmes, Macmillan, London, 1969.
Tory and Whig: The Struggle in the Constituencies, 1701–1715, W.A. Speck, Macmillan, London, 1970.
Robert Harley and the Press: Propaganda and Public Opinion in the Age of Swift and Defoe, J.A. Downie, Cambridge University Press, Cambridge, 1979.
Robert Harley: Speaker, Secretary of State and Premier Minister, Brian W. Hill, Yale University Press, New Haven, 1988.
The Making of a Great Power, Geoffrey Holmes, Longman, London, 1993.

On the literary context

The Eighteenth Century, The Context of English Literature Series, (ed.) Pat Rogers, Methuen, London, 1978.
The Eighteenth Century/The Intellectual and Cultural Context of English Literature, 1700–1789, James Sambrook, Longman, London, 1986.

On literacy

Literacy and the Social Order: Reading and Writing in Tudor and Stuart England, David Cressy, Cambridge University Press, Cambridge, 1980.
Printing Technology, Letters & Samuel Johnson, Alvin Kernan, Princeton University Press, Princeton, 1987.
Dublin's Trade in Books 1550–1800, M. Pollard, Oxford University Press, Oxford, 1989.
The Practice and Representation of Reading in England, (eds) James Raven, Helen Small and Naomi Tadmor, Cambridge University Press, Cambridge, 1996.

Index